TWO SISTERS

TWO SISTERS

A SPIRITUAL LEGEND

GRAHAM ADRIAN

A record of this publication is available from the British Library.

ISBN 978-1-910027-32-5

Typesetting by Wordzworth Ltd
www.wordzworth.com

Cover design by Titanium Design Ltd
www.titaniumdesign.co.uk

Cover image *The Leaping Horse* by John Constable (1825)
by kind permission of the Royal Academy, London

Published by Local Legend
www.local-legend.co.uk

**LOCAL
LEGEND**

For Jan Dower,
whose mediumship over the years has provided suggestions
for many of the scenes described here.

www.local-legend.co.uk

ABOUT THE AUTHOR

Graham Adrian has walked spiritual pathways throughout his life and the accounts of an afterlife given to him through mediums proved, he says, "so evidential that they just could not be ignored." He then turned his mind to a dedicated study of spiritual phenomena, becoming a book reviewer and columnist for Mind, Body & Spirit publications and gaining widespread respect for his wisdom, thorough research and profound historical knowledge.

Over the years, the desire grew to make more use of what he had learned and to write something creative of his own. Why not, he thought, write an adventure story from the perspective of both sides of life, the higher world intertwined with this earthly one?

"In our illusory and often violent physical existence, the spirit world can appear remote," says Graham, "but in reality it is never more than a heartbeat away. And I am convinced that there are consequences for our every thought and action, not just here but also hereafter."

This, then, is the theme of Graham's wonderful debut novel *Two Sisters*, a story set in a true historical context whilst spiritually very much for our times. Every reader will identify with the good intentions, yet passionate recklessness, of our heroine Nance and follow the twists and turns of her adventurous life with baited breath...

ABOUT THIS BOOK

In 18th century England, life is tough for the Auldfield farming family but they are proud, hard-working people. Nance's sorrow at her sister's death is eased a little by falling in love, but this only begins a sequence of devastating events that only seem to lead to one place – the gallows!

Unknown to her, she is guided by her sister's loving spirit, finding new life and love herself in the afterlife and trying desperately to avert the consequences of Nance's reckless, if well-meaning, actions.

The author's debut novel, based on a Suffolk legend, is a brilliant, historically accurate description of Georgian times including genuine dialect. But, far more than this, it is a truly exciting adventure story that also inspires us with beautiful, erudite writing to consider the possibility of an afterlife where our spiritual efforts on Earth are rewarded.

CONTENTS

ILLUSTRATIONS

CHAPTER 1

THE CONDEMNED
AND THE VISIONARY

Nance Auldfield had dreaded the crowd even more than being hanged. But now her growing fear was not that there would be 'nothing' beyond the drop, but that there might indeed be another world, a parallel existence where her sufferings would continue and perhaps increase. In the twilight, she had glimpsed something in the water basin, before shrieking and sending it flying with a fist. A face! In the moonlit cell, a disembodied face gazed back. Yet it was no reflection but her sister's face – a sister dead for many years.

Her tortured mind shifted back to the crowd as the noisy chatter from below, wafted on the evening breeze, told her that people were already gathering. In a few hours she would be paraded before the whole of Ipswich and the very people with whom she had lived and worked. Yes, there may be a friend or two to offer a prayer, but most would be 'honest citizens', there by right to see justice done. The truth was that they wanted their morbid curiosity satisfied and their pious expectations fulfilled, by way of entertainment. After all, executions were intended to draw spectators. "If they do not," Dr Samuel Johnson had declared, "they do not answer their purpose."

All day the gaol had rung with hammer blows as the gallows was erected. She heard they were building it high up beside the outer gate to give everyone a better view, and she knew that as she dropped her skirts would open... That would surely amuse the crowd, that raucous, unruly, derisive, gawking multitude. Throughout her life people had stared at her, whispering, nudging and drawing their own false conclusions. Now they were determined to accompany her to the bitter end, having witnessed her trial and stalked the carriage returning her to gaol. Tomorrow they would be standing shoulder to shoulder, clinging to treetops and clambering onto roofs, to watch her swing.

The balladeers and poets would be out in force too with their usual moralising doggerel as the black bag was placed over her head and the noose about her neck. There would be a prolonged drum roll, a brief silence and then the local Jack Ketch would complete his dreadful work.

How had it all come to this? Had her family's love, toil and sacrifice and a life of poverty and servitude been for this? Had the sincerest love for another, dearer than self, been for nothing, nothing but this? In the past, the family had been together and there had been security of sorts, a sense of belonging and a purpose in living however hard life was at times. There had always been an expectancy of something better. And then, one mistake – stealing a horse – which her mistress had long since forgiven.

The family was almost all gone now and she missed them terribly, especially her elder sister, dearest Sarah. She was the first to go and it had been a sobbing Nance who held her as she breathed her last. At first Sarah had seemed so calm as though resignation had gently prepared the way for her. But then she had fixed a moist, quizzical eye on Nance that seemed to penetrate to her very soul, her expression inexplicably changing to one of unbridled horror – a look that still haunted Nance. What had she seen, she for whom death held no terrors? Sweet, spiritual Sarah. Her second sight had offered many warnings to Nance. If only they had been heeded, she would surely not now be living out her final hours in the condemned cell.

As the light faded, she heard the turnkey's footsteps as he began his evening rounds. She lit the stub of a tallow dip to read aloud the chaplain's prayer for forgiveness, but only heard again his stern, unfeeling words.

"Oh Nance, had you but served your God with half the passion you served another, He would not have led you into temptation and abandoned you when most you needed Him."

The spluttering flame wreathed a smoky, sulphurous aura about her as she knelt in prayer. Moonlight filtered through the barred window, the rays lengthening on the flagstones as she read aloud. Then the tallow-flame gave up the ghost and the scrawled inscriptions of former and late guests of His Majesty on the stone walls faded from view. The turnkey's footsteps, the rattling of keys and rasping of bolts grew distant and ceased. Between the gloaming and the murk, a solemn stillness reigned as though the very world itself was in repose.

A calming, otherworldly presence now descended, bringing a certain peace and consolation. Had Nance the inner eye to see, the form of her sister, insubstantial yet pulsating with life, had appeared beside her. So many times she had tried to show Nance that life is forever continuous and that, come what may, all would be well. Now, fearing that she had only made matters worse by revealing her face, she sought to ease Nance's torments in subtle ways by placing an incorporeal hand on her shoulder. There it remained as Nance felt its healing influence, bringing her rest, her moist eyes closed in slumber, her head pillowed on the straw-covered stones.

Sarah was left to contemplate ruefully the events of the last years: a rejected true love and a blind, unquenchable passion for one unworthy of it, that had led to so much suffering and finally imprisonment.

One day in Georgian England, the parson pronounced Zebedee and Beth man and wife, and they made their home in a tied cottage not far from Amberslea and a few miles from Ipswich. In those days, the lanes wound their narrow, unhurried way around blind corners, between tall banks and weather-worn fences. On the approach to Piper's Vale a canopy of majestic, towering elms shaded the sand and stone cart-way, gaps between the trees offering views over glebe, meadow and pasture of the beautiful blue Orwell. There, deep in the Valley of Alneshbourne, was the Harvey estate where the Auldfields worked; further on, nearer the river and encircled by more elms, lay the Abbeyfield Farm where Nance would later work. Originally a priory, the farm still retained many medieval features including an encircling moat, fed by a stream that flowed onwards through a waterlily mead by the Orwell. Nearby was a white gothic-style barn from an earlier century, fashioned from the ruins of the old priory chapel.

A crooked pathway led from the lane through a vegetable patch to the Auldfield's white, lath and plaster cottage. Twin oaks towered above its sagging roof, their branches entwined in a protective embrace. Amberslea was then a cluster of cottages in front of the parish church of St Mary, its rubble exterior like Abbeyfield Farm, almost unchanged from medieval times. The church stood within the bounds of Amberslea Hall and a gate in the church wall was the private entrance for the park's owner, Squire Roker. To the north of the village – screened discreetly by trees – were the Poorhouse and the House of Industry for paupers.

Zebedee rose to become head ploughman on the Harvey estate. Nance was the baby of the family and her brothers John, Albert and Mark worked the farm and helped their father with the ploughing, a thankless task as Old Zeb was famed for his meticulously straight furrows, up to a quarter of a mile in length. Suffolk farmers, otherwise noted for their meanness, paid extra for the best handiwork. When a well-meaning son ploughed furrows he considered equally straight, it was only to be reproved by his father for having been "bodged agen" and being "all outta kilter." Unlettered and never travelling beyond the county, Zebedee spoke in dialect loosely related to English. The occasional 'furriner' – that is, anyone from outside the county – was wise not to enquire about agriculture. Listening to Zebedee's detailed reply, such as the comparative merits of bawking, bouting and back-striking, he either had to pretend to understand or be thought 'sorft' and have it patiently explained all over again.

Master Zebedee and Dame Beth, as she was called being the wife of a master, were well respected by their employers the Harveys and by all in the village. A daily "How are yew diddlin', bor?" from Mr Harvey would produce a cheery response from Zebedee and some sage advice on agricultural matters. When the day's long 'jahney' was done, he liked nothing better than to lean on the wicket gate by the lane and pass on news, often older than his home-brewed ale, to all who paused to chat as they returned from the fields. Hard working and prematurely aged with his hoary hairs and knowledge of country lore, he was honoured as the village statesman.

Sarah, Nance's elder sister, was an incurable invalid, subject to frequent fevers and often obliged to do what little work she could from home. When she was confined to bed, Nance became her nurse even as a toddler. Though unlettered like her father and physically infirm, a strange and powerful intuition elevated Sarah above mundane things. Over the years she gained increasing insight into the mysteries beyond life and death, those deemed devilish by the religious, impossible by the ignorant and unknowable by the worldly. Gradually she came to know the spirit world intimately, a place kinder, more inviting and strangely more real than the earthly one that brought mostly toil, hardship and suffering.

Her favourite retreat for contemplation was beside a spring in a hollow beneath a willow. Often at noontide she would recline on its mossy margin, ruffle the mirror-like surface with her fingers and moisten her feverish brow. As the ripples receded and dancing sedge and foliage reappeared, the water sometimes misted over and then cleared to reveal a panorama of evergreen woodland, purling streams and flowery meadows. A strange sunlight, although the sun was never visible, shed a benign lustre from an azure sky of pinkish-white clouds, whilst gardens overflowed with soft blossoms around many picturesque dwellings. An all-pervasive sense of peace and heightened consciousness overwhelmed her in these moments. Sometimes she would even see the cottagers themselves, spritely and ageless despite being what the world would term 'dead'; indeed, they were very much alive, far more than she had ever been.

Well, so much the better, she thought, for she sensed that sooner rather than later she would take her place amongst them. Certainly those folk were not drenched by vernal showers, scorched in the dog-days, wearied by moonlit harvests and chilled by winter's boreal blasts.

All too soon the vision would fade to be replaced with muddying water, marish grass, numberless flies and hours of toil and sickness until the embrace of an ever-welcome night.

Old Widow Perkins was a sickly, dying woman, and Sarah had done all she could to make her last days comfortable. So as she approached the woman's cottage one morning, she was astonished to see her wave blithely from the window, apparently restored to health. Sarah waved back, promised to call later and completed an errand for her mother.

"I've just seen Widow Perkins, Ma," she cried excitedly, "an' she be har owd self agen." Beth's reaction was incredulity and profound shock.

"Yew cont not have done, darter."

Now it was Sarah who was puzzled. "Why iver not?"

"Widow Perkins died yesterdi'. I've just heard."

Beth wrestled inwardly with the shock of her daughter's announcement. Widow Perkins, a firm believer in folklore and like Sarah blessed with second sight, was said to wait every April 25th, St Mark's Night, in the church porch. It was believed that, come the witching hour, the apparitions of those who would suffer some possibly fatal complaint in the year ahead would walk up the path and into the church. If the apparition reappeared, the person would recover with the time spent inside the church an indication of how long recovery would take; but if it did not reappear, the person would die. This last April, Widow Perkins had duly waited and indeed a spectral figure had glided up the pathway; as it drew level with her its face became visible, that of the widow herself. On it glided through the locked door and into the church and, though she had waited until cockcrow, it did not reappear.

Sarah, never one to argue, thought for a moment, appeared satisfied, shrugged and said she would collect pennies for the funeral. She was questioned no further for her mother had never known her be untruthful. If she said she had seen the widow that morning, then in some strange way she had – though Beth could not begin to fathom how. Certainly, Sarah had an uncanny ability to see things others could not. Some called it witchcraft, and witches were still prosecuted.

6

"Yew marn't tell noo one, maw," Beth told her daughter, "not niver! Stick ta readin' the tea leaves. There's none as minds tha'!"

Nance was born a few years later at Brandeston but was raised in the cottage near Amberslea where she grew up quickly. The region was famous for the best barley in the county and as Barsel approached the farmer would drop his breeches to squat on the virgin soil. If it were neither damp nor too cold for a bare bum, it would be 'comfortable enough' for his precious barley. When Nance was carried into the fields at such times, wrapped in her mother's shawl, it was not for long that anyone had to "watch out for the wee mawther." In no time at all she was away with the weeding dames, scampering between the rows of tender shoots with a hoe, eagerly filling basket after basket. Soon she would be just as eagerly raking and pronging through the long days of Haysel and, as she grew older, tossing the dried hay ever higher onto the groaning wain. She would watch in fascination as ropes were thrown over the tottering load to secure it, to cries of "Pull agen, pull agen! An' agen!"

When the waving golden harvest was ripe, she was away in the fields at first light, toiling with the rest, sometimes far into the night beneath the soft white radiance of a harvest moon. At gleaning time, when the bell was rung, she was always first through the gate and could pick up nearly a comb of wheat, enough for her mother to bake bread well into winter.

One day a fourth brother arrived, Matthew or Little Matty. Nance rejoiced in her new brother and, when Beth was absent and with Sarah increasingly indisposed, cared for him as mother as well as sister.

The seasons came and went but rural life in Suffolk continued unchanged as it had for generations. Elsewhere, the wooden parts of the plough were replaced with iron, but here nothing changed. After all, why had God made ash trees? The seed-drill, too, was not to be found in Suffolk, seed being sown in a broad cast by hand during the waxing moon.

'One for the rook, one for the crow,
one to perish and one to grow.'

The 'dark satanic mills' were beginning to appear in faraway places. The labourer, the servant and even the master might come and go, but the Auldfields were a fixture, as though they were the real stewards of the land. Horses were almost as important as people here – Mr Harvey was a noted breeder of the Suffolk Punch – and indeed Zebedee treated his ploughing team with as much care as though they were human. On winter nights he would rise every two or three hours, take a lantern and some oats and creep into the stable to check that all was well. Then at seven o'clock, with a tinkling of chains he led his team away to the fields and worked until late afternoon, by which time he had walked eleven miles. He steered them as much with words as by pulling on the cords, and not so much spoke to them as sang. In early morning, as he began to navigate a field, using an old coat on a fence as a marker, and with gulls and rooks beginning to follow in his wake, his song mingled with the calls of the shepherd guiding his flock to pasture.

Nance loved these horses from her earliest years and relished the task of carrying the workers' vittles, known as 'elevenses' and 'fourses', into the fields. Zebedee would take his beloved daughter in his arms and place her on one of the horses. From sitting while her father and brothers ate and rested, she progressed to riding as they made their way back to the stables; and from being led, she was soon walking them herself. Carthorses are normally the most difficult of mounts, stubborn, resentful and independent and, released from the tram, are prone to kicking, rearing and plunging – in short, everything likely to throw even an experienced rider. When one did rear, however, it only increased Nance's delight and she never suffered a fall. By watching other riders and by experience, she taught herself to control the horse by the position and movement of her legs and body alone, without a saddle or even a proper bridle. Instead of a whip she used her hands or simply snapped her fingers. She mastered the trot and then the canter, listening for its three distinct beats, and finally, when out of sight and certain father was not watching, the four beat gallop. By the age of twelve she was working for Mr Harvey, delivering and collecting his prized horses.

On such an errand, a year or two later, as she cantered a carthorse bareback up the long carriageway leading to Amberslea Hall on her way to the stables, she caught the eye of the owner, Squire Roker. He was captivated by the extraordinary sight. Her curly black locks fluttered becomingly over radiant cheeks while intelligent, dark and darting eyes explored the way ahead.

"Young Miss Auldfield, in't it?"

She brought her mount to a snorting, rearing halt and gazed awe-struck at the young country gentleman, dressed for his afternoon walk in a black, gold-buttoned coat, white silk stockings and gold-buckled shoes.

"If it please, yes, sir."

"Come down, m'dear," he said, offering his hand. Shyly she took it, slid to the ground and made her dop, watched in surprise by an approaching groom. It had been drilled into her that a command of social graces impressed the best people. "Charmed, m'dear," he said with a smile and a slight bow as though welcoming a genteel Miss rather than a labourer's daughter.

Seeing her ride so expertly and mindful of her reputation, he could imagine her, with the right training, leading the field at the Ipswich races. More to the point, he might pocket a handsome wager. After all, who would bet on a mere slip of a girl to beat professional jockeys? What odds would his sporting friends offer – a hundred guineas to one, certainly, even five hundred perhaps, if not a thousand? What a capital wager!

"Won't you come inside, Miss Auldfield, and take tea?" he asked, leaving the puzzled groom in charge of the horse.

He led her through the imposing entrance of the palatial Gothic, redbrick pile and into a magnificently panelled hallway. From there she was shown into a room, so large and splendidly furnished – a single window was the area of her father's cottage – she thought that only a king might live like this.

"Not quite, my pretty," he smiled. "Don't be impressed by all this! *Aude, hospes, contemnere opes!*"

"Beg pardon, sir?"

"Dare, my guest, to despise wealth, or rather convention. It's people who are important, don't y'know. Now, pray be seated." Nance sank

9

into what seemed like a gilded throne. A liveried footman entered, looking curiously even more resplendent than his master. Other footmen followed carrying everything, or so it seemed to Nance, for a feast. "How d'you come to ride so well, m'dear?" asked Master Roker.

"I just dew as I wants an' the hobly allus kinda does it."

"But you must have learned – who taught you? And do drink your tea."

At this point he was beginning to think that some education would not go amiss; what a pity such a damnably attractive and talented wench expressed herself in a manner barely intelligible.

Modestly, with no thought of trying to impress him, she told him of life on the farm and how she came to master the art of riding. Soon a second wager had occurred to him. Who amongst his friends would not also bet against his turning this artless maiden into a desirable nymph, with all the attributes a gentleman could want?

"Amazing!" he exclaimed. "I'll strike a bargain with you. You ride the winning horse for me at the Ipswich races for a wager – not that hack of course, a thoroughbred – an' I'll pay you handsomely. An' I'll make a lady of you to boot. Well, what say you, my pretty?"

"Me a laday?" she queried, a little alarmed and suspicious of his intentions. "Now sir, yew be a-teasin' I. An' I'm noo jockey."

"Hmm, we'll see about that. Have you had any schooling?" She had not. Her father's cottage stood on extra-parochial land and she had not therefore been entitled to such schooling as the parish might provide. "Then you shall. I'll speak to your father."

And at church the next Sunday he was as good as his word. The Sabbath, a day when only essential chores were done, saw the Auldfields promenade like the gentry, dressed in their finest. Old Zeb wore a tricorne and an ageing coat a size too large, having first visited the neighbouring fields to inspect his peers' ploughing handiwork, whilst they just as carefully inspected his. Beth eased a remade dress over tightly-laced stays that reduced somewhat her spreading girth and trimmed an ancient cap with a bow and cherished piece of lace. Their sons, with an eye for the maidens, preferred tight-fitting breeches and high-collared coats to emphasise their fine physiques. Sarah did not usually accompany them on the long walk, but made sure that

Nance had a serviceable gown. Thus turned out, they could confidently return a greeting from the gentry with a doffed hat and a bow or a deep-sinking curtsy.

They attended Evensong and, being unable to afford a seat in the white box pews, stood dutifully at the back. They listened in wonder to an interminable sermon of how the Almighty had ordered the positions of the high and the low, the one being subject to the other, and heard the dire warnings of what awaited the unrighteous and ungodly, especially the "wicked and slothful servant." They sang gustily as many of the hymns as they could remember, while the church band accompanied on fiddles and recorders, flute, trumpet and a rumbling serpent.

After the service, Robert Roker rose from his pew and walked over to where the Auldfields were standing near the fount, bowing politely in front of Nance and waited to be introduced. Not only did he converse heartily with the family, he waved away his carriage and accompanied them on their way home. Beth had never felt so honoured, being escorted like this, and Zebedee's face showed his humble pride at being the valued retainer of the gentry.

Roker suggested that Nance spend one day a week at the Hall, with himself making up the difference of what she would have earned on the farm. A model of civility, he nevertheless framed his polite requests in such a way they seemed orders that lesser mortals felt obliged to obey. So Nance received her first schooling from the servants at Amberslea Hall. It was there, too, that she used a saddle and bridle for the first time and soon a new rider in male attire was to be seen, racing the grooms around the Hall's spacious parkland.

One day, on an errand for her master at harvest time, she rode up to his homestead, stabled the horse and entered via the 'backus' to find Mistress Harvey unconscious on the parlour floor.

"She's dead, she's dead!" screamed a young maid. Nance bent down and felt her pulse: she was breathing, but only just.

"She's not dead an' she's not a-dyin'," said Nance confidently, then added cautiously, "not wholly, noo how." She turned to the maid. "Help me get her in the chair. Will yew bend yar backs an' help?" she added sharply. Together they hoisted the plump woman into the chair and Nance loosened her clothing, thrusting a hand inside the gown to untie the constricting stays. Then she massaged the woman's wrists and gave instructions for her to be kept upright to aid her breathing. Satisfied for now, she announced she would ride to Ipswich to get the doctor.

She went to the stables, took down a halter and walked out the young Suffolk Punch she had just ridden. At fourteen hands, the colt was already a fine specimen, chestnut in colour with white pasterns, its coat so beautifully groomed that it rippled as though polished. Its ears were cropped and the tail 'bunged' after the modern fashion but a natural forelock brushed the forehead and a black flowing mane sprang from the crest and covered the withers.

Nance fastened the halter, mounted bareback and set off through a landscape of crop-waving fields, grazing herds, ivy-clad pollards and white, red-roofed buildings. It was market-day and the narrow Amberslea Road carried riders with saddlebags and pedestrians with baskets, all filled with vegetables, flowers or fruit. There were large-wheeled carts, carriages and gigs and drovers with cattle, sheep or pigs, all going to Ipswich. She set off at a trot, keeping carefully to the right of the track and sometimes off it, to avoid people and livestock. To guide the horse, she used the commands taught to every Suffolk work-horse, calling "wheesh" to turn right and "camether" for left, speaking firmly yet pleasantly and patted its neck so lovingly that it reciprocated in the only way it knew, by lowering its head until its muzzle touched the chest and moving its quivering cropped ears back and forth.

Soon they abandoned the road and cantered up a lane and onto the heath, across the furze and russet scrubland in the direction of Ipswich. The high-spirited colt could hardly believe its luck. Instead of being yoked to the usual lumbering cart, here it was with a light, well-seated rider it knew well and whose only fault was not going fast enough! In no time it was at the gallop. At one point Nance thought she heard her name called but, leaning as far forward as she dared, she kept her eyes dead ahead for all that mattered was getting to the doctor as quickly as possible. The caller was Squire Roker, himself on horseback.

"Nance, Nance! What's up, I say?"

He touched the horse with his whip and gave chase to what was demonstrably a swifter mount. On and on Nance galloped, keeping her lead. Weary reapers paused in their labours to watch her thunder past and a shepherd, reclining after his nightly vigil, rubbed his eyes and gazed in wonder. As numerous birds shrieked, flapped and took wing, a fowler, angry at first then astonished, relaxed his grip and lowered his useless gun. By now she was approaching the race track and was soon pounding the sacred turf near the Gentlemen's Stand and passing the winning post. As she swept on towards Bishop's Hill, Roker slipped farther behind. Eventually he gave up, drew rein and cursed his luck.

"She'll kill herself. An' Gad blast and sink me, there goes my thousand guineas!"

The spires, towers and lush greens of Ipswich soon lay below in the dell, bordered by the shimmering Orwell to the south, and Nance began to descend the lane leading to St Clement's Church. Letting the horse choose its pace, she merely shifted her weight backwards and let it negotiate the precipitous incline at speed, its soup-plate hooves churning up swirls of dust. The end of the journey was almost at hand and now much of the long, winding street was already dotted with tethered horses, carts and carriages. Crowds of people were making their way on foot towards the market on Corn Hill, some pausing at the Neptune Inn, and hearing the rhythmic thunderclap of hooves and seeing a female rider making no attempt to check her speed they scattered hurriedly, turned and gaped in disbelief.

A girl riding bareback, "crowdin' an' gooin' loike blazes" it was said, her skirts fluttering wide, had never been seen before. As she passed, they followed until the street became filled with eager spectators surging forward. Finally she pull on the halter, cried "Woo-ah! Camether" as they turned into Stepple Street, then "wheesh, wheesh" and "woo, worre, woo-ee!" The colt reared, dropped its head, reared again, took a pace or two forward and halted. Nance sprang down, secured the reins to a post and made for the door of the doctor, George Abbett. The housekeeper appeared and stared at her, capless and covered in dust.

"Mistress Harvey, she got the... vapours!" said Nance, struggling to remember a medical term for a state of collapse.

"Nonsense, child," replied the housekeeper. "Women of your class don't have the vapours!"

"But she be Mr Harvey's wife, ma'am, an' she be wholly sick!"

"Your mistress, you say?" The housekeeper looked at the horse with its reeking flanks, again at the dishevelled rider, and decided the call was indeed urgent. She showed Nance into the parlour where a handsome young gentleman laid aside his newspaper and rose to meet her. Short in stature but with a straight back, he had the ruddy cheeks of a countryman and the sharp, intelligent eye of a scholar. Inclining his head towards her, his voice was soft and kindly.

"How may I be of service?"

Hearing what had occurred, he ordered his gig and sat beside Nance with the colt in tow. The milling throng still packed the street and for the first time she became aware of being the object of their attention; pointing fingers, sidelong glances, the odd snigger and innumerable eyes followed her as they trotted past. Nance kept glancing back to ensure that the precious horse was securely tethered, and only now did she begin to worry whether or not she had done right in taking it. Horses were valuable property. They were solely for the master's work, not for the convenience of servants. Riding on the estate was one thing, but going beyond the gates without permission was something else entirely, tantamount to stealing.

"I'm afeard wha' Mr Harvey ul say fur taakin' the hoss," she confided. "D'yew reckon ul be riled?"

"Of course not," said the doctor. "You've shown great courage and presence of mind. See, we are nearly there and scarcely one hour has elapsed since your mistress was taken ill."

Twenty-five year old George Abbett had an appetite for the finer things in life and the leisure to pursue them. Both doctor and surgeon, whether one suffered from a mild upset, a life-threatening disease, a toothache or was in need of an amputation, he was the man to see. His wealthier patients virtually paid for the practice whilst the less well-to-do contributed what they could; for the very poor there were home visits, treatments and remedies without charge.

A lifelong, enthusiastic horticulturalist, he was also a crack shot and his greatest passion was for shooting game; as this was days into the grouse season, Nance had been lucky to find him at home. According to the season, he was as likely to be found with his fowling-piece at a shooting party, surprising wildfowl on the Orwell or stalking heath and woodland for something to shoot, as in his surgery. Unsurprisingly, his practice suffered and he never quite achieved the reputation and rewards his medical skills merited.

As he listened to Nance's account of her ride, of which he thoroughly approved, and the care she took of her sister Sarah, he formed the opinion that she had an unusual and spirited destiny. He told her that should she ever be in need of a friend she should not hesitate to call on him.

They found Mistress Harvey, who had suffered a fit, somewhat recovered and out of the danger she would have been in had she been left on the floor. He dispensed the necessary medication and, as was normal at the time, applied leeches for bleeding. Having explained to the lady how brave and diligent her young servant had been in bringing help so quickly, he left to call at the Auldfields' cottage. Examining Sarah, he silently concurred with her detectable though unvoiced opinion that she was not much longer for this world.

Nance and her ride to Ipswich became the talk of every parlour, coffee house and wayside inn for weeks to come. The young object of everyone's admiration developed a shyness she had never known, embarrassed by being stared at and pointed out wherever she went. She came to realise, for the first time, that women who rode astride rather than side-saddle were mocked, with a crude suggestion of what it would do to a certain part of their anatomy. Then she became angry. So that was what all the fuss was about, that was why everyone pointed, winked and nudged. More to the point, that was why Squire Roker wanted to exhibit her, as some sort of freak for the amusement of his friends.

From that day on she stopped riding, declaring that she would "ride a hoss noo more, not niver." She remained true to her word. At least, it would be many years before that terrible, fateful day when she had to mount one again.

CHAPTER 2

LOVE AND DEATH

Nance's family decided that a change of scene would be beneficial for her. Accordingly, she was found a place in the dairy of an estate some six miles distant, and saw it as a welcome escape from all the unwanted attention. The only drawback was her being away from Sarah so it was made a condition of service that Nance be allowed to visit her if her condition worsened and the end seemed nigh.

So the day came when Nance left home for the first time. She made her farewells to each one in turn, but the most tender was to Sarah.

"Fare ye well, dearest sis. I'll allus remember yew in my prayers."

"An' fare ye well too, Nance. We've learned yew all we can. It's only fitten yew be a-maaken' yar owen way in life." They embraced and Nance kissed the moist brow of her sister, perhaps for the last time. Then she took up her scrip, tied it to a stick, tossed it over her shoulder and set off to join her new master as a dairymaid.

Sarah was deeply touched by the warmth, affection and devotion shown by her little sister. So much so, she resolved that when her worn-out body was finally cast aside, wherever she found herself and in whatever form, she would by Heaven's grace find a way to repay that love. Inevitably, her physical condition worsened until finally, a year or so later, she took to her bed not expecting to leave it. The time had come for Nance to return home.

It was now Eastertide. Dame Chenery, a family friend, had given birth to another child and Sarah was to have been a godparent. This was no longer possible so Nance was asked to attend the christening in her sister's place. After the simple ceremony, the party repaired to the Chenerys' cottage. The older guests drank their host's health in ale and munched her bread and rusks while the younger ones slipped away to join in with the fiddle's merry jig, dancing and whirling about with stamping feet and grasping hands.

Nance had joined the party late from an errand, entered the dance and spun round to face a handsome, smock-frocked youth. They hadn't met, but she recognised him as Jethro Merryridge, a labourer from the Abbeyfield Farm (and also her secret admirer). Now face to face, his heart beat wildly and his cheeks reddened as kindly eyes looked shyly into hers. He had been standing apart from the jigging couples, but now Nance's enquiring eye and outstretched hand was the invitation he'd hoped for. For her this was simple, honest fun, far removed for once from stern parental looks; but for Jethro it was serious stuff indeed. Beside her for the first time, he felt a strange warmth that rekindled the embers of passion that had smouldered since he first set eyes on her. She had an intoxicating fragrance too!

Fifteen year-old Nance, however, her head full of gaiety and blissfully ignorant of the effect she was having on the boy, jigged ever more vigorously, her hopping feet seemingly more in the air than on the ground. Jethro wished they could dance and dance, but all too soon the fiddler ceased. A flushed Nance promised to return as soon as she had paid her respects to Dame Chenery, unaware of the plaintive, adoring eye that followed her to the cottage door.

At this very moment, Sarah began to experience strange womanly sensations that could only be her sister's. The closeness of their bond and her heightened sensitivity meant that she could feel what Nance was feeling even at a distance. Now there was a deep, stomach-turning glow that could only be the warmth of love. Beside her daughter,

Beth could not help noticing the reaction and wondered what was happening. The answer was simple enough for Sarah, yet incomprehensible to her mother.

"Nance's met the man ul marry!" A moment's reflection and she sank back on the pillow, her inner mind contemplating what the future might hold until, eventually, a knowing smile lit up her haggard face. Whilst she herself would never know a man's love (in this world, at least), her sister would; and she rejoiced in the happiness she foresaw for her.

Beneath Nance's childlike excitement, womanly feelings had indeed been aroused although she was unconscious of their true meaning. She exchanged greetings with Dame Chenery and cradled fondly the family's latest addition. Another guest, a relative of the Chenerys, was Edward Cabern, a waterman who plied the ferry between Harwich, Walton and Langer Fort. With him was his twenty year-old son Robert, an apprentice waterman. Together they had walked the seven or so miles from Felixstowe village. While she was talking, patting the new infant and pulling faces, she noticed Robert staring at her.

"Alawk, tha' be my good fur naun nephew, Rob," said her hostess. "If he ant broken some poor mawther's heart a-riddy, then sure it's not fur want o' tryin'. Watch yarself, maw!" He continued staring, Nance thought to the point of rudeness yet, mildly curious, she smiled back. "Yew've met yar match this time, Rob," muttered the dame as she strode past. He edged his way through the throng towards Nance and, unusually for that humble company, bowed respectfully.

"Do I have the honour of addressing Miss Auldfield?"

She nodded, rose to the occasion and bobbed. "An' yew are?"

"Robert Cabern, at your service."

She was attracted at once to him, the interesting partner of moments before now forgotten. Moreover, she now felt the beat of her heart as Sarah had sensed, but it was responding not to Jethro but to Robert. They fell into conversation, she flattered to be the object of all this male attention, he in awe of the lass whose skill with horses was still the talk of the county. As they exchanged pleasantries, Nance began to feel a growing ardour that went beyond mere attraction, stealing through her every limb with enchanting pleasure. In time this would prove as irresistible as a candle flame to a moth – and just as deadly.

She gazed into his penetrating blue eyes in a face already lightly weathered and sporting a dark, trimmed beard. An apprentice who would sooner be at sea and visiting distant lands, he affected a seaman's dress with his hair in the traditional queue. Like Jethro he was attracted and also empowered, captivated by her ebony locks, rose-red lips and milky-white bosom. When she was jostled and stumbled against him, he felt those ebony locks sensuously brush his cheek whilst Nance, to her own surprise, found herself wishing to be jostled more so as to end up in his arms, her head against that sturdy shoulder.

"Have you always lived in Amberslea?" he asked.

"Since 'bout soo high."

"And you are Master Zebedee's daughter?" She nodded proudly.

"There's none as ploughs a straighter furrow in all Suffolk."

Their pleasantries continued about nothing in particular, though each glance, sigh and silence acquired the eloquence of love that words can never give. Around them all the while, ballads were being sung and old tales retold, strong men arm-wrestled and children chattered and danced by the cottage door. No-one noticed this little head-to-head except a lovelorn Jethro who, with his nose pressed against a clouded windowpane, marked every glance and gesture. That very afternoon the couple were beginning, silently, to consider a permanent union, even though it might be years before they could save enough to furnish a cottage and begin married life. Cabern, more desperate than ever to make his way in the world, now knew that nothing was more important than having Nance at his side permanently.

As the guests departed, he promised to catch up with his father on the walk back to Felixstowe, and accompanied Nance homeward. A devastated Jethro, helpless captive to love, watched them stroll together through the village and disappear from view. The air was pregnant with the promise of spring, hedgerows and overhanging boughs newly green with foliage as rooks swooped and combed the fields for the swelling grain. The honeysuckle and hawthorn were in flower, bees avidly seeking the gooseberry bushes and a first butterfly alighted on the Lady's Smock before dancing along the violet-clustered greensward. Decorum dictated that Nance walk a little apart from Robert, but not so carefully that she couldn't occasionally trip or stumble on the potholed cart-way.

He, of course, lost no opportunity in grasping an arm, steadying her and offering his support.

This longing that she felt for his embrace was something entirely new. Although men had noticed her and been attracted, it was simple affection rather than with any intentions, since she was still little more than a child. Moreover, employers discouraged any followers of their younger servants, so Nance hadn't experienced even a flirtatious male friendship. Her only love had been for family and, above all, for Sarah. The idea of sharing her life with a man was not something she had given any thought. Now here was one who treated her as a grown woman and whose eyes looked directly into hers with a certainty that she alone was the one for him.

For his part, Cabern had been impatient to finish his apprenticeship, dreaming of bigger and better things. But now that he had met Nance, he couldn't help wondering what it would be like to have this exciting, bewitching and adorable lass with him always. As the gathering dusky shadows lengthened, they continued on their unhurried way and watched the last glimmers of day settle on the uplands and lonely heath as the first stars appeared. Only the wan light from a crescent moon guided their final steps to the wicket gate leading to the cottage.

"How is it we've never met?" said Cabern, above the hissing of the guardian geese. "And shall I see you again, Nance?"

"Tha' yew can, if yew's a mind ta," she said coyly. Their hands touched.

"Then right minded I am to call on Nance Auldfield."

He took her hand in his, squeezed it gently and put it to his lips. With their faces almost touching, and keeping hold of her, he leaned forward for a chaste, parting kiss on her cheek but, impulsively, with her free hand she tugged him closer and pressed her lips against his. A thrill shot through them both from head to toe and he returned with an even bolder kiss, then more, while she hung about his neck and nuzzled his cheek. As he held her fast in his broad arms and squeezed firmly, perhaps a tad roughly, her heart raced and her chest heaved. She responded with hot kisses in a spontaneous and breathless, not to say careless, passion.

21

"Well Nance, I'd best be a-going," he murmured reluctantly at long last, releasing his grip. He turned and paused awkwardly, as if uncertain how to leave.

"Yew'll want a light fur yar lantern," she whispered, regaining her breath.

He unhooked it from his belt and handed it to her. Inside the cottage, her parents, having grown anxious about her long absence, watched her take a candle and hold it to the flame in the fire. As she did so, they noticed an expression on her flushed face of pure, innocent joy as the candle flame flickered brighter. She replaced it in the lantern and carried it almost reverently back to the gate. Sarah had heard Nance's return and gone to the dormer window, looking down on the pair together. As Cabern took the lantern from her, both their faces were illumined and for a moment they remained transfixed, spellbound, inches apart in a halo of light. Sarah did not recognise him and felt a growing unease, an intuitive conviction that somehow this was not the man destined for her beloved Nance. Something had gone wrong, very wrong. From that moment, all the happiness she thought she had foreseen for her sister vanished and an ominous cloud hung over the future.

"Haps I really should be going," said Cabern at length.

"Well, if yew dewn't get a-gooin' soon, Robert," she smiled, "yew ont be a-coomin' back!"

"I'll be back!" His reluctant steps began the long journey homeward. Nance's eyes followed as the receding figure grew fainter, turning for a final wave and a blown kiss before rounding a corner.

He returned often whenever work permitted and the old weather-battered cottage beneath the oaks with its low, oak-beam ceiling and stony floor, became a lovers' bower. Another young man, Jethro Merryridge, passed the cottage as often as he could in the hope of glimpsing Nance but, with a sense of irrevocable doom, he saw Cabern entering or leaving instead.

The family took to Cabern as one who was a step or two higher than their station in life, with his promising future as an educated man. Although he had sailed no further than the German Sea, he had been regaled by seamen with yarns about life in foreign parts and, as he retold them, he gave the impression he would soon be seeing them for himself. John, Albert and Mark were impressed to the point of envy and demanded to know more about those strange lands and peoples across the water. For this family who seldom left the village and knew little of life beyond it, Cabern's boyish humour and exuberance passed for wit, his skill in mathematics and navigation seemed like wisdom. The way that he flattered women, especially Nance, being always respectful and diffident to the point of shyness, made him seem sophisticated. He said that he loved her and thought only of her happiness, and it was with such sincerity that no-one, including Nance, doubted him. Except, that is, Sarah.

Her life had been a losing struggle for many weary days. Aware of the dark folk tales about death, such as coffin-shaped cinders shot from the fire and candlewicks curled in her direction suggesting a winding-sheet, she lived each day as though it were her last. No longer awakened by the lark to work in the fields, she felt useless and a burden. Yet she possessed a sharp and growing perception of the way people conducted themselves and whether they meant what they said or not, backed up by unfailing intuition; this made her more than equal by far to those the world deemed 'clever'.

In particular, she noted in Cabern a confidence that bordered on arrogance and a disposition to find easy ways rather than right ways. He would be easily led and, moreover, the outcome of a thing would matter more than the means to achieve it. She saw in him one who was self-centred and too opinionated. That he would act honourably towards Nance and marry her, she had no doubt; but what he might do when her back was turned was altogether another matter. There was something about him that was not quite respectable – and if he were careless with his own reputation, how could he safeguard another's? Unmarried women in this community aspired to domestic service and employers felt that a servant with a sullied reputation reflected adversely on themselves. 'Honest and trustworthy' was a necessary part of a poor servant's references.

Sarah begged her sister to be more cautious and, at least, to insist on a long courtship, which in any case was usual for persons in their walk of life. Nance thought her wrong about him but promised to take care, asking her not to be fearful. Sarah did once manage to speak privately with Cabern, but her warning about the consequences of not taking life more seriously came to nothing. Had he been willing and able to hear, he might have hesitated to involve himself in certain undertakings already in the offing…

In her worsening sickness, more out of the body than within it, and clearly dreaming increasingly of people and places of another world, the hour came that she knew intuitively would be her last. She would have preferred simply to lie back and drift peacefully into a last sleep, but struggled to stay awake until all the family had been summoned. A blackbird pecked ominously at the windowpane while chattering lapwings, squabbling geese and the joyful cries of children were mocking reminders of life, when all that awaited her was death. Only when everybody was present did she finally release her tenuous hold.

"Oh Nance, Nance, hold me… I feel kinda dizzyfied."

"Yew'll get better," was the unconvincing reply.

"Noo, I'm a-gooin'."

Nance put an arm round her, kissed her cheek and moistened it with tears. "Dewn't be afeared!" she sobbed. "Yew's gooin' ta a better place. Loike the parson says, yew's a-gooin' ta live in God's garden."

The family sighed, wrung their hands and wept as Zebedee recited the Twenty-Third Psalm. Sarah beckoned her sister closer and whispered a final warning about Cabern. Then, seized with a sudden convulsion, she looked fearfully and deeply into Nance's eyes, as though able to see into her soul and read some terrible destiny. A moment before, she had been relaxed and calmly awaiting death's approach but now her face showed only dread, not for herself but for her beloved Nance. To the family, however, this meant only that the Grim Reaper was come, as in the Bible, to 'sever the silver cord and shatter the golden bowl'.

She rose slightly and made an effort to speak, but it was too much. Her muscles relaxed as her spirit prepared to depart and a pall of darkness descended until she could scarcely see those about her. Then

24

a funnel of light appeared, like a sunbeam through darkening cloud, and at the foot of the bed a stranger's smiling face beckoned.

"Nance... who be tha' thar man?" she whispered.

Nance saw no-one but just spoke words that came to mind.

"Why, tha' be one o' God's angels, come ta taak yew ta live with 'em."

"Fare ye well, then," gasped Sarah.

In a moment or so, her eyes stared blankly as the life force ebbed from the body. Nance closed the lids, clung to her sister, kissed her and buried her head in Sarah's chest. The family stood or knelt with bowed heads in silent prayer and heartfelt grief.

Sarah felt herself floating as though in a dream, then rising and being able to stand. The kindly-looking stranger beckoned her toward him and took her hand. As she glanced back, she saw herself cradled in her beloved sister's arms and everyone around overcome with sorrow. It saddened her too, but the stranger gently led her away. In his eyes was the sort of look that suggested he knew all about her, even though she knew nothing of him. She noticed, too, that what had seemed a funnel of light was an aura about this being. In workaday clothing, he had the appearance of an older man yet with the vitality of one far younger.

Silently and slowly, they entered a cavernous gloom pierced by a distant though ever-growing light that resembled a wan moon when night covers the Earth and robs everything of colour. Onward they glided through increasing brightness to emerge at last into the full light of day. Before them a pathway wound through a wavy meadow like the ones of her visions, rich in flora of translucent colours with mellifluous scents. Above them, somehow familiar feathery, white and pinkish clouds floated in an azure sky and a benevolent light.

The stranger led her toward a temple-like building over which a rainbow floated, predominately of blue, indigo and violet. The polished marble columns of the portico reflected the blue hues into the vestibule, painting it in living colour contrasting with Sarah's sickly, pallid features and dull aura. She hesitated on the threshold but the man gave her hand a reassuring squeeze.

"It's all right, Miss. Please goo in. Yew's expected."

Still she hesitated, her eyes questioning: was he an angel as Nance had said?

"Law bless yew, I'm noo angel, Miss," he chuckled. "I lived in Amberslea too, though many years afore yar toime. I heard yew wuz a-coomin', an' as yew wuz on yar owen, loike, I asked ta be the one ta coom an' meet yew. Haa'ter all, us Suffolk Puds should stick together, eh?"

"Thus wholly kind." She managed a smile, despite the dreadful tiredness that was overwhelming her. She could have slept for a century there and then.

"Say noo more fur now, Miss," he said, kindly. "Us has a place a-riddy prepared fur yew." He led her through a pastel atrium to a room with a couch covered in the softest linen, with a perfume of rose petals and lavender. As she sank into a downy cushion, sweet and longed-for sleep overcame her at last.

Cabern too mourned Sarah or, rather, assumed the mask of mourning that convention demanded. In truth his only real regret was the temporary halt it brought to his courtship of Nance. However, this gave him the space to take up an invitation to meet with one Captain Diamond who might, he was told, change his life for the better. Exactly what the wealthy merchant was offering, he was unsure of; but he would not refuse, given the promise that it would be much to his advantage. There were warnings from his father about the man's reputation for smuggling, but they went unheeded by the ambitious and spirited young man.

A summer's evening found him at Lower Walton, south-west of Felixstowe village, walking to a meeting with Diamond at the Ferry House Inn.

The inn stood in fields just north of Langer Marshes and, apart from the occasional cart or carriage, the only sounds were of screeching gulls wheeling above and cackling marsh fowl. Its crooked, sagging and many-gabled roof, the irregular wood and mortar walls and sunken windows all showed its age. Within, whitewashed walls and sanded stone floor, neatly hung displays of pewter and clay pipes, a caged canary and blackened oil paintings all gave the appearance of a respectable place. In the parlour at day's end, any seaman or labourer, clerk or servant, could sit on a bench near the welcoming hearth and enjoy good company. The ale was dispensed by a plump young maid in a mobcap, bunched-up overskirt and décolleté gown that begged to be pressed.

As Cabern approached the low-beamed door, the orange glow of the late sun reflected in the window lattice, painting the ancient hostelry with a smile of welcome. Curiously though, he noticed a lantern being waved slowly from side to side at an upper window. Wondering if it were a signal for someone further along the lane, he glanced in both directions but saw nothing except a distant glow in the field opposite that also moved as though in reply before vanishing. He shrugged and stepped inside and, being expected, was shown into a private parlour, its door unlocked for him. Lit by a silver candelabrum and furnished with armchairs and a linen-covered table, the room was reserved, it seemed, for select company.

The gentleman seated opposite wore a plain coat and tight-fitting breeches stuffed into stout riding boots, showing him to be a man of action. Still in his early thirties, with dark curly hair and bushy side-whiskers, Diamond's face was friendly enough, with keen eyes; but that expression could easily become the opposite, as Cabern would discover. The man's authority was confirmed by the evident deference of his companion, clearly a seaman, whose calculating looks and slightly menacing presence marked him out as an officer of sorts, if not a captain himself. Both had the quiet confidence of men who knew that what they ordered could be enforced, if not by threats or beatings then by something more permanent.

Diamond was indeed a captain but one who spent more time on land than at sea. He owned a number of ships that carried every type of cargo, mostly between northern Europe and English ports. Most of this trade was legitimate and earned him a reputation for reliability and honest dealing; yet his ships also carried other cargos that paid more handsomely, being duty-free. Cabern had come to Diamond's attention as someone who could be an asset to the business, being an apprenticed waterman who knew the coast and tides. He was respectable and had a father who both worked for the government and was, reputedly, the most skilled pilot of the coastal waters. Robert was also known to be ambitious and discontent with his present situation. As he entered the secluded parlour, the captain rose from his seat and greeted him not so much as an apprentice as an experienced seaman, beaming heartily and seizing his hand.

"Welcome, me lad!"

This surprised the young man who had intended the customary bow, but now instead remained upright and merely inclined his head as he shook hands.

"Your servant, sir."

"An' a good and trusty one too, by all accounts. An' one who, if I reckon aright, is minded to be a master."

"You think too highly of me, Captain, sir. I'm plain Robert Cabern, son of Master Edward Cabern, waterman and pilot. I have yet to make my way in the world."

Diamond's outward show of admiration and respect concealed a thoughtful and hidden motive.

"Edward Cabern! A finer pilot with a truer heart ne'er feathered an oar. I'll wager he can still pull a match with any man!" He gestured towards his companion. "Cabern, meet Mr Rackhem, *Kathy O*'s first mate."

This time it was Cabern who extended the hand first. Mad Jack Rackhem took it but eyed him closely, weighing him up before arriving at any favourable opinion. A smile even flickered over the tanned, leathern face.

"Jack Rackhem, at your service," he said with an abrasive accent that was not local, perhaps of Essex or London.

Diamond motioned them to be seated and at that moment the door opened as the maid entered with three brandy goblets on a tray balanced delicately above her shoulder. With a flourish she swept it down before them, leaning forward in a way that made her ample cleavage even more prominent. Diamond grinned, waited until she had left and closed the door.

"Cabern, I'm a blunt man and I'll come to the point. How'd you like to work for me as *Kathy O*'s acting cap'n? I carry all cargoes and pay well. Every merchant from Cornwall to north Britain knows me.

Why, a few voyages and you'll have enough profit for a cottage of your own and a nest egg – enough to marry that lass I hear you're a-courtin', if you've a mind to."

"I'll think on't, sir."

"And that's only the beginning. You carry an extra cargo for me, a little free trade, so to speak, and as cap'n you can carry your own goods as well. As long as you mind my interests, you're at liberty to pursue yours."

"Free trade?" Robert inquired naïvely, still wondering if he had actually heard the word 'captain'. Diamond dropped his voice.

"Oh, just a little brandy for the parson, tea and lace for the ladies and the like."

"You mean moonshine?"

"An' here am I thinking all along you're a gentleman who understands these matters," said Diamond, looking genuinely surprised and hurt. "What's the harm in a little free tradin'?"

"Well, I don't rightly know."

"The gentry and esquires that live so much better than the rest of us – do you really think they're that scrupulous? Why, there's precious few as would object to a barrel left agin the stable door in return for a small favour, such as borrowing a horse for the night, provided he didn't have to stick his own neck out. Then there's the squire's lady with her fine silks an' gloves, that'd cost a pretty penny if 'twas all bought regular. An' there's even a parson I know, not twenty mile hence, for whom Smith the smuggler is almost as regular a caller as Jones the baker, even if 'tis at the witchin' hour."

How long Sarah's sleep lasted, she couldn't tell. Eventually, she awoke more refreshed and rested than ever, with dim recollections of angelic beings beside her. In place of her old clothing, a simple white robe now covered her, tied with a cord. The man who had led her here reappeared, took her by the hand and they entered the pastel-blue atrium, walked its length and paused beneath a colonnade overlooking a garden. It was far beyond anything even the visionary Sarah had dreamed of. Everywhere, everything pulsated with vibrant colours while a central fountain poured crystalline waters into a canal that irrigated the floral borders and encircled the garden. Beyond this were paved terraces ringed with oaks, their wreathed branches overhanging in a canopy of shade. Birds perched in them and chorused sweetly or swooped through the blossom. There were people, too, strolling along the mossy pathways, reclining in shady arbours or sprinkling their faces with droplets from the fountain.

In the middle distance rose mountains, their peaks emerging through silvery clouds that showered a soft, light rain. Pendant terraces of shaggy boulders supported serpentine trees while tapestries of flowers covered ledge and slope or overhung precipices. Light blue rills undulated through crevices and gullies, feeding vaporous waterfalls that emptied gently into the fountain that watered the garden. Between the mountains there were valleys and cottage-dotted hillsides, lakes, woodlands and innumerable meadows, far into a distance with no horizon. The man spoke, although Sarah heard him within her mind.

"Is it not bootaful?" he asked. She could only smile agreement in silent wonder. "I wuz head gardener at the Big House in the owd admiral's time."

"Yew mean Admiral Vernon?" He nodded.

"I lived for tha' garden. Niver wanted ta dew nothin' else."

"An' yew's from Amberslea too?"

He nodded. "Jed's my name."

"Not Ole Jed Winterbottom?"

"The very same."

"My pa spoke o' yew. Yew's still talked about in the village."

"Why, Lor bless 'em, I didn't think as any'd remember." He drew back his powerful shoulders and surveyed the garden with loving pride. "Yes, I wuz head gardener. Still am."

"Yew are?"

"When I came over, the owd admiral met me an' put in a word for me. Now I'm gardener here. Come along, Miss. I'll show yew round paradise." Together they ambled along one of the mossy pathways, their steps releasing clouds of herbal scent, and she watched him cast a fond though not uncritical eye over the borders.

"It's all soo perfick!" was all she managed to utter and was surprised to see him shake his head wistfully.

"Not soo! Yew see tha' owd tree fudder along the path?" She nodded. "It's grown soo big, it's fare obscurin' the prospect. Us ul have ta move it."

"Yew move trees?"

"Not on my owen!" He laughed. "I have ta get permission from the master an' have help." They continued on their way. Now and then he stopped to finger a flower that especially caught his eye.

"Can I pick one?"

Jed was shocked and silent for a moment, then shook his head.

"Lor bless yew, noo, Miss. We dussent dew tha' har. We just dussent!" They continued walking. At length he paused beside a burgeoning rosebush, its petals soft and dewy. Beneath it, all but dancing, were the crimson specks of the Shepherd's Sundial.

"If yew wuz ta gather up the most bootaful blooms of Earth," he observed, pointing at the flowers, "an' cover 'em wi' gowd and set in 'um the most costly gems, there's none as could rival the humblest flower in God's garden. Some Earth folks get a glimpse of our world while still in the body – I believe yew did – but none's niver allowed har."

"Why soo?"

He stood for a moment, sage and thoughtful.

"'Cos none'd iver want ta leave."

How long she stood there, gazing about her and lost in rapture, she knew not. Tellingly, however, time for her family was passing all too quickly. For Zebedee, the strain of constant toil began to tell, called to the plough at too early an age his health was damaged beyond repair. The younger brothers took on more of the ploughing, whilst Beth too was of an age when a life of travail and subsistence living had also taken its toll.

Sarah's reverie ended only when Jed gently informed her that a home and garden of her own awaited her. Surprised, she followed him across a meadow populated with charming cottages like those of her earthly visions. One of them attracted her so much it might have been made for her; but, of course, such an idyllic little cot was far beyond the expectation of anyone in her lowly station. Nevertheless, it was to that very wicket gate beneath a spreading apple tree that Jed guided her. Lavender tumbled over the stony pathway and hollyhocks towered above the picket fence, whilst around the door and windows climbed roses. From the tree, a blackbird piped its greeting.

"Well, aren't yew a-gooin' in?" said Jed, opening the gate and indicating the garden in which he himself had taken a loving hand.

"It cont not be fur me!" she cried.

"There's noo mistake, Miss. Pleased wi' it?" Her face positively sparkled.

"I'm wholly spiflicated! Its soo wannerful! But Lawk, I cont niver afford it."

"Then why dewn't yew axe the man?" Jed chuckled.

"What man?"

A tall figure in a brown monkish robe appeared beside them. Although mature and authoritative well beyond youth, he showed no signs of ageing. As he watched her blink and contemplate the beautiful haven, his smile grew broader and he cast a fatherly, tender eye on her that seemed to know all about her.

"I assure you, Miss Auldfield," he said with a slight bow, "every brick, board and flower is yours. It is yours because you have earned it."

She was dumbstruck. No one had ever treated her with such deference. It just could not be true! Even Jed's reassuring smile as he took his leave could not convince her. Still puzzled, yet embarrassed at being so absorbed in thought as to forget her place, she bobbed and stood with head bowed. He continued addressing her, not as a superior but more as a father would talk to a beloved daughter.

"You have earned it with everything you have ever thought, said and done. Everything has gone into the making of your new home. Everywhere you look, you will find a reflection of you – not perfect, but then none of us is. Some parts could be smoother while others are rigid when they should naturally curve, because they have been forced. Others seem to stand apart instead of blending in with the whole. You will notice there are even weeds in the garden, which represent your less careful thoughts. When you think more positively they will be transformed into flowers. Indeed, the very building will change with the way you think." Again she shook her head in disbelief.

"I still reckon thus har coterage the best I iver did see."

"I will leave you now to settle in. If you need me, just think of me and I will come to you. My name is John."

"Yew's soo very kind." She added nothing, but a further question was in her mind.

"You wonder who I am? I have watched over you since your birth and I have walked by your side. Whenever I could guide your steps aright, I did. I tried to lessen your sufferings too where possible, but I could not interfere in the life that – well, as you will come to understand – you chose for yourself. I am here to help in any way you need and I can still guide you, but I cannot live your life for you, any more than I could on Earth. So, now enjoy your new home. It is yours. You have earned it."

CHAPTER 3

MOONSHINE AND LIES

When the creeping shadows and fading light signalled an end to the working day, Nance was in the habit of placing a posy of wild flowers on Sarah's grave. As the churchyard yews merged with the gathering gloom and smoke curled from a dozen cottage chimneys, candle light gleaming in as many windows, she knelt solemnly with her tribute. She could also not shake off a certain foreboding, for when her sister's body had been laid out for burial it was still supple, believed to be a sign of another family death before long.

As she knelt there one late evening, two men arrived with a lantern and spades. Unaware of her presence, they commenced digging several yards away. She could not see them clearly in the darkness, but heard their voices and recognised that of her brother John. Encouraged to see the world for himself by Cabern's tales of foreign lands and peoples – albeit at second and third hand – but having no inclination for the sea, he had considered enlisting in the army. Without any formal education, he was taking elementary lessons from one of the few locals who could read, write and add up, the parish sexton; being unable to pay for this tuition, he helped out with the grave digging. Ole Nick, as he was known, was a cheery soul whose years of grave digging had made him quite philosophical.

"How fares it with Ole Zeb, bor?" he asked. "Still got the nasty owd tizzick?"

"'Em's fare grumpy an' proper poorly," replied John. "'Em's laid up with the rheumatics."

Nick shook his head sadly. Nance watched as, silhouetted against the setting sun, he lifted a few clods of earth on his spade and offered them to John for inspection.

"Tha' be the only cure fur the owd screws," he declared authoritatively, "graveyard mould!"

An owl hooted, angry at having her silent vigil disturbed, and a nearby guard dog bayed a warning as the men resumed the task of preparing the last resting place for a gentleman of the cloth.

"Why," asked John, "do us bury a parson arse about face?"

"Soo as on Judgement Day, when all arise, ul be a-facin' his flock."

"But this one's in amongst 'um," objected John. "'Ul have his back ta half of 'um!" The other stopped digging, rested on his spade and looked at him reprovingly.

"Dewn't yew taak the roise out of I, young man!"

They resumed digging. Nance, still hidden and not wishing to be thought eavesdropping, stayed motionless and silent. John became even more thoughtful.

"Dew yew reckon thar's any har as ul – well, yew know, resurrect?"

The older man, his face now visible by the lantern's gleam, shook his head.

"There's not none of 'um coomin' back. Haa'ter a few years, I smashes 'um up good an' proper – the pauper plots tha' is. Has ta, ta make room." His words fell as heavily on Nance's ears as a blow from his spade. How could anyone be so heartless? Her poor dead sister had been laid there to rest, not to be dug up in a few years, her gentle body broken into pieces. Oh, how wicked, so very wicked! What sort of a world was it, where not even the dead were left in peace? The tears welled up and stained her cheeks as noiselessly she stole away. But even Nick seemed to think the conversation a mite gloomy, for as she departed she heard him cheering up John with his graveyard humour.

"Wha' be the difference 'twixt a washerwoman an' a sexton?" John did not know.

The old boy chuckled. "The washerwoman stiffens the collars an' the sexton collars the stiffens!"

"But what if—?" began Cabern.

"You're caught?" anticipated Diamond. "Bless you lad, whose goin' to peach on you? That fine gentleman you're obliging, or his good lady? If they did, d'you think I don't have enough on both to ensure they'd be up afore the beak as well? Or the Justice's clerk with his ounces of backy? Or the shopkeeper with his tea? Or the fisherman who landed the stuff, the post boy who ran it and the farmhand who hid it? An' if ever you did come afore a jury, d'you think there could be found in the county twelve good men and true who'd never been involved in free trade themselves?"

"But there're those as would say it's agin the law." A sound escaped Rackhem's lips which his hastily raised hand managed to disguise as a cough. The captain, however, was a more patient man.

"The great an' good who rule this land – what do they impose taxes for? For the likes of honest working folk, like that lass o' yours an' her kinfolk? To provide 'em with the necessaries in times of need? That father of yours, for instance, as honest an' hard workin' a government man as ever plied the Ipswich water. Supposin', God forbid, he took ill an' couldn't work, an' were left wi' nothing but a rag o' canvas to weather out his days? Would there be ought for him but parish relief? Ay, an' that paid grudgingly. And is there ought in the way of a pension for any of the lower orders, besides the workhouse? Well, what are taxes for, if not for the likes of us." That was not a question.

"Government says," Cabern observed thoughtfully, "we might have to fight the French again soon."

The captain held up his goblet to the candelabrum and warmed it. Then he sipped it, savouring the taste.

"By government, d'you mean that corrupt bastion of wealth and privilege – Farmer George and his sycophantic friends – gentlemen amateurs the lot of 'em, whose ineptitude and stupidity just lost us half the empire?"

Cabern was taken aback by the sudden change in tone. "You mean the American colonies? But what about India and the rest? The French still mean to take it from us, if they can."

"We are not at war with France."

"Government declares they might become a serious threat again soon," Cabern protested.

"That's only to prepare us for a war they've already decided on." He leaned forward and spoke in earnest. "I'll tell you a thing or two about the French, lad, and their warmongering monarch. There's bloody revolution afoot, mark my words. A few years or so, an' the French will rise up and do the job for us."

"But if we're threatened, we must fight for our country's sake."

"Let the patriots have their war." Diamond's tone was contemptuous. "I fight with no man that doesn't threaten me. I work only for profit and consider no man my enemy that doesn't regard me as such. If he does, then I play the very devil. Otherwise, blood is an unnecessary expense."

A glance at the young man's indignant face, however, made him realise that politics was losing the argument. He drained his glass and motioned to Rackhem who rang a bell to summon the maid. Quietly, he asked for more brandy yet in a way that conveyed a different, subtle order. Her raised eyebrows and slight nod showed that she understood. As she whirled around, she caught Cabern's eye and brushed him with the hem of her raised skirt, confident his gaze would follow her to the door. Diamond relaxed and grinned again, looked into his empty glass and tried a different tack.

"Old England's the best place to be anywhere on Earth, but you must mind your own interests. Nobody's goin' to do it for you. It's up to you to provide for yourself and that young lady... may I say, the future Mrs Cabern?"

"Ay, you may, Cap'n, if she'll have me."

"Then there you are lad, there you have it!" he declared, banging his fist on the table. "An' will you marry her on a 'prentice's wage, an' navigate blindly through the shoals of penury? Or will you plot a different course altogether an' stand arm in arm afore the parson as Captain and Mrs Cabern?"

The reply was a moment or two in coming. "Cabern the smuggler? Well, I dunno."

"Nay, lad! Cabern the wealthy merchant captain, dealing in the finest tea and liquor for gentlemen and ladies of quality." With Cabern still appearing undecided, there came a sharp, double rap on the parlour door. "Happen I was wrong," declared Diamond, standing up. "I thought you a man of spirit and enterprise. Come along, Mr Rackhem, I see we're wasting our time. Good day, Master Cabern."

"Wait! Let me think on't."

"Good day!" was the curt yet still civil reply.

Cabern was left alone in the parlour but with the door open. As he watched the captain and first mate walk away it was apparent, by the unusual silence and the way the locals, mostly seamen, were suddenly grouped in alarm by a window, that something untoward was happening. From outside came a hammering on the hastily bolted front door. Diamond paused as Rackhem peered through the window.

"What the devil is it, Mr Rackhem?"

"Press-gang, Cap'n!"

In the dim light beyond the window, seamen could be seen wielding clubs, at their head a naval lieutenant with a cutlass hanging at his belt. Their mission was to take men for His Majesty's ships, by force if necessary. In practice that meant anyone, seaman and landsman alike, any able-bodied man of the labouring classes between eighteen and fifty-five whom they might clap in irons, especially after dark.

"How d'you fancy another spell aboard a man-o-war?" cried one customer despairingly.

"My liberty pass is still good," said another confidently, feeling in his pockets. "But hold on, damn me if I don't 'ave it with me!"

"What about my wife an' child?" declared a third. "Who'll provide for them? It be a cruel law as'd drive a pregnant woman an' child to poverty." The door began to succumb to the kicks rained upon it.

"They're on the breakers already! Haps they'll take pity on us?"

"Pity's not among the articles of the press-gang."

Now, Cabern's trade was exempt but that was no use without the written pass – and that was back in Felixstowe. Without it he would more than qualify for service. He thought quickly and, as Diamond and Rackhem prepared to leave, stepped forward.

"May I have a word with you, Cap'n… sir? I've thought on your offer an' happen I was wrong."

A glow came to Diamond's eyes. "Is it a bargain then?"

"My hand on it," said Cabern with a purposeful look. The two men faced each other squarely. "I mean, ay, ay, Cap'n."

Diamond spat on his hand, struck it with the other, extended it and grabbed Cabern's.

"So you are a man of spirit, I knew it. What did I tell you, Mr Rackhem? Come on, then." he said, quickly retracing his steps. "You too, Cap'n Cabern. It's time we stashed the patter, cut cables and were away."

"But the press-gang?"

"That's a fate for lesser mortals, not captains."

As other men dashed past them, heading for the rear of the inn, Cabern followed the two men through one door and then another into a tiny room with a revolving bookcase, on the other side of which was a descending spiral staircase. Outside, they could hear the clatter of boots on the stone floor and the cry of, "Halt, in the King's name!" The few who made it to the rear of the building only found it guarded by more sailors and Cabern heard the sounds of scuffles and blows, punctuated by expletives.

Rackhem took a lantern and led the way down the staircase whilst Diamond closed the bookcase door behind them and secured it. They descended into a low vaulted cellar where startled rats scurried and dashed into the shadows. Rackhem walked to the far wall and put his shoulder against it. A section of it moved and interlocking bricks parted as it turned, revealing a passage beyond. Illumined by the glimmering lantern that threw grotesque shadows across walls and ceiling, they eventually arrived at what seemed a dead end, beyond which flowing water could be heard. As Cabern's eyes grew accustomed to the gloom, he could see rows of locked cages, piled high with casks and boxes. Hidden behind these was a reinforced, iron-studded door which Rackhem opened with a key.

They stepped through into an old, echoing drainage tunnel, cut into the chalk, along which water dripped into a running stream a few inches deep. After some quarter of a mile they reached a barred grating through which Cabern saw winking pinpricks of light, the floating beacons of Harwich harbour across the estuary. Roughly hewn steps led up to a second reinforced door for which Rackhem again produced a key. Here was another cellar like the earlier one, with more locked cages. Another ascent through a trap door and they were in the basement of the Ferry House.

Had there been any doubts in Robert Cabern's mind about Diamond's operations, these were now wholly dispelled. The three men retired to a room and for the next hour or so the young man was acquainted with the tasks he was expected to perform as *Kathy O*'s acting captain. Pointedly, little was said about ports and harbours, a lot about bays, coves and rivers. The talk was friendly enough – there was no going back now – and included a supper of roast beef and ale provided by the ferryman's wife.

When Cabern finally left, with a hearty handshake from Diamond, he had a new confidence. Not only had he found an employer but also, he believed, a fatherly comrade who would stand by him and had his welfare at heart. Had he been as perceptive of human nature as Sarah, he might have been more wary.

True, he could navigate and he knew the coast, but he was not an experienced seaman let alone fit to captain. But then Rackhem, as he would quickly learn, was the real captain. The true reason behind the offer was that in Diamond's smuggling operations it was the captain who handled negotiations, arranged deliveries and extracted payments. So whilst the crew mingled anonymously with other seamen and dispersed to safe cottages, the captain's name became known throughout the land. Soon, every magistrate and riding officer would be on the lookout for Rob Cabern…

After carefully checking that the press-gang was nowhere about, he bent his way home by a circuitous route across the marshes. Glancing across the estuary from higher ground he saw, with a sudden thrill, a

ship in the moonlight. It was no merchantman, but had the unmistakable raised stern of a sleek, tiered, three-masted, cannon-carrying
Cornish lugger, built for speed. His first command!

Sarah stood awhile looking at cottage and garden and trying to comprehend everything the man had said. When she turned round she
saw a young, good-looking woman trailing a pleated silk gown and
beaming joyfully beneath a huge hat. She seemed somehow familiar
and the woman greeted her as an old friend. Sarah smiled back but
was still puzzled.

"Will this jog your memory?" said the woman, bending her back,
hunching her shoulders and contorting her face until she resembled a
sick, elderly woman, racked with pain and about to breathe her last.

"Widow Perkins!" gasped Sarah.

"The very same, only I'm a widow no longer… at least, I'm with my
husband again. I don't know if we'll stay together, mind. Come on, give
me a hug!" The blackbird in the tree warbled another greeting, whilst
thrushes alighting on the cottage roof and a passing linnet joined in.
A playful collie that on Earth would have been chasing the lambs in
a nearby field, played happily at the women's feet. A delighted Sarah
thought the other's hug would surely crush her, then the woman hung
on her neck and planted a kiss on her cheek.

"You don't know how good it is to see you, Sarah! When I heard
you were coming, I had to be the first to welcome you." She stepped
back, young and attractive as she had been a moment earlier. "And now
we're neighbours again. Well, what do you think of your new home?"

"I dewn't know. I've not seen inside yet."

"Lord bless you, here am I chatting away when you'll want some
time to yourself. We'll have a good gossip later, then. I live just over
there." She indicated a white cottage in a flowery glade beneath a beech.
"Do let me know when you're settled in."

"Haps 'amara then?"

"Why yes, except there's no tomorrows now."

"Soon then, Widow Perkins?" The woman nodded.

"I'm Mollie now. An' remember, I'm a widow no longer." She grinned, patted Sarah's arm and strode across the meadow, pausing only to turn and wave to an overjoyed yet perplexed Sarah. What had happened to Mollie's voice, saying "tomorrow" instead of "amara"? What was wrong with plain English? And why so ladylike with that enormous hat? No doubt time would tell…

It was such a relief not having to lie on a hard bed when feeling ill, or to toil from dawn till dusk when well. She still needed to rest awhile, her mind adjusting to such changes, and there were still vivid dreams of her old life now, especially of when she was young. But then she desired nothing more than to explore the surrounding meadows and enjoy her beautiful little garden and the company of her old friend and neighbour. Indeed, there were many other neighbours who she discovered, strangely enough, were very much like her. It was as though they were all of like mind.

Inside the cottage, as John had said, every stick of furniture and every ornament reflected something of herself. Even the pictures on the walls, added thoughtfully by him, showed the rural scenes she had always known. And before long she discovered that she no longer needed rest. Moreover, although she picked apples from the tree to eat, she realised that she wasn't hungry. The strangest thing of all was that there seemed to be no passage of time – no early morning rising, no sunset at the end of a day, in fact no sun that she could see. 'Now' was both yesterday and tomorrow – how could time be measured?

There was one thing, however, that spoiled her otherwise contented existence and that was the ever-present thoughts of her poor sister Nance and the terrible fate Sarah felt sure awaited her. She determined to ask John if 'something could be done' for her.

Her fears proved real enough. One morning, while it was yet dark and the family were asleep, a horse and cart, the hooves and wheels bound with sacking, trundled silently along the lane and halted at their cottage gate. The driver alighted, lifted out a large scrip and carried it up the path to place it by the door. An anxious Nance, awakened by the honking geese, threw a shawl about her shoulders and hurried down-stairs to open the door just as the man was walking back to the cart. The stranger had hoped to depart unnoticed but introduced himself as a friend of Captain Cabern who had asked him to leave some goods. No, he could not stop to explain. At the mention of Cabern's name, an inner heat ran up Nance's spine like a burning flame, setting her heart ablaze. She had received no word of him for some weeks.

"Cabern, d'yew say?" she gasped. "Yew have news o' Rob Cabern?"

"Don't you be a-troublin' yourself over him, Miss," he replied, head down. "He's in good health and business couldn't be better. That's why he asked me to leave you a small present, as a token of his affection, so to speak. Well, I has to be orf."

"Thank yew, Mister—" began Nance, but the stranger was already mounting his cart. He attempted a friendly, awkward wave; but a shaft of moonlight revealed a crooked smile and sharp, unfriendly eyes. Nance would come to know and dread him as Cabern's henchman, Mad Jack Rackhem.

That morning 'brefkust' was delayed while the family gathered round the curious scrip that Nance had placed on the table. A signed note was tied to the handle and John, who by now had enough learning to read the alphabet, spelled out the letters.

"R – O – B… Rob," he announced.

"Rob Cabern!" breathed Nance quietly.

"Well, aren't yew a-gooin' ta open it, darter?" asked her father.

"Haps I might, Pa."

She unfastened the clasp and took out a number of items, care-fully wrapped in waxed paper. As each wrapping was removed there were sighs and gasps. There were numerous bottles containing brown or yellow liquids, tobacco, lace, silk handkerchiefs, gloves and the prized commodity of tea. It would be some days before all the bottles were identified, and the family had no idea what value to put on them. It seemed unlikely that this odd assortment had been obtained honestly.

"Who does Rob work fur, Nance?" said John. "Cap'n Diamond?"

"I hear tell," said Zebedee, "as how tha' thar Diamond has many friends, some of 'em gen'l'men an' magistrates."

"True," sighed Nance, as the realisation of what Cabern was really doing dawned, "but it's not them as ul swing if Rob be caught."

"Diamond's a respected merchant," Zebedee reasoned. "Eawer Rob won't be scaling cliffs or fighting battles with riding officers. Some of 'um are in on it 'umselves anyhow! Noo, he's a merchant cap'n now, just doin' a bit o' free tradin'."

"Yes," she added, 'in the shadow of the gibbet, more 'n likely."

"Time wuz," her father reminisced, "whole villages slept by day 'cos they'd been a-runnin' and hidin' the stuff by night. The owd ridin' officers seldom got a look in. There wuz even parsons in on it," he continued. "They'd hide the stuff in church vaults an' belfries, called it parish relief."

"Tha' wuz in times agon, Pa. Yew know the penalty now, even fur assemblin' ta take part in a run." She indicated a stretched neck.

"Then again," John objected, "it's agin the law, but not natural law. There's many had been honest an' upright citizens, had not the law made tha' a crime nature niver meant ta be."

"It's noo use talkin' 'bout times agon," replied Nance in despair. "It be a vicious business now an' well yew know it. Threats, beatin's, murder even. Pardons are handed out ta them as turns King's Evidence an' rewards paid ta informers." She paused and looked at them sternly one by one. "Besides, how's the government ta raise money? Us dewn't pay noo taxes loike the gentry. Tea be five shillin' a pound an' we can dew without."

"Tea's just pennies, if yew know the right person," laughed Mark. "An' this be wholly free! Trouble with yew is, Nance, yew's too bloody good."

Nance swept the articles into the scrip declaring that she wanted nothing to do with moonshine, so the family hid them. Silence did not come naturally, however, and it was not long before their close friends, the Chenerys, knew the secret since the families visited each other's cottage. The Chenerys kept a small shop in one of their rooms offering the necessities of everyday life. They reasoned that what the Auldfields did not want might appeal, at a suitable price, to others, albeit below the counter; this way, the Auldfields and a reluctant Nance also profited from the silks, lace and spirits.

Soon Nance found a place as servant-of-all-work at Abbeyfield Farm, and when an incredulous Jethro Merryridge laid eyes on her he watched her longingly whenever she was about. A girl no longer, she was growing into an attractive woman with sparkling dark eyes and sun-kissed cheeks, now quite tall with a well-proportioned figure. She was lively and energetic, wore the low-cut gowns then fashionable that emphasised her cleavage, and had the air and agility of a healthy country woman. Her polite and modest demeanour was a legacy of her time at Amberslea Hall. However hopeless the matter, she was even more irresistible to her love-sick and still secret admirer.

Jethro was the educated son of Josiah Merryridge and the younger brother of Garrow, a riding officer. He had taken the lowly job of labourer to learn as much as he could about farming, with a view to owning a farm himself one day. Now he imagined that Nance's employment at Abbeyfield Farm was proof of their destiny; taking fresh heart, he contrived to be always on hand to open a gate for her or shoulder her burden.

One summer afternoon he overheard Mrs Knoller sending Nance on an errand to another farm on the outskirts of Ipswich. This could be his chance to speak with her without others' prying eyes. He calculated how long it would take her to walk there and back, so late evening found him in the woods bordering Piper's Vale, gathering sticks for lops. Seeing her approach from a distance, as she walked beside the Orwell with a basket of freshly-picked produce, he emerged from the trees, for all the world a woodcutter.

"Hello Nance, I never reckoned on seeing you. Why be you out so late?"

She pointed to the basket. "Some garden stuff fur Mistress Knoller."

"The mistress thinks mighty well of you, doesn't she? Certainly, we all do."

"Kind of yew ta say soo, Jethro," she smiled.

At last he was alone with her, walking the path together. She wore a seductive, plum-coloured gown that all but fell from the shoulders, with a linen cap perched saucily on dark, curly hair – and she was smiling! Surely this meant that she felt kindly toward him at least? In his mind, the battle was half won before a single skirmish had been made.

"Nance, I've been minded to speak with you."

"Yes, Jethro?"

"There's a cottage coming free this side of Mansbrook Grove. It's a sheltered spot near the riverbank surrounded by trees. Mr Knoller wants six pounds a year."

"Will yew hire it?"

He shook his head. "More than I can afford on my own, at least for now." They continued walking as the setting sun glowed red on scattered clouds and lengthening shadows began to merge. A keen breeze off the river made her shiver, so he slipped off his coat and placed it around her shoulders. "Mind you, I could recoup some of the rent in other ways."

"How?"

"Well, it's woodland, but Mr Knoller doesn't object none to some clearance. I could dig a small plot an' grow garden stuff. An' I could fence it in an' build a hin-as for fresh eggs an' keep goats in the woods. They could forage and drink from the stream while I be at work."

"Would it pay the rent?" An embarrassing silence followed.

"Well," he began awkwardly, "I could milk 'em, an'... sell the milk... or turn the curds into pressed cheeses. There's none round here sells goat's cheese."

"But how can yew be a-dewin' all tha', when yew's workin' on the farm?"

Now he had to force the words out as a deep reddish tint came to his cheeks.

"Happen a wife could."

"Yew thinkin' 'bout taakin' a wife, Jethro?" she asked, her interest aroused. "Yew's someone in mind?"

"As I said," he continued awkwardly, "I could get back some of the rent. There're fruit trees there an' I could plant more an' grow taters, cabbage, peasen an' beans."

"Enough ta support a wife?" Now her face reddened too as it began to dawn on her that she was the wife he had in mind!

"An' plenty fruits," he added hastily. "There'll be gooseberries as well as musharune to pick, an' matured apples to eat in winter an' the juiciest pears, all watered from the brook. Father will make a present of

milled corn, an' Mr Knoller will let us glean all the wheat we need…
an' we could rear a pig."

"Soo who's the lucky mawther?" she enquired teasingly, certain that
he meant her. His embarrassment was now total. The long moments
of evasion were at an end.

"Folks say as how you're spoken for… to Rob Cabern. Are you,
Nance?"

"I've promised ta wait fur 'em," she replied guardedly.

"An' there can be no other?"

"I'm spoken fur, Jethro." She walked on a few paces, stopped and
prepared herself for what might be coming, something the head would
rather not hear. But strangely, as the memory of a carefree dance and
an inner warmth came to mind, perhaps the heart knew differently.

"An' a fare good wife you'll make him, I'll be bound."

He struggled to withhold a tear, so unpractised in the ways of
rustic courtship. Heavens, even a butterfly flitted about her and rested
on her sleeve, lowering its head and folding its quivering wings, as a
humblebee hovered nearby too. If only he could be as close. Finally
he managed to find his voice enough to speak, haltingly, some lines
memorised from a romantic novel.

"But if ever you should change your mind, here's one who will fall
at your feet and worship you for ever, if only you will consent to be his."

With dismay he saw that his words caused the flicker of a smile.

Yet this was not what he feared. His eyes were filled with such
earnestness and devotion that Nance had no doubt of his intention to
love and care for her always, and it was a look she would never forget.
In her heart of hearts, she felt a growing fondness for him – not the hot
passion with Cabern but something more pleasant and sweet. Had she
known this all along? If Cabern had not appeared at the christening,
perhaps she would indeed now be courted just as happily by Jethro,
even eagerly. But she checked herself.

"Please, Jethro, let us speak noo more of it. I cont be noo more ta
yew than a friend, but yew'll not find a truer."

He would have liked to die there and then, his life in ruins and an
eternity of misery before him. Somehow, though, he was able to voice
the longings of a simple, loving heart.

"I will say no more, then, 'cept that I will love you always. I'll live in hopes an' come what may, whether I live an' die here, or change my sky for ever, I'll love none but Nance Auldfield."

He turned his face to the river, yet the courage and resignation of a martyr awaiting execution welled up in him. By Heaven's grace, if he were to be hanged, let it not be for a lamb but something far more precious – one heavenly kiss. Turning back, he clasped her hand tenderly, put it to his lips and leaned forward to press them against her cheek… but she withdrew, startled and quite overcome. She put down the basket. No, no, she told herself, she could not do this, certainly, she must not kiss him.

Too late, for her own passion was aroused. No, she would offer her cheek to be kissed, that was only fair, and leave it at that, but then the kiss was so sweet and loving that she could not object to a second, even a third. Now she was aflame as she had been with Cabern, although this was different, not so much forceful as ethereal.

Modesty dictated that she resist so she stepped back and lifted an arm to keep her distance. Yet something else was in control. Offering just one kiss in return, she pursed her lips to press against his cheek, but his lips found hers first, imprisoned them, and ardour proved too great for any further restraint. Now they were in that incorporeal realm known only to lovers, beyond space and time, grasping each other's waist and melting into each other's embrace. Decorum was lost on the chilly gusts of night air from the Orwell, careless of any watchful eyes.

At length he picked up her basket and walked her homeward with unwilling steps, an arm snugly about her to keep her warm. Though shivering slightly, she was also in no hurry and wanted like him to prolong this special hour together. All too soon, their slow steps brought them to the farmhouse and the bridge over the moat. They crossed to the farmhouse door, embraced and exchanged a final kiss.

"I'll never forget you, Nance."

"An' I'll niver forget yew, Jethro, fur yar kindness ta me an' the love yew bear me."

He would have bargained his very soul for more kisses, but though her dark misty eyes looked back at him lovingly, he feared this love would all too soon be again for Cabern.

"Now I'd best get a-gooin'."

He held open the door and whispered after her, "Good night, Nance." Turning to walk away but weakened by emotion, he slumped and grabbed the handrail, fearful that he might faint and pitch head-long into the water.

Sarah was pottering happily in her garden, still enchanted by it all, when she noticed some children walking past in a crocodile behind a woman. As they approached she waved and they waved back, though they seemed strangely subdued. One even leaned on a crutch and all of them looked longingly at the garden.

"Can they coom in?" she asked the woman. The woman looked young yet authoritative, even rather prim, with short, parted hair and studious eyes. She nodded and showed her charges through the gate that Sarah held open. It was clear that all these children were suffering some ailments or troubles. The woman smiled pleasantly enough but in those eyes, if one looked deeply enough, could be seen much experience of deprivation, brutality or horror. The children, it transpired, had been foundlings, beggars or cripples, little mites who had walked the streets in rags and starved or died of cold, or been exploited, even murdered. Death had taken them without anybody noticing.

"You're wondering," observed the woman, "why they are still suffering? Because they seek the love they were denied on Earth."

"But yew love an' care fur 'um."

"I do, but I was privileged," she murmured, introducing herself as Emma. "I had a life of comfort and learning. The compassion of the heart and the prompting of the soul do not come easily to me, though I do try. The truth is, they need more than I can give, someone to touch and heal their souls. They need the hand of one who knows love and has suffered enough to understand."

Sarah knew at once what was required of her. Kneeling down, she took one of them in her arms, then another and another, and soon she had squeezed and cuddled them all and asked each one their story. They were pitiable, telling her of horrors she hadn't known existed. All shared the common thread of an absence of love. Suddenly, she also recognised something that hitherto she hadn't dared to admit even to herself. She was alone here herself, and lonely, thinking of dear Nance and her family.

"Dew yew be a-coomin' back now!" she said to the children as they turned to leave. "Promise, now!"

"We promise, Miss."

"Haps we can goo explorin'?" she said, looking to Emma for confirmation.

"I can't walk far," said the boy with a crutch.

"Course yew can," said Sarah, taking him by the hand. "Yew needed yar owd crutch afore, but not now. Yew can walk wi'out it in this place. Let me show yew." She took it from his hands, held him up gently and guided his unsteady steps. "There yew be, yew can walk."

"Yes, Miss," said the little boy, smiling now as he took his first steps unaided.

"An' dewn't call me 'Miss', Sarah's my name. Remember yar promise now, all o' yew."

"We will," they chorused.

Standing unnoticed beneath the shading oaks, John smiled.

CHAPTER 4

LOVE AND BETRAYAL

In Amberslea, the shorn fields of autumn gave way to frosty furrows, wintry gales and the first dustings of snow. Fowlers stalked the whitened heath and bare-bough copses, their scattered reports bringing a leaden death to lapwings and woodcocks. Open-jawed beagles cornered innocent hares whilst huntsmen winded the horn in pursuit of foxes.

At daybreak, the Auldfield brothers would break the frozen surface of their pasture with an unwieldy beetle so that the cattle might graze, and loosened the nourishing turnip roots for them. Then they inspected the sheepcote and its guests, huddled behind a sheltering furze or osier-lattice hedgerow. They chopped logs for the fire, broke the brook's ice for water and, when there was time, patched up the puddled, potholed lane.

The disagreeable task of flail thrashing continued in the barns and there were always trees to be pollarded, ditches to be dredged, gates and fences to be mended. Their labours continued until eventide. Only then would they bend weary steps homeward toward the welcoming glow of a candle in the cottage window.

When the sexton tolled the distant curfew, they would rake the kitchen fire and cover it with ashes, then take to their beds for winter's only respite, a deep, dreamless sleep. Restful and refreshing though the nights were, the family welcomed winter's decline when increasing daylight meant a saving in candles.

'Come Candlemas Day, sow beans in the clay,
throw candles and candlestick right away.'

More presents arrived at the cottage, silently and under cover of darkness. Local men, including Albert and Mark, began to help the smugglers by running the goods and hiding them. Whilst Rackhem and the crew lived and moved about anonymously, Cabern began to be known as 'the good captain', a potential friend who would always see you right. Farmers found their unlocked stables entered at night (if locked they would be burned down) and the horses in a lather. Beside the door would be left a keg of brandy as a 'thank you' for their being 'borrowed'. Albert and Mark, who had previously drunk nothing more intoxicating than ale, acquired a taste for this brandy. Their only previous hangover having been after harvest-home, they began to lie longer in bed until sober enough for work.

The Ploughs of Suffolk

Blissfully unaware of all this, Sarah busied herself with home and garden and by chatting with Mollie and the neighbours. The children returned and in a happier state. One by one, Sarah learned the troubles that afflicted them just as a mother would, since they represented the children she would have liked to have. Gradually she persuaded each one that their troubles were in the past and could be let go, just as the boy had his crutch. Soon her garden rang with shouts of childish excitement as they scampered along paths, climbed the tree and inquisitively touched and smelled each flower.

Emma was also deeply moved by Sarah's love for the children and she too now radiated a warmth of her own. Freed of her own anxieties, and as though by way of a gift in thanks, she taught them – and a bemused Sarah – how they could move instantly from one place to another by thought alone, now that they were no longer hampered by earthly suffering. In this way she led the children on expeditions beyond meadows and woodland to distant plains and mountains. It was a revelation to discover the various other inhabitants of this new world, either in solitary dwellings, scattered hamlets or small towns.

For the children, the most magical spot of all was actually quite local, yet hidden from their normal view, having neither pales nor an entrance. Emma showed them how to get there by using their minds. One moment they would be in a meadow, the next in an arboreal, emerald-carpeted valley. At their feet was a quiet stream with violet and flame-shot lilies, winding its way between banks of flowers and overhanging trees before gushing over rocky waterfalls. Crystals in the rocks reflected the light as brilliantly as Earth's brightest day, whilst the waters echoed through the thickets and hollows with dulcimer tones.

In the stream appeared flashes of scaly red and silver as fishes, sensing the human presence, surfaced in welcome. The children knelt, dipped their fingers into the water and watched fascinated as the finny tribe circled and leapt playfully over their outstretched hands, even at times landing on a moistened palm.

"This is 'fishing'," said Emma, "except that we don't catch them, we play with them."

Leaving the children to play, she led Sarah deeper into the valley. In a meadow there were peaceful sheep, lowing cattle in the shadier areas and horses roaming freely on the upper slopes. Fed by numerous tributaries, the stream swelled in an ever-widening flood and became a flowing river that plunged over a cataract bathed in a film of fine spray. From a high bank, an enthralled Sarah looked over the white waters to see a creeping wildwood and asked her friend what lay beyond.

"You wouldn't want to go there. You just wouldn't," was all Emma would tell her.

Some time later, curiosity – or perhaps a guiding power instinct – prompted Sarah to return alone to the 'secret kingdom', as the children had named it. Transfixed, she again stood above the cataract, wondering why that enticing sylvan view was supposedly out of bounds. Yet even as she contemplated this, she found herself in an instant transported to that very place. The entangled wood's leafy perimeter seemed at first impenetrable until she noticed a mossy, dappled pathway leading onward. Tentatively, she made her way along it between tapestries of leaves beneath a low roof of interlacing greenwood; but the further she ventured, the more dank and foreboding it became.

Undeterred, she continued walking even though the way grew gloomier. This was no wood after all, she realised, but a dense, unbounded forest. Eventually, only occasional glimmers from a louring sky were able to penetrate the canopy, revealing a zigzag footway around tree stumps and fallen rotting branches, the forest floor becoming enveloped in dense, Bible-black shadows. Moreover, some strange force seemed to be opposing her now, as though the very earth were grasping at her heels to prevent her every step. The air became fetid, overpowering, and soon a noxious mist hovered about her.

The path had disappeared and she didn't know which way to turn. In keeping with her surroundings, her mind began to give way to a deep melancholy, forcing her to think back to her poor sister's fortunes and weighing her down with increasing despair. What strange impulse had prompted her to come here, she thought, on the point of turning back. But just then, John's voice whispered in her mind.

"Keep straight ahead and do not be afraid."

His encouragement uplifted her flagging spirits and gave her a sense of purpose, of being on an important mission. Moreover, although no light penetrated the canopy above, a new light seemed to radiate from her inner being now as though her very soul had become a lamp to light the way. Putting aside all her anxieties, she trod wherever this light led, picking her way bravely around decomposing stumps and heaped debris of fallen branches.

Eventually, a foggy, invasive mere came into view, fowl-smelling and undisturbed by so much as a ripple, and she could just make out the figure of a man wreathed in mist, reclining on a log and staring blankly at the surface. At first glance he seemed elegantly clothed, similar to the fashion she remembered from girlhood. Closer examination revealed a threadbare justaucorps, grubby waistcoat and shirt and a battered tricorne. His hands were thrust into worn breeches, whilst his laddered stockings and gold-buckled shoes were caked in mud.

She stepped forward. The man became aware of her but continued in his self-absorbed reverie. Approaching carefully, her shoes sliding and sinking in the ooze, she stood unsteadily a short distance away.

"Why be yew sittin' thar, all on yar owen?"

"Why do you ask?" He turned to face her and blinked. "Oh, I see you're a creature of light. You have a family, I suppose, whilst I have nobody… nobody."

She shook her head. "I dewn't have noo family either. I mean, 'um's still in t'other place."

"But you can go where you like, can't you?"

"Why cont yew?"

"I don't know. No light can penetrate here – and in the darkness one place is much like another anyway."

"Dewn't be sappy! This har's a terrible, rum owd place. Dewn't yew have noo bein?"

"What?"

"A bein, a hoom, the place yew be in."

"No."

"Everybody has a hoom, or summat called hoom!"

"I have a tumbledown ruin but it's certainly not home. It's filthy, rubbish everywhere, nothing's in the right place. I tried sorting it out but it just went back to being what it was." As he spoke, he raised a hand to shield his eyes. "That cursed light of yours hurts my eyes."

As if in response, the glow about her dimmed, leaving just enough to glimpse the ground at her feet.

"Dew yew mind if I coom an' sit by yew?"

"If you like."

The man was visibly relieved at the light's withdrawal. Sarah sat on the log beside him. He removed his hat and she could just discern his features, pleasant enough, even handsome, or rather they had been; now the eyes were much older than his years, haughty, and his mouth curled in a cruel sneer. He had a look of corruption, as though too much wrongdoing had been compressed into too short a life. She also thought that he might prove dangerous to know.

Just then, across the mere and unnoticed by the man, another figure appeared. She recognised John's familiar face and brown robe. He winked at her and nodded encouragement. Her confidence returned.

"I be called Sarah. And yew are…?"

"Just call me Thomas,"

"Where be the place yew say's not hoom?"

"Not far."

She stood up and looked round for John but he had vanished.

"Let's me an' yew get a-gooin', Thomas. Where be the house?"

"Over there, on the other side of the forest. It's some walk."

"Oh, noo! I cont walk it. 'Sides, there's a gainer way. I'll show yew." As she clasped his arm with a tender but firm hand, he became aware of a penetrating warmth, gentle and pleasingly feminine. "Just think yew's thar, an' thar yew be!"

He shrugged and pictured to himself the gloomy, ruined pile he had been only too glad to leave earlier, and was somewhat surprised if not overjoyed to find himself standing once more beneath its decayed, lichen and ivy-clad walls.

"You see," he said squinting hard, "it's just as I told you. An' now there's this terrible light too. It's penetrating to the very soul. Gads my life, it's agony!" As he spoke, he pulled his coat over his head, sank to the knees and crossed his arms as though in a shield, cowering and defensive. "Swounds, I can't bear it!"

Sarah wasn't sure what to say, even feeling somewhat guilty for bringing this light into his home. John would know… but he was nowhere to be seen now. Yet she felt inspired to speak and words poured out without thinking, her voice somehow deeper.

"Yes, you could bear the light, Thomas. You could open yourself up to it if you really wanted to and let it brighten up your life. It's only your own mind that's stopping you. Look at my little light. Then try to imagine what it would be like to open yourself up to the great spiritual light that shines everywhere else. Breathe it in deeply. Come on, Thomas, try it for me."

What had she said? This was not the simple, uneducated Sarah. Thomas was just as astonished, both at the sudden change in her voice and her perfect English. Yet he stood up, eyes shut tightly and grimacing, as Sarah, feeling an increasing fondness for him, impulsively placed a hand on his arm and touched his cheek with her lips. A rush of warmth and affection flowed through him that he had never known from a woman, and an unfamiliar sense of love stirred. A moment before, she had touched him with words and now she had touched the heart.

Dutifully, though without understanding, and since he had nothing to lose, he lifted the head. So brilliant was the light becoming, even with closed eyes, he thought it would surely blind him. He tried as best he could to breathe it in, for she deserved this, and somehow the light became more benign and bearable. There was a growing lightness of the heart too, that he had not known since arriving in this strange land.

"Now breathe out the light!" Sarah instructed him gently. He did as he was told and, for the first time, saw through squinting eyes the green of the grass and foliage around his home. After a few more breaths and exhalations, previously unseen flowers came into colour, swaying in the gentle breeze. The house itself, too, looked rather more imposing, yet still exuding decay in every brick and blanketed by thickets.

"Well," said Sarah, finding her own voice again, "aren't yew gooin' ta ask me in?"

Thomas led her up a weedy, broken path to a portico entwined with ivy, turned the blackened brass doorknob and put a shoulder to the rotting timber door until it opened.

"I'd better go in first," he said apologetically, "you might fall over something."

"Dewn't be sorft! Yew cont fall har."

Inquisitively, she slipped inside past him but struggled to see beyond the dark vestibule. Everything reeked of mustiness and decay whilst peeling plasterwork and giant cobwebs hung from a vaulted ceiling over a rickety stairwell. At her feet, brick dust, broken stair rails and a fallen beam littered bare floorboards. She trod cautiously along a hallway and paused before the open door of a room, its only light being a meagre ray that penetrated a chink in the window shutters.

"Wha' be in har?" she asked.

"My study. Gad, it's chock full of stuff. I've tried tidying it up, but it just goes back to being what it was."

"Course, it does. The room is yew," she said intuitively. "Yew cont not change the room without yew change yarself."

She stepped warily across to the window, pulled apart the shutters and knocked open a grimy window. Light poured in, turning the rising dust into gilt-speckled clouds. Upon an ancient desk were an armillary sphere and a drinking cup fashioned from a human skull, whilst on the floor was a broken globe of the world. Bookshelves covered every wall, groaning under hundreds of weighty tomes with peeling bindings and bare spines testifying to their being well-read. Above the higher shelves were yet more books, jammed against the ceiling and draped in cobwebs. Awestruck, she wondered how she could possibly communicate with a man who apparently had the sum of all human knowledge crammed into one room. How could she begin to discuss any subject when she was not even literate?

She stepped forward, selected a book at random and withdrew it; a spider darted out and scurried for cover. Blowing the dust off the book and opening it, she hoped, as she could not read, to see a picture of something. But the only illustration was a coat of arms pasted onto the inside cover. She guessed that the book had belonged to Thomas in earthly life and that the coat of arms was his.

"Is this yew?" He nodded. "Would yew like ta read me wha' it says?"

"The Right Honourable Lord Edgecombe."

"Soo yew wuz someone important!" She was impressed and slightly amused as well, aware of entering uncharted waters and being already way out of her depth. "Wha' be the book about? Dew tell me, for I cont read – only the odd word, an' this be all dashes and squiggles."

"It's ancient Greek. But don't worry, I've discovered that you don't have to read in this world. Just hold the book, place your fingertips on the page and you will be able to sense the contents and the personality of the author. With practise the books even come somehow alive – that's the only way I can describe it. You can see and hear the events described as though you were there as they actually happened. Sometimes that's not as the author thought they had happened, or had been told, or simply wants you to believe. Go on, try it!"

As she ran her fingers over the first page, mental images started to form of a strange land in a faraway time and place, a land of marble colonnades and temples and avenues of painted statues. There were rocky islands with white cliffs and sunlit beaches on which she could hear waves breaking. She heard verses too – Homer's no less – of "black ships sailing on a wine dark ocean" and "the dawn rising with fingertips of rose." This was no paradise, though, for another volume described the citizens quarrelling incessantly as city fought city and warfare was common. This second author had an exalted mind yet, in turn, clearly revered another even wiser man. This one declared that a life not carefully examined was not worth living.

The writer went on to describe an ideal city where men and women followed whatever calling most suited them, and where there was justice overseen by rulers who protected their people instead of exploiting and oppressing them. These rulers led by example and prepared their people for 'a higher life to come'. Surely, thought Sarah, he meant the very world they were now in.

"'Em knew all about this place," she said in surprise. "I niver guessed as how one head could hold soo much!"

"Yes," agreed Thomas, "that's Plato, writing about Socrates."

She picked up the next dusty volume and sensed it in the same way. "Ah, thus be the same man. Only now tha' man's on trial fur his life, in spite of being called the wisest man in Greece. He talked o' life haa'ter life to any as'd listen… but the jurors, they judged him impious, and said as how he'd corrupted the youth. Blas more, they condemned 'em ta dead. But he was the best an' bravest o' men, an' said as how thinking and doing right wuz more important than life itself. An' he went to his death willin'ly cos I reckon he knew he'd be a-coomin' har!"

"That's Socrates right enough," said Thomas, remembering grimly the countless hours spent at school, construing such texts on dog-eared, ink-stained pages and being punished for every mistake. After all, the Classics were a necessary part of a gentleman's education.

Another volume described a huge empire where people were never happy. Some important man was talking about the foolishness of trying to hold on to what was transient, while ignoring what endures forever.

"Here be a man," said Sarah, "who reckoned care o' the soul more important than ruling his empire."

"Marcus Aurelius."

Yet another book, once she had brushed off the dust, disturbing another spider, told of a man whose grandfather had been a great hero in life. The man travelled in his sleep to meet him.

"He saw our beautiful world an' wanted ta stay. But his owen father told 'em this life's a reward tha' maun be earned an' ta goo back and dew his duty."

"Cicero's Republic," Thomas sighed.

"An' as fur this one, well…" She paused and continued to 'read' in silence. "This one's more real, he coom har while still a-walking the Earth… Lawks, he wuz a strange 'un… He says sometimes people har went to 'em on Earth and told 'em things an' then he left his body an' coom har ta talk with 'em… He saw happy places an' others a kinda Hell, all dark an' gloomy an' barren – jus' like where I found yew."

"That's Swedenborg," he told her. "But I believe there's a natural justice in this place. We make our own Heaven and Hell. This place," he made a gesture to indicate his home, somehow just a little less dark and untidy than before, "is my own doing, I know. But people don't continue to suffer when the fault is not theirs."

"Noo?" she objected, telling him about the children.

"But you were there to help them."

"True, I was, I s'pose," she agreed thoughtfully. Then she added, "I reckon as how you understand a lot more'n you let on."

Cabern was enjoying early success in his smuggling career. The cargoes were landed at night, mostly at Walton Ferry, and carried through the tunnel to the Ferry House Inn, either into the cellars or up to the stables for a run. From upstairs windows a candle would be waved, either vertically to warn of danger or horizontally to confirm that the coast was clear.

One damp night, Cabern, with Rackhem and a handful of gang members on horseback escorted a cart from the inn on a run. They left the Felixstowe Road north-west of Amberslea, dismounted and waited at the foot of a hill, the agreed rendezvous for the handover of goods. Sure enough, as well as the occasional barking dog and bleating sheep, they soon heard the trotting hooves of half a dozen or more horses. When the trot slowed to a walking pace, Rackhem made the hoot of an owl. There was no response. He tried again but there was still nothing. He turned to Cabern.

"What boats be foul here?"

Then they saw the riders emerging, half a dozen shadowy figures strung out in the pale moonlight, all but one with the plumed helmet of a dragoon. They formed a line and trotted towards the smugglers.

"It's the Revenue!" snarled Rackhem and cupped his hands to his mouth. "Ahoy there! Show your reckoning."

"Stand to, in the King's name!" demanded their leader, drawing a cutlass and quickening the horse's pace. He was Riding Officer Garrow Merryridge – Jethro's elder brother, no less – of the Preventive Service and he'd been hunting Cabern and his crew for months. Rackhem aimed a pistol at him and fired, but hit the horse. As it stumbled and fell, Merryridge rolled clear, then he sprang up and charged at Rackhem in a fury. The dragoons discharged their carbines, dismounted, drew swords and attacked.

The moon withdrew as though in fear as the hitherto silent heath rang with a cacophony of shouts, baying dogs and lowing cattle. Cabern, cutlass in hand, lunged at Merryridge but only succeeded in skewering his cloak. As he fell back, the officer turned his attack on Cabern while two sword-wielding dragoons attacked Rackhem. Fighting back to back with his first mate, Cabern launched a kick at Merryridge who gasped and doubled up, allowing Cabern to slice viciously through his sleeve followed by a thrust to the side of the body. Merryridge retired to the shadows.

Cabern then turned to the dragoons fighting Rackhem. As one man turned to face him, Cabern kicked him in the shin making the man gasp and stagger back, the bone broken. Rackhem lunged at the other soldier, wounded him and saw him withdraw. But now Merryridge reappeared, not as badly wounded as he feared, raising his sword high with his one strong arm and knocking Rackhem's blade from his grasp. Seeing him without a weapon, one of the wounded dragoons advanced again, this time brandishing a carbine. Rackhem had to retreat with the man in pursuit. The other gang members had been fighting hard, but gave ground and attempted to draw the soldiers away from each other.

The field was left to Cabern and Merryridge. It was a desperate encounter, both for the soldier who risked life and limb to uphold the law and the smuggler who faced execution if caught. They duelled alone as the moon came and went, one moment illumined by its pale glow, the next stumbling around, struggling to find each other in the darkness. As they closed in, Cabern gouged the other's face but Merryridge, reeling and slashing wildly, managed to kick out, damaging Cabern's knee and making him fall. He followed up by cutting Cabern's sword-arm and then a powerful thrust aimed at the neck caught the forehead, cutting it to the bone.

The fight would have been over had not Rackhem, rescued by a companion and re-armed, returned to the fray. Their blades crossed and re-crossed as each sought an opening. Merryridge lunged forward but Rackhem parried, stepped aside and delivered a blow to the head with his pistol-butt, a final kick finding Merryridge's jaw and leaving him unconscious and bleeding.

By now the rest of the skirmish was over. The gang knew the heath well even in darkness and had disappeared into gorse and hollows, only to reappear to attack a pursuing dragoon. Soon all the soldiers had either been wounded or overpowered. The gang returned to where Rackhem stood breathing heavily, between the outstretched forms of Cabern and Merryridge. Some of them wanted to take a final revenge on the officer but Rackhem forbade it; he had enough wisdom to know that, bad as things were, nothing much would change as a result. The authorities would tolerate the threat posed by Cabern and his men as long as the matter didn't go too far. Murder would mean the smugglers facing the threat of the militia on land and the navy at sea. If caught, the penalty was execution and hanging in chains. Far better, he reasoned, to lick their wounds.

Peace reigned once more as creatures of earth and air settled back down to rest. The men lifted Cabern onto the cart and drove back towards Walton as stealthily as they had come, on the way lowering most of the contraband down the well of one of Diamond's safe cottages. The rest, spirits in casks, they sank in a pond. By the early hours, they were back in the comparative safety of the inn.

Cabern was badly wounded but Rackhem dared not call in a physician. Then he remembered Nance and her strong influence on his captain. Why not bring her into this? She could be trusted to nurse him and not betray him; afterwards, perhaps she might even be persuaded to join them. Without delay, he wrote her a letter and handed it to the least villainous-looking crewman with instructions to place it in her hands. When the man arrived at Abbeyfield Farm the following morning and handed her the letter, with a pleasant "Aatanune, Miss", she handed it back and asked him to read it.

"Law noo, Miss, I cont read proper, noo how. But Rob's hurt bad – not wholly, but as needs physic and good carin'. Says as how yew's ta coom ta the Ferry House Inn."

"Alawk! Rob in trouble?" gasped Nance, her heart in her mouth with a dozen imagined fears. "Haps I should coom at once." The man shook his head.

"Haa'ter dark ul do fine, Miss. Best if yew coom alone, an' noo one sees yew. At the inn, ask for Moll."

Nance stood, troubled yet excited too, by the door. Rob's very name made her tremble with a mixture of joy, uncertainty and stomach-churning fear. Yes, she would at least see him soon – so much had happened since their last meeting – but how badly hurt was he? She only knew that he needed her and she must go to him.

In the evening, she made her excuses to her mistress then tied up her scrip and, with a glance at the threatening Noah's Ark clouds in the darkening welkin, wrapped a cloak tightly about herself and lit a lantern. On the way, she stopped at her parents' cottage to tell her father of her mission.

"Noo good ul come o' yew an' tha' Cabern, yew gatless mawther!" said a despairing Zebedee. "Mark well what I say, noo good!"

As she shrugged and walked away, her mother called to her from the upstairs window.

"Bless yew, Nance!" she shouted above the gathering wind and rustling leaves. "Yew mind those ruffians dewn't harm yew none. An' coom back safe an' well ta yar poor owd pa and her as bore yew!"

It was well into night and scything with rain by the time she arrived at the inn. She held the lantern high to light the way until the path from the road became visible, the wind lashing her cloak and making it flap like a sail. Entering the inn, she shook the water from it and extinguished the lantern. Immediately, a woman introduced herself as Moll Stanton who was at pains to hurry Nance away from the regulars and up the stairs. They passed through a door at the far end, which Moll locked behind them, and went over to a panelled wall. One of the panels slid back to reveal what looked like another wall, but was in fact a folding staircase. When she had drawn down the steps, she climbed them followed by Nance. They entered a low-beamed chamber with a single window in which stood a candle with a reflector. On the bed, heavily bandaged about the head and clad in only a nightshirt, Cabern lay fast asleep.

"You'll both be safe here," Moll assured her and pointed to Cabern. "He's suffered a nasty gash to the head. He's concussed, lost a lot of blood and has a fever. You'll find everything here you need – bandages, herbs, vinegar."

Nance stood silent, unsure of herself. "What if—" she began.

"If you need anything," Moll anticipated her thoughts, "just knock the floor with your shoe. Oh, an' if you have to take a walk, just push down the steps and slide back the panel. Best you don't leave the inn, though, not 'til this business is over." She turned and left them alone, raising the folding steps behind her and closing the panel.

Nance was finally alone with Cabern although in circumstances far removed from romantic. His nightshirt and bed linen were soaked in perspiration. All night she sat by the bed, wiping his fevered brow and dabbing it with vinegar but on the few occasions when his flickering eyes opened they showed no recognition. She made fresh herbal poultices for the open wound, into which salt had been rubbed, and forced water a drop at a time through his parched lips.

The rain continued unabated and dawn revealed vast sheets sweeping across the marshes and drumming against the roof and windowpane. Water poured from overflowing gutters and, in one or two places, dripped from the ceiling. Moll returned and together they changed Cabern's clothes and bed linen. The landlady could not but be aware of Nance's obvious care for him and marvelled at how she sat for long hours, refusing all but the briefest rest. Moll was a mistress who ran a bordello along with the smuggling den at the inn and thought she knew all about the intimate goings on between men and women; but never had she come across a situation quite like this. Surely, she thought, an angel from Heaven, if there were any such thing, could not show more selfless devotion. Angel or simple-minded fool?

The storm passed and so eventually did the crisis. Cabern finally opened his eyes to see an exhausted Nance at the foot of the bed, herself asleep at last.

"Is that you, Nance?" His voice was a faint whisper. "Nance?"

She awoke. "Oh, Rob!" She drew herself up and shuffled unsteadily to his side. "Rob, at first I thought yew a gonner." She sank to her knees and took his hand in hers. Their eyes met and remained so while, gradually, he came round.

"What happened, Nance? Why am I here with you?"

"Yew've been wholly sick. They sent for me – yar friends, Rackhem and Moll. Thus all I know." She could hold back her fears no longer. "Oh Rob, why dewn't yew leave this trade? Let this be a warnin'. I dewn't want yar gifts, they've brought us nought but sorrow. I just want ta see yew safe an' in honest work." She related the events of the past year or so and the increasing sufferings endured by her family, her parents' ill-health and the growing recklessness of her younger brothers.

"I'm so sorry, Nance." he said at length. "What can I say?"

"What's done cont be undone! I'm loosin' 'em all, but I dewn't want ta be a-loosin' yew!"

"Nance, trust me. Just one more voyage. It'll have to be a long one after this – then I'll have done with it."

"Have done wi' it now, Rob, Now's yar chance. Yew was dollop't near ta dead. We'll put it abroad yew is dead, then yew can be someone else. Yew can get other work, happen on land."

"What would I do, Nance? I'm no landsman. No, one more voyage and I'll have money enough to set up in business on my own."

"Money ont dew yew noo good when yew's dead."

He thought for a moment and then shook his head.

"As you say, perhaps it would be better if folks thought I was dead. I'll think on't."

Moll approached with a breakfast tray. As she quietly opened the secret panel she heard their voices and paused to hear what was said. It only took a moment to convince her that Cabern needed a different visitor, if Diamond were not to lose him for the sake of this silly child of the soil. She trod loudly as she ascended the steps and entered the room to express heartfelt joy at his recovery. As soon as she left, however, she sent word to Rackhem to be ready that night.

The day passed agreeably enough with Nance having no inkling of what was afoot. Cabern slept some more and ate his first proper meal. As darkness fell, Moll entered the room, lit the candle with a reflector and waved it repeatedly across the window. Soon a light from the Ferry House was waved in return. Only when Rackhem and his crew entered did Nance realise what was about to happen.

"Oh, dewn't not taak him, please dewn't!" she begged. "He's still weak."

"Now don't you worry none, Miss," began Rackhem. "The Cap'n can't stay here. The Preventive's abroad. It's too hot for us an' we'll not leave him to the halter."

"It's for the best, Nance," said Cabern, rising to sit on the bed. "I'll be back when things have settled down and I'll get word to you soon as I can." She took his hand, then his arm and clung to him in a last tearful embrace. "Cheer up, Nance." He rubbed a clenched fist against her chin. "I just ran aground an' shipped a little bilge water. Cheery now, be cheery! It isn't every squall as capsizes a boat."

She squeezed him tightly in her arms, desperately forcing her lips over his. The old fire rose in her again as her kisses were returned, kisses that might so easily, so cruelly, be their last. Finally, the impatient crew prised them apart and Moll stepped in to restrain her as she tried to hold him back, even as the crew lifted him up and bore him away. Down the steps they carried him, along the corridor and down into the cellar where they placed him on a litter to carry him, wading along the tunnel to the Ferry House. There, from a window in a room visible only from the water, a candle was waved back and forth.

A boat appeared alongside and Cabern was helped aboard. Then muffled oars pulled the boat away as silently as it had come.

CHAPTER 5

BETWEEN TWO WORLDS

The light seemed to follow Thomas as he shuffled across to a rickety chair and flopped onto its dusty upholstery. He lowered his head and rested it in his hands.

"I always thought there was something more to life, but I did nothing about it. Truth is, I was so busy enjoying myself in the other place, I never found time to enquire more about this world."

"So yew knew sommat about us?"

"A little at any rate."

"From the books?" He nodded. "An' yew kept it all ta yarself?"

Now he was shamefaced. "I read them long ago. We had to. One won't go far in life these days without Latin… and a gentleman must have Greek."

"An' they didn't mean noo more ta yew than tha'?"

"They did – but I didn't think much more about it. Now I begin to see what you mean."

"Be thar other books loike these?"

"Not that I can think… oh, wait a moment, yes, by Gad, the Church Fathers and their so-called prophets, but—"

"But what?"

"Well, they weren't very scholarly. They wrote Vulgar Latin and sloppy Greek. Besides, no-one bothers much with them nowadays, even the papists. I mean," Thomas continued haltingly, "they were the most awful plebeians, certainly no gentlemen. They fashioned doctrines as the mood took them and led their followers by the nose – and they weren't above attacking each other, sometimes bitterly."

"Maybe so. But on this particular subject they agreed, didn't they?" Nance had no idea where her words were coming from now, but she did sense John's presence again.

"No matter, the Church rejected their prophets."

"Only because their prophecies didn't agree with Church teaching. But the scriptures were always written long after the event and carefully edited by the Sadducees, then again by the Romans four centuries later." Her voice was becoming deeper, more masculine, and Thomas was looking at her incredulously.

"Whoever you are," he objected, "where is all this leading us?"

"Did not one of them write, 'Our maidens utter divine oracles, see visions and say the holy words that are given them to speak'? Then again, 'Others forewarn and see visions of things to come, still others lay hands on the sick and make them whole… and the spirit speaks in many tongues' – just as I am speaking to you through this woman. Even Augustine found spiritual gifts being practised in his day."

Thomas, sitting bolt upright and attentive now, stroked his forehead and searched his memory. "Come to think of it, I did read something of the sort."

"You did, while you were in Italy on the Grand Tour. Only your mind was elsewhere at the time and philosophy could never compete with the serious business of wenching and collecting indecent statuary – a naked Venus from an excavated Pompeian brothel, I believe?"

"That was an antique," Thomas protested. "And I did buy the books of the authors you mention too. I had them crated and shipped to England and added to my library when I returned."

"And promptly forgot about them." John's voice was addressing him belittlingly, like a schoolmaster confronting a dull pupil. "The martyr Justin wrote about 'guiding spirits' speaking through the prophets – where do you suppose those spirits lived? Hidden away in some dark forest perhaps, or in a mountain cave, or floating in the clouds?"

"Here, I suppose," agreed Thomas sheepishly, "in this place, the world we are now in."

Sarah – or was it John? – drew back and the censorious facial expression relaxed. The voice remained masculine but grew a little warmer. "Do you not see? This is the stumbling block, the darkness you created for yourself. You had access to all this knowledge yet you failed to embrace it, let alone share it with others who were thirsty for the truth. So this house we are in mirrors your mind exactly – a tumbledown monument to your hopes and ambitions, a museum of all those things begun but never finished, and a mausoleum where your spirit shares a similar fate to your body.

"You could help people, you know, a lot of them, if you so wished. There are many here who wander about in ignorance and darkness, just as you have. You could help them. As a gentleman you'd do it well, charming them and reminding them of things they've forgotten. Why do you think you've been given such a big house and grounds – do you think you deserve all this for yourself? It's time you began doing the work here that you should have done on Earth."

Thomas submitted himself to this admonishment, coming as it clearly did from a higher authority.

"But Gad save, how could I possibly invite anyone here? It's not even a mausoleum, it's a ruin, it's filthy."

Sarah came back to herself again and grinned impishly with a girlish twinkle. He watched, charmed, as the light played on her ruddy cheeks, soft hair and, indeed, on the simple white robe that failed to conceal her strikingly womanly figure.

"Then let's me an' yew get going an' clean it through an' through."

Nance returned from the inn to Abbeyfield Farm late in the evening and went straight to her garret. As she lay down to sleep she reflected that the following morning it would only be a matter of time before she saw Jethro again. She buried her head in the pillow as though to hide the shame and confusion she felt. What was she doing? Thoughts of an injured Cabern flooded her mind and filled her with guilt: he had been risking his life for their future happiness – as he saw it – while she had betrayed him, flirting shamelessly when his back had been turned. Even worse, was she falling in love? No, that must never be and she must never be alone with Jethro again.

Having made this resolution, and feeling drained and exhausted, she closed her eyes and fell immediately asleep. Yet in the realm of dreams her inner spirit told a different story and she was back in that ethereal evening, enfolded reassuringly and lovingly in Jethro's arms. When daylight roused her and the guilt returned, she groomed herself and soberly went about her duties.

Meanwhile Jethro wavered between being resigned to losing her one moment and hoping for the impossible the next. When they did meet, she simply smiled politely and busied herself with her tasks, yet her affected and unconvincing courtesy merely encouraged him and rekindled his smouldering expectations. He followed wherever she walked and was nearby whenever she halted. Seeing her trying to hide behind a barn door on her way to the dairy, he dashed up to open it. She raised her arms defensively, pulling as stern and disapproving a frown as she could manage, but he grasped her hand and put it to his lips.

"Dearest Nance," he begged, "just one more kiss before I lose you for ever."

"Noo Jethro! Happen someone ul see us!"

She tugged her hand away but the response did not deter him. He clasped both her arms and, with his face just inches away, she again resigned herself to letting him kiss her cheek – several times. As his trembling lips hovered near hers, she could not control herself and grasped him about the waist, pulling him inside the barn away from prying eyes. Now her kisses were just as eager as his. Yet, curiously, she remained at peace; this was nothing like the fiery, animalistic passion she felt with Cabern. There was something transcendent about being so close to Jethro, as though together they entered a higher state of being.

Jethro was no longer his own master but her helpless devotee, whilst Nance, alternately cautious and passionate, both avoided him and submitted to his ever bolder advances. Every day now saw them walking, embracing or lying in each other's arms in groves, meads and cornfields, lost in the warmth of each other's company.

All too soon it was harvest-time and Jethro's days were spent either tying the sheaves or wielding the sickle. Only once, late in the evening, a chance errand to the farmhouse give him the opportunity to slip away to the garret where a faint candle glow under her door indicated that she was still awake. He tapped the door softly and she opened it, still dressed. A little shocked, she quickly pulled him inside.

"Jethro! If Mr Knoller catches yew har…" Her voice was hushed as though the walls had ears. He lifted her up in his brawny arms and carried her, struggling but only mildly, to the bed where she sat like a nymph as he knelt beside her and reverently clasped her hands. Bringing one hand to his lips, he then pulled her closer, daring to rest his face on her breasts. She sighed, her heart thumping, and cradled his head with trembling hands. Should she submit and become his? The parson would marry them with no fuss and little ceremony, as he had her parents, and then there was that desirable little cottage by the river that could now be hers… No more sleeping in a garret and no more hedge-school for lovers.

But wait, what was she thinking? Had she not promised to wait for Rob? At that moment heavy footsteps ascended the stairs and the sudden terror of discovery, and the ruin it would bring, brought them to their senses.

"Jethro, hide! Quick! Mr Knoller ul kill yew if he finds yew har," she hissed, looking helplessly for a hiding place in the sparsely furnished room. "Out o' the winder – goo on, hurry!"

She blew out the candle. The footsteps reached the landing and were just feet from the door when Jethro reluctantly squeezed himself through the dormer window. With his feet on the sill, he reached up to grasp the ridge of the triangular roof and hoist himself clear. There he hovered, draped over the pantiles, hanging by the elbows. At the knock on the door, Nance slipped out of her gown and threw a shawl over her stays, punched the pillow and dishevelled her hair. After the third knock she opened the door a few inches whilst giving a huge yawn, with every appearance of being roused from a deep sleep. There, in a nightshirt and holding a candlestick, stood Mr Knoller.

"I thought I heard voices," he began awkwardly.

"I didn't hear nothin', Mr Knoller. I've been fast asleep." She gave another yawn and pulled the shawl tighter.

"Are you sure there's no-one here?" he added, a little gruffly. "Mind if I take a look?"

"Why, Mr Knoller," she cried indignantly, "how could yew even think such a thing? Taak a look."

She opened the door wider and stepped aside, the perfect study of injured innocence. Yet even as she spoke, she could see beyond the window a tell-tale dangling foot. And if she could see it, so would Mr Knoller. To distract him, as the flickering candle moved in an arc and his eyes traversed the room, she let slip the shawl. He could not, being a man, help noticing her exposed breasts and looked askance in embarrassment, missing the window in his search. Seeing no-one, he scratched his head and mumbled an apology while Nance pulled the shawl back into place, her exaggerated modesty suggesting that it was he who was at fault for disturbing an innocent woman at such an hour. No sooner had he closed the door and begun descending the stairs, she raced to the open window and looked up. Above her dangled a pair of legs.

"Jethro," she hissed, "coom on in, yew sorft ninny." She guided his foot to the sill and helped him clamber back inside. "Mr Knoller nearly caught yew," she whispered. "Yew'd best stay awhile 'til the coast's clear."

Even as she spoke, her thoughts and feelings switched again to Cabern. Whatever his faults, he was no clumsy ninny and he hid from no man – not riding officers, not dragoons and certainly not a busybody farmer. Not only would he defend her honour with his life, he was a bolder lover too – a tad rough, but strong and protective. No, she was Cabern's woman. Jethro's clumsiness had nearly cost her job not to mention her honour. And what sort of a life was he offering anyway? Working all hours for a hired cottage on a small plot of land and with an uncertain future… Jethro laid a gentle hand on her shoulder and grinned meekly.

"Where shall I sleep then?"

"Which iver side o' the floor's more comfortable," she said coldly. It seemed that love's powerful yet tenuous spell was broken, as she flopped onto the bed, turned over and faced the wall.

"What's up Nance?"

She did not respond. He had begun to dream that they were going to marry after the harvest. But he knew whose shadow had come between them again and did not need to speak the name. He had lost her, after so many throws of the dice and when he'd seemed to be winning. As Nance's eyes closed, the memory of Rob's first overpowering kisses by the cottage came suddenly as fresh to her mind as when she had stolen upstairs that night to lie beside her sister, whose second sight already knew it all. Cabern had left her with a lovesick mind that would give her no rest until she was again in his brawny arms. This time her dreams were filled with images of him, commanding his ship and fighting dragoons, as her other would-be lover snored peacefully a few feet away.

"I wouldn't know where to begin," sighed Thomas.

"What's this, then?" she asked, picking up the skull-cup.

"A relic of a misspent youth. I used to drink toasts from it. At times I was far happier seeking oblivion than facing bitter reality."

She remembered a wicked little verse from childhood.

"Ashes ta ashes, dust ta dust, if Heaven ont have yew—" She picked up the skull and held it above her head.

"Careful with that!" he cried, starting towards her.

"—the Divil must!" She hurled it to the floor where it shattered into fragments, sending several more spiders scuttling for cover. Kneeling down, she scooped up the fragments, held them in cupped hands and he watched in astonishment as they came back together to form a skull again, with no sign of breakage.

"Death," she teased, "does it exist?" Next she picked up the armillary sphere. "An' what does this round thing dew?"

"It shows the different zones of Earth, like the Equator, the tropics and so on. But it doesn't work here, nothing does." He looked around at the settling dust, slumped against a bookshelf and placed his head in his hands.

"Things work right well fur me. Why dew't they fur yew?"

"Because you're different. You only accept what you know is true, not what others believe is true and try to impose on you. Like most people, I believed what I wanted to believe, especially if it pleased other people and was of benefit to me."

"How easy it is," replied John's voice again, "to believe in the rightness of everything and know the truth of nothing. This woman was sufficiently evolved to ask questions and seek the truth. Belief is for children, the first stop for the credulous and the last refuge of the ignorant – not to mention the justification for every selfish, greedy desire and depravity known to humanity."

"I should have been more inquiring," he admitted, crestfallen. "'Seek and ye shall find, knock and the door will be opened.' Well, I didn't knock and the door didn't open. Too busy looking to my own interests."

"It is difficult to cultivate a meaningful, philosophical life when you are only interested in a pleasant one. Yet had you tried, your life could have been so different. After all, you did meet someone very much like this woman, the sort that Tertullian wrote about. What was it…? Oh yes, 'We have among us a sister blessed with the gifts of revelation… she sees and hears mysterious communications… sees visions and understands the hearts of men…'"

"I don't remember. If I did, she didn't show me anything."

"Of course she didn't. You were only interested in seducing her so she fled."

"Damn my eyes," Thomas groaned, sinking to his knees, "now I remember. A pretty wench she was."

"Yes, damn them indeed. She had the gift of second sight and you could have seen something of the greater reality through her eyes had yours not been so blind."

"Ah, I wasn't very kind to women," he agreed, shamefaced.

"I know," said Sarah, back to herself. "We cont hide nothin' from noo one har."

"Then it's all up with me, I suppose." He stared glumly again at the floor, but saw in surprise that it was now free of dust.

"Don't be sappy! Look about yew. The room isn't dusty noo more, even the cobwebs are gone – and the spiders. Remember," she added, inspired, "this be a world of thought. It was yar thoughts tha' created this place, a mind full o' cobwebs!"

Not only the cobwebs but, even as they watched, every speck of dirt vanished too, the paintwork brightened and the furniture gleamed as though polished. A light breeze from the open window wafted in with the scents of flowers that were already replacing the weeds and brambles. Thomas' appearance was also altering, from an apparent threadbare vagabond to the immaculately dressed gentleman he had once been, whilst the jaded, etched and prematurely aged face softened into the kinder, even foppish features of his youth.

Before he fully understood what was happening, his attention was drawn to the open window and the fast-fading light outside. He saw a darkening welkin in which stars were appearing as everywhere became hushed and still.

"Have yew not seen it afore?" she asked, noting his puzzled expression. "The nights kinda pull in quickly har, but in noo toime it'll be morning agen."

"Look," he said in wonder, pointing upward and taking her hand, "there are Castor and Pollux and, beyond them, Orion and Taurus. The Great Bear must be overhead. And way over there, the Dog Star. I've never seen them as bright as this." He looked back into the modest eyes of the fresh-faced, guileless young woman. "Will you be my friend?" was all he could manage.

They walked for a while in the soft light of the night, around his garden and beneath trees, no longer dense and threatening. As Thomas began to feel less troubled about himself, he began to be aware that there might be something important troubling Sarah. What had she said about not being able to hide anything? She smiled readily enough, but her smile failed to conceal a certain sadness; looking more closely, he somehow divined that, deep within, she did indeed bear some kind of heavy burden. He took her hand.

"You say you have no family here?"

"Noo, as far as I know they're still livin' – I mean, they're still in t'other place."

"I think there's more to it," he observed, holding her hand more firmly. "Would you like to tell me?"

Her mind flew instantly to the family cottage beneath the entwining oaks, to the fields all about and sandy banks of the Orwell. She pictured her father labouring hard at the plough and her dear Ma, always busy but with a ready smile. Life had always been a struggle but somehow they'd been contented, at times even happy. But something was very, very wrong. She could sense it. What had happened to change everything? All the worries and anguish about Nance poured out now.

"Thar's a man, Cabern," she sobbed. "Rob Cabern. My sister Nance loves 'em. She'll dew for 'em what she ont dew fur noo one else. She's blinded by passion. Noo good'll coom of it an' I'm soo afeared. Tha' man ul ruin har, all of us..."

Thomas listened patiently before speaking, surprising himself as much as her.

"It is possible we can help her."

"How? I cont even see har. How can I help har if I dewn't know wha's a-gooing on?" They came back to the house and she sank into a chair, clean and comfortable now, waiting anxiously and hoping for the impossible.

"I believe there's a way we can return – it is permitted. Bear with me while I tell you what I know. See, the difficulty for me was in leaving the Earth at all. I was murdered. I'd been out carousing with friends and we parted in the early hours outside a club in St James's. I strode off alone but two footpads with daggers waylaid me demanding money, so I drew my sword but I was too drunk to notice a third man behind me. I felt the blade enter below my heart and pierce my lung. That was me done for.

"The extraordinary thing was that I was able to get up, apparently none the worse. Of course, I hadn't realised I was snuffed out. So I carried on walking until I reached home and somehow I just walked through the door. A footman was in the hallway but he just ignored me and other servants were up and about, showing not a glimmer of recognition. It was like one of those awful dreams, where you find yourself in a place with no recollection of how you came there but can't leave. And everywhere was becoming so gloomy.

"Finally, the notion came to me that I must be dead – but then how could I know I was dead? At some point I heard horses' hooves and carriage wheels and saw a moving light, and a coachman with a lantern appeared and asked me to go with him. I climbed in and took a seat, and as we drew away I saw there were other passengers. I realised they were dead too yet somehow – and this is the weirdest part – they knew where they were going, which was more than I did. It was a night-time journey along a silent road until eventually we emerged into the light like dawn breaking.

"I could see people in the distance I recognised, family and friends whom I knew were long dead, so I waved and I wanted to stay there, but the coachman forbade it. He brought me here instead and said it was to be my home. It looked like it was about to tumble down but the man said that was all that could be done with the materials I'd provided. Then he left.

"As you know, it was dirty with dust and cobwebs everywhere and the place literally seemed to be falling apart. I felt so tired now that I just lay down and slept and dreamed, my whole life passing before me like nightmares, one after the other. Eventually I awoke only I couldn't bear to stay in here with this damned, overpowering light. It's just as I told you," he went on, squinting hard, "it penetrates to the very soul. Gads my life, it's agony!

"So I threw my cloak over my head and set off to explore. I stumbled through that forest and finally reached those swampy, turgid waters where you happened upon me. It was the only place where there wasn't any light."

Sarah listened carefully but it was a while before she spoke.

"What was the year o' your death?" He told her. "But when I coom… Why, yew've been here ten years, yew poor, lost, troubled soul."

"No, don't pity me, Sarah," he said earnestly, coming over to kneel beside her chair and take her hand. "It's only as much as I deserve. But the point is this, as I was saying, I believe there's a way back. As I sat there on that foul, muddy shore, I kept thinking about my former life. And I found that if I thought about it vividly enough, I became heavier… heavier, that is, until I seemed to belong more to the old familiar world than this place. Then I began to see, just as though I were actually there, the forms of places and people I knew. It wasn't clear at first but, truth is, somehow I was there. With practice, I found I could visit my old haunts and even stay awhile. Still, what was the use? I couldn't speak to anyone and, of course, no-one knew I was there."

"How would that help me?" sighed Sarah.

"Well, it would be different for you. You have close family, especially your sister, and I believe you could be near her if you so wished, walking beside her and perhaps even influencing her. As for me, I'm not that close to anyone. I can't blend in with them, if you see what I mean."

She glowed at the prospect of seeing Nance again, and looked deeply with gentle eyes into his.

"Yew have a friend now, Thomas."

"Thank you, I'm very fortunate." His fingers squeezed her hand, a gesture she found pleasing, and in return she placed her hand on his, stroked it and rested her head on his shoulder.

"Will yew show me how I can goo back to my family?"

"Yes. Even better, I'll come with you. You've helped me far more than I deserve. Now I'm going to help you."

"First of all, you must think of earthly things – the weariness, the travail, frustrations and disappointments, the sickness, and the grosser things like overindulgence."

She pictured herself rising weakly once more from her bed, for the unpleasant chores of emptying pisspots, collecting the night soil and drying it for compost. Then she thought of her sister and how she had clung to her as life ebbed away, as though trying to hold back the departing spirit.

"Do you feel heavy now?" he asked, taking her by the arm.

"Wholly soo." It was as though she were in her old body again.

"Then think carefully about where you want to be."

The very atmosphere felt oppressive as a thick vapour enveloped them, and she realised they were no longer in his room. In her mind's

82

eye she pictured her old home. Her body felt denser and she passed through, with a tingling sensation, what seemed like layers of cobwebs but which she then saw was the door of the Auldfields' cottage. They found an interior unnaturally opaque, like a marsh mist, at least to their eyes, for plainly it was still light outside. So thick was it they could scarcely see or move around. Sarah in particular was aware of an almost unbearable heaviness as well now, as though weighed down by an unshakable burden.

"You'll become used to it," said Thomas, encouraging her.

She made a determined effort to find her way about and see what was happening. Her mother was sitting by the smoky hearth plucking… what, a pheasant? An unheard of luxury, perhaps a perk of some kind or a 'thank you' for some special service rendered. More likely poaching, a capital offence.

As she thought this, sequence of pictures and sounds of her worst fears flashed into her mind. She saw her brothers Albert and Mark with a sack and a spring-trap net, hiding in thickets and hollows and wriggling snake-like beneath fences. Guiding each other in the pitch black and mimicking the cries of beast and bird, they were spreading their net and waiting. When rustling noises indicated the presence of creatures, they sprang the trap; each animal or bird was being despatched and stuffed into the sack. The night's work done, she saw them steal away like prey themselves, avoiding spring-gun booby traps and gamekeeper alike.

After a while, a distraught Sarah saw Matty enter followed by his father. Old Zeb walked with a stoop and lowered himself into a chair with the weariness of one far older than his years. Sarah stood beside him and tried to stroke his hoary locks and kiss his furrowed brow to comfort him, but now his only reaction was to shudder, as though from a sudden draught. Yet a strained expression did show some relief and his eyes glowed brighter. If only she could be back in the flesh to care for him now…

She turned to Beth and saw a deep weariness there too, along with sadness. Approaching her mother, she instinctively put a hand on her shoulder as though to comfort her but it passed right through her, as though through smoke. Beth shuddered. Sarah was becoming distressed by what had happened to the family. Where was John, and where indeed was dearest Nance? Before long, the door opened and they both entered. Nance, visiting for the day, wore a simple linen dress and apron, her eyes were tired and her features drawn. She hugged her parents and then looked at her brother Matty slumped in a corner.

"Haps yew'll goo an' give Ma a hand, seein' as how yew only works chance-time now an' seein' as yew've had another restful day, courtesy of Rob Cabern. That's if yew can put down yar precious brandy. If I had ought ta dew wi' it, yew'd not get it noo more."

So that was it. Sarah might have known who was behind all this, her worst fears confirmed.

"Dewn't goo on soo, Nance," slurred Matty. "Us niver meant noo harm. Us be just havin' a little owd drink."

"While the rest of us slaves all day an' half the night. An' if we dewn't work, the Harveys ul turn us off an' we ont have noo roof over our heads."

Sarah and Thomas remained while the family prepared and ate their meal. There was one thing more she had to know – was Nance still besotted with Cabern? She waited until everyone had gone to sleep before going to the bed they used to share where she knelt beside it. With her talent for divining her sister's secrets, she quickly learned what she feared, that Nance was indeed still in love with Cabern, and madly so. What fate was this, that had rendered her a smuggler's doxy?

"Nance, dearest Nance, it's me, Sarah," she whispered. "I be a-tellin', an' just yew be a-hearin'. Nance, I'm not dead! Nance, dewn't have noo more ta do wi' Rob Cabern, not now, not niver!"

Her words could not be heard yet something of the thought within them penetrated. Her sister stirred, her eyelids flickering, and she put out a hand as though to touch Sarah's bodiless form.

Sarah did indeed feel a hand, an all too firm one – John was at her side.

"We must go, Sarah," he urged. "You cannot stay." His tone was authoritative yet compassionate, for her face was a picture of misery. Surely something could be done for her poor sister? Her tears and objections were of no avail as John took her by the arm, motioned Thomas to follow, and led her away from the cottage.

Nance's fears for the family's future materialised soon enough. John, the most sensible and responsible of her brothers, had decided he had enough rudiments of education from the old sexton. Encouraged by Cabern's tales of foreign parts, he considered enlisting in the army and left for Ipswich. Then scarcely had the family bade a sorrowful farewell than Albert began to experience the ill-effects of his new love for brandy, delirium tremens, in the form of menacing spiders crawling out of the wall. Staggering drunkenly homeward one snowy night, he had collapsed and died of exposure. He 'lay against the wall' in his parents' cottage the next day, Sunday, the family only too aware of the old saying, 'If one lies against the wall on a Sunday, another will lie in the same place afore long.'

The fatal night for Mark had come when a harassed gamekeeper set a trap in an Orwell Park depleted of game. He armed and stationed servants in the woods, ensuring that each had a clear field of fire, then tethered several wildfowl to low posts, leaving them to peck and squawk. Hours passed until the keeper heard an owl's hoot close by, followed by another, so deliberate that they had to be human. The keeper had a call of his own and made a signal to his men to prepare for action.

The poachers, attracted by the noisy, squabbling fowl, attempted to deploy their net, whilst the sable clouds high above parted a little, allowing enough pallid moonlight for the keeper to pick out a human form.

"Stay where you are, you blackguards!" he bawled. "Stand up and show yourselves!"

For Mark and his pals, the sudden shock of discovery turned to gut-wrenching fear then blind panic. The keeper saw another indistinct mass rise up and perhaps a third.

"Fire!" he ordered. There were flashes and the deafening discharges of half a dozen muskets echoed through the wood as all nature erupted. Every bird and beast shrieked, yelped and flapped against foliage then bolted through it in terror. The keeper's party had advanced through the choking smoke, quickly joined by others bearing flambeaux. They found only the abandoned net and dark blood stains on a pathway.

It was still dark when Beth was awakened by raps on the cottage door. Opening it, she screamed as Mark staggered in, pitched forward and lay motionless, his shirt and coat soaked in blood. A musket ball had passed through his chest, piercing the right lung and breaking a rib. As he was laid on a bed, a terrified Beth told Matty to ride in all haste for Dr Abbett, but a barely conscious Mark had grimly accepted his fate.

"Kiss me, dearest Ma... I'm done fur!"

He lingered in agony a while longer before the eyes flickered and stared sightless in death. For the second time in a few months, a humble cortege wound its mournful, solemn way from the cottage to the church. Another mound of earth was heaped to mark the spot where Mark's remains had been laid beside those of Albert and their sister.

CHAPTER 6

HARVEST HOME

At Abbeyfield Farm it was now harvest-home. For many a weary day every available man, woman and child had been labouring intensely, sometimes well into a moonlit night, to bring in the harvest. Finally, the longed-for day arrived when all the fruits were gathered in and the sickle had shorn the last field.

On this day, the last sheaf of corn, representing the spirit of the fields, was placed on the last load of the harvest wain and decorated with green boughs, flowers and ribbons. The mowers and tiers, including Jethro, clambered aboard and with a cry of "Hold ye!" were driven to the barn where they were greeted by whistles, huzzas, fiddle and horn. The Lord o' the Harvest, the elected headman, waved a leather bag containing largess, the shilling coins solicited by the weary reapers from passers-by. Solemnly, he placed it on the ground. All gathered in a circle, as custom dictated, while he stood a few paces away and hallowed it.

"Holla lar, holla lar, holla lar-jees!"

The rest inclined their heads and accompanied him, drawing out the "o" sound then holding onto the final "lar", lowering their voices before throwing up their heads and yelling "jees!" as loudly as possible. Afterwards they thanked each donor by name before the younger men raced around the fields shouting, "Lar-jees, lar-jees!" From neighbouring fields, farms and hamlets the cry was returned, "Lar-jees!"

This was also the day when the farmer invited all the harvestmen for a harvest-home supper, known as the horkey. Rank was absent from these gatherings and master and servant sat at the same table, jesting and singing until the early hours. At Abbeyfield Farm the supper was held in the back parlour. Nance's task had been to help prepare and cook the gargantuan meal with other servants and some of the wives. Whole carcases were turned and roasted on the spit, whilst every available pan, trencher and skillet crowded the hearth and pots and cauldrons hung from hakes over the curling flames. Bellows fanned the wood-fired oven as tables and dresser groaned with every kind of seasonal dish, pudding and fruit.

Several dozen people, including Jethro, squeezed around the tables. Mr Knoller said grace, and when everyone's horn cup was charged with strong harvest ale he proposed the farmer's toast, thanking Almighty God for the bountiful harvest and wishing health and prosperity to all in the year ahead. The Lord o' the Harvest responded in song.

"Here's a health unto our master,
the founder of the feast!
I wish, with all my heart and soul,
in Heaven he may find rest.
I hope all things may prosper
that ever he takes in hand;
for we are all his servants
and all be at his command.
Drink, boys, drink, and see you do not spill,
for if you do, you must drink two – it is your master's will!"

He was then crowned with a pair of ram's horns, painted and decorated with flowers. Nance and the other maids brought in the first course of cod and lamb to loud cheers and a second followed of roast beef and then a third of poultry, including the harvest-goose, every dish accompanied by vegetables and as much ale as a man could swallow. Plum puddings, the horkey cake, custard and apple pies and pyramids of fruit brought the feast to an end.

Mrs Knoller led the wives and children into the front parlour for tea and left the men to their ale, where the Lord o' the Harvest divided up the largess. Then it was time for the serious business of singing, to the sound of the fiddle, by the parlour minstrels.

> *"Come all you fine ploughboys, come help me to sing,*
> *I will sing in the praise of you all.*
> *An' if we don't labour, how can we get bread?*
> *We shall sing an' be merry with all.*
>
> *There be April an' May, there be June and July,*
> *what a pleasure to see the corn grow.*
> *An' when August draws nigh, we will reap shoofs an' tie,*
> *go down with our sickles to mow.*
>
> *Oh, it's when we had mew an' tied every shoof,*
> *we shall sing, feast an' drink humming beer!*
> *We'll make no more to do, but to ploughing will go*
> *an' provide for the very next year.*
>
> *Then at night we retire thro' clouds an' thro' clay,*
> *no comfort at all can we find.*
> *We shall sit down an' sing, an' drive away care,*
> *we will leave the wide world to repine."* [1]

For a few blissful hours, everyone's cares and troubles were forgotten and every man sang and drank as though the night would never end (and he would not have to rise and go to work on the morrow).

But one man, Jethro, could not forget his cares, Nance and her rejection. Had she at least loved a worthier soul he might have resigned himself more easily to his fate; but that he, an honest man who laboured every hour the Good Lord sent, should be rejected in

---

[1] *The Ploughboy's Glory*

favour of a criminal was altogether too grievous to bear. He knew now that his only chance of somehow living life without Nance would be to leave his home and seek a better fortune in some other land. As his companions revelled noisily, he took a foaming cup and slipped away unnoticed, wandering out into the sunset to drown his sorrows. Then, across the moat and a few dozen paces from the farmhouse, he disappeared amongst the elms.

After Sarah's enforced return from the cramped confines of her old home, Thomas's refurbished palatial mansion gave her the joy of a snared bird regaining its freedom.

They stood in his study, an odd-looking couple: he immaculately dressed, she in plain linen, her artless hair trailing over shapeless shoulders. Welcoming light poured in and beckoned them through the French windows and onto a newly-paved terrace overlooking the garden... and what a garden it was now. When last they had seen it, beds of budding flowers and sprouting grass were starting to replace the weeds. Now the flowerbeds were a kaleidoscope of dazzling colours, bordering a cadmium lawn that swept over an incline down to a tree-lined avenue. As the pair entered the garden, a carolling of birdsong and a fluttering of wings greeted them from overhanging branches.

Taking in the scented air, the pair sauntered along the terrace and descended a flight of smooth marble steps to the garden. Waiting for them there was Zebedee's late plough-horse, the joy of her childhood, with flattened, quivering ears and a welcoming whinny. It nuzzled her hand and then trotted away happily to rejoin its companions in the pasture beyond the avenue. As Sarah contemplated the ethereal beauty about her she wished so much that, somehow, her Nance might come to know that this wonderful world awaited her too.

Thomas needed to explore his newly transformed home, especially his books, and Sarah could see how important this was for him. So she shrugged and slipped away back to her own cottage. As for those nagging fears for her sister, what better way to occupy her mind, she reasoned, than by tending her own garden. It was now growing so fast that it all but hid the cottage walls.

No sooner had she begun working than the children, as boisterous as ever, dashed up and wanted to play. Then Mollie called and wanted to chat – perhaps for an hour or two, or was it a week? The neighbours also descended on her, prompting visits to their homes in return when she was not playing with the children, until she became entirely distracted from her troubling thoughts. Every person here was of the same mind, all were friends with no formalities, something that Sarah had never experienced. It seemed only a moment ago that she had stood beside Thomas in his study and she resolved to visit him again – but then someone or something always distracted her.

Yet she couldn't stay away for long. She found him as she had left him, surrounded by piles of books. Unlike the rest of the house, little had changed in his study; yes, the room remained free of dust and spiders but books were still piled high on every available space up to the ceiling. Her unexpected appearance surprised him and he arose, greeting her apologetically and bowing (though with his mind, she felt, still elsewhere).

"Gad save, if it in't Miss Auldfield come to rescue me a second time! Look, I've tried, how I've tried to sort this lot out and find those perishing Fathers, but I've got nowhere… nowhere." He took her hand and kissed it. "I'm so awfully sorry. Forgive me, I should have called on you." She put a finger to his lips.

"Yew marn't apologise. If any should visit, it's me. I meant ta coom many a time, then summat allus coom up an' I ended up forgettin' ta."

"I'm glad you're here. Perhaps it was for the best anyway, you needed some time to yourself and I wanted to sort things out. Not that I've done any good, mind."

"The garden's grander than ever."

"Is it? Egad, I'd clean forgot."

"You forgot the garden?" She was incredulous. Nature is surely more important than any house, however grand.

"Perhaps I should take a look." He offered his arm and together they strolled onto the terrace and down the steps. Everything was as she remembered, except… Towards the end of the lawn had appeared what she believed gentlemen call a folly. It was a mysterious temple-like structure with four Ionic columns on a lofty podium supporting a portico with a finely-carved frieze on the pediment. There were three statues on the podium and two smaller friezes running around it, but, curiously, no steps to be seen and no means of entry.

"Good heavens, it's a tomb, Hellenistic I'd say," mused Thomas. "But what on Earth is it doing here?" He noticed, too, a grotto with a human skull on a pedestal and, a few yards away, what appeared to be a freshly dug grave with a ladder protruding.

Sarah's attention was already elsewhere, drawn to an ornamental rock pool to one side of the garden. Droplets from a waterfall, fed by a bubbling rill, sang like the strings of a harp on its rippling surface. Waving flags shadowed part of the pool, which was surrounded by an herb-scented, mossy margin. With surprise, she realised that it was similar to the humbler pond she used to gaze in when meditating in her earlier life, glimpsing the world she was now in. Like her new cottage when she had first seen it, this pool somehow seemed made for her.

"Is this not paradise?" said a familiar voice. She turned to find John standing beside her.

"Far better than tha' muddy owd hoss pond back home!" Awestruck, she looked about her and drank in the surreal beauty.

"Do you think," he went on, "you could work here with Thomas?"

"Work here?" she gasped. "Me? But I'm jus' a ploughman's darter."

"Not at all. You will come to realise that you're an old soul whose spirit has evolved through many lifetimes. You have helped many others already and can do so again. The choice is always yours, of course."

Thomas had come over to them and, meeting John in person for the first time since their enforced departure from her parents' cottage, bowed respectfully in deference. He looked at Sarah with new eyes and suddenly realised how much he would rather be in the company of this adorable creature than alone with his books. Why had he not seen it and spoken up before? Playfully, he slapped her on the back.

"I'd be honoured to have you with me, old gal! As soon as I've sorted out things inside, we'll get started."

"Oh no," smiled John. "It's not that simple. In your case, you had a lifetime to sort things out and you accomplished nothing. One cannot reap what one has not sown."

"But Gad, my library—"

"No excuses! The library can wait. You're here to do the sort of work you should have been doing in the other place. There's time enough for books." As his smile broadened, his words became deliberately intriguing. "We have in our libraries here everything of importance ever written, including the lost—"

"What, the library of Alexandria, the one that was burned to the ground?"

"Indeed, we have everything from Alexandria and elsewhere, scrolls and papyri, all the wisdom of the ancients – everything from cuneiform and hieroglyphs to Attic Greek and Latin, from Plato and Cicero to Augustine and Swedenborg." He paused, looking a little more stern. "But in your case, the right to pursue these studies must be earned. Do you understand?"

"What is it you require of me, sir?" he said respectfully, realising now that this was the same voice that had spoken through Sarah earlier.

"Many a lost soul will be coming your way, guided by the light and beauty of these gardens, those who wandered in darkness just as you did. Some think they are still in the other place, whilst others are trapped in an existence they've imagined for themselves. They don't know where they are or which way to turn. You can help them – if you agree to this."

"Yes, yes, damn me if I don't. My word on't as a gentleman. Only—"

"What is it?"

"May I… that is, I wonder, would it be possible to see my family, sir? I glimpsed them from afar when first I arrived, but that's all."

"They're happy and well – more than you might appreciate at present – and, yes, they look forward to being reunited. But they dwell on a higher plane. You will too someday, but you must earn it, you must evolve to their level. Do you understand?"

Thomas nodded, looking a little crestfallen, as John now turned to Sarah.

"And you, Sarah? What do you say, would you like to work with Thomas?"

Thomas squeezed her hand as she mouthed a 'Yes'. Yet the joy she felt at being so honoured – not to mention of being alongside this man whom she liked more than she cared to admit – could not dispel a continuing inner sadness. If only, she was thinking, she could help poor Nance too.

Meantime, near Downham Reach, a small sailboat was braving the choppy evening waters. Its lone sailor steered for the shore, downed sail, beached the craft and dragged it clear of the mud. Looking like a fisherman in wide-soled mud-splashers, he wore light blue trousers and a red conical cap. Around his legs and arms, however, and hanging from other parts of his body were rings, amulets, horses' bones and a human rib – that of Margery Beddingfield, strangled and burned on Rushmere Heath for her husband's murder. The man wore these to ward off the evil forces that were as much a part of his world as the river and its people. Adding to the trinkets and fastened to his clothing were written spells, charms and verses. Finally, to protect the precious craft, his only means of livelihood, in his absence, a horseshoe was nailed to the masthead.

He took up a basket of fish and a lantern and, as dusk fell, set off up the bank to take the path to Abbeyfield Farm. This man was Sorcy Solomon, known locally as the Sorcerer because of the infernal beings that were believed to accompany him. A jack-of-all-trades, he had been a mail-coach guard, militiaman and journeyman before turning to fishing to scrape a meagre living, catching and selling fish to local houses and businesses.

His leaky and much repaired peter boat was probably the most dangerous that ever plied the Orwell. His own handiwork, it was made of makeshift materials since his poverty preventing him from obtaining the proper ones. Its single sail was made of pieces of canvas sewn together and the boat creaked, listed badly and sometimes shipped water under its owner's weight. The only reason he entrusted himself to it, setting sail in practically all weathers, was his confidence in the power he wielded over the demons he was convinced tormented him.

A firm believer in the dark arts and demons, his enemies were twofold. First, some witches at Needham Market had set a curse to torment him, using amongst other execrable matter the bones of Mrs Wilkerson of Felixstowe, also executed at Rushmere. Second, his mind had become an open door for mischievous Earthbound spirits, trapped in their twilight existence, who wished to contact the physical world. Solomon was a sensitive being through whom they could experience the only reality they knew, thereby continuing to influence human affairs.

He was forever seeing them, either mentally, or as will-o'-the-wisp figures in the corner of his eye. They spoke to him too. At times they were unintelligible but they also gave clear warning of storms and other dangers, either imminent or not far away. Why they should do this was quite clear to Solomon: they protected him and kept him alive, solely so that they might continue to torment him. But as he was no more inclined than the next man to meet his Maker any time soon, he resolved to let them continue. His powerful charms and spells kept them at arm's length, making life at least tolerable. For their part, they would never let him drown on any of his hazardous expeditions, he reasoned, since that would deprive them of their pleasure.

Now, as he set off for the farm, he became aware of the piercing eye of his chief tormentor fixed steadily upon him and a clear voice urged, "Danger ahead. Go back!"

What possible danger, mused Solomon, could there be at this hour, safe ashore and without a soul about? From around his neck he took his most powerful charm, Beddingfield's rib, and, holding it before him, cried, "Begone in the name of the living God an' by the spirits of the undead, I conjure thee. Get thee hence, Satan!" The phantom vanished and he resumed his journey.

In the smoky and sweltering kitchen, an exhausted Nance contemplated the piles of dishes, pots and utensils that would take the rest of the night and all next day to scald, scour or polish. Added to this, she had to continually recharge the revellers' ever emptying cups of ale. It was when she entered the parlour for this purpose that she noticed Jethro's absence.

"Where be Jethro?" she asked. The men looked around the room and then at each another, trying to remember when they had last seen him, before announcing between hiccoughs that they didn't know. She returned to the kitchen as the older men now left to join their wives in the front parlour and one or two maidens slipped back the other way to be with their lovers and enjoy an embrace or a jig. When Nance returned later with more ale and again enquired about Jethro, some noticed the worry in her voice. One remembered seeing Jethro taking more than a passing interest in Nance, whilst another had been nearby weeks before when they had returned from Piper's Vale, walking side by side.

"Yew know wha' I think?" said one, leaning across the table and thrusting his face in front of the Harvest Lord. "I think Jethro Merryridge be in love wi' Nance Auldfield."

"Eawr Nance?"

"Yes, Nance. An' what's more, haps har be in love with 'em."

A few cups of ale more and everyone became convinced that the two were lovers. One banged his cup on the table and began to sing.

"Youth's the season made for joys, love be then our duty;
she alone who this employs, well deserves her beauty.
Come be gay, while we may, beauty's a flower despised in decay.
Youth's the season made for joys, love be then our duty.
Let us drink an' sport today, ours be not tomorrow.
Love with youth flies swift away, age be naught but sorrow.
Dance an' sing, time's on the wing, life never knows the return of spring.
Let us drink an' sport today, ours be not tomorrow."

All the while, Jethro had been sitting on a log beneath the elms consoling himself with ale. Apart from chinks of light from the curtained windows and the muffled din within, all was darkness and silence. Then he heard sounds, scarcely audible, like a trotting horse and cartwheels and, sure enough, the indistinct shapes of horse and cart loomed into view. It halted in the lane only a few yards from where he sat. Linen-wrapped hooves and wheels meant only one thing – smugglers. One man alighted and walked stealthily towards the bridge and the farmhouse.

Inside, Nance was becoming increasingly worried about Jethro. Determined to look for him, she took a lantern and stepped outside, closing the door behind her and crossing the bridge.

"Jethro?" she called. "Jethro, are yew out thar?"

He rose at the mention of his name. But as she held up the lantern it revealed a shadowy man approaching. He addressed her in a husky whisper as the light fell upon his seaman's jacket and trousers. Rob Cabern! She would have cried out had he not leapt forward and cupped a hand to her mouth, grasping her hand and kissing it.

"Nance, my darlin', everything's all right. I've come for you, just as I promised."

He looked into her dark eyes expecting his welcoming grin to be returned. Instead, overcome by her old passion sparking like gunpowder, she stood there trembling and helpless. She swayed and might have fainted had not Cabern caught and steadied her. He looked closely into her eyes and saw the love of old but also, he realised, an anxiety.

"Rob, Rob, tell me yew's noo longer involved wi' Diamond and Rackhem," she pleaded.

"Nance, I'm almost done with them. One more voyage, that's all, an' we'll have enough to buy a business, settle down and work for ourselves."

"Noo, Rob! I've told yew afore. I'll marry yew but I ont be noo smuggler's wife. I'll keep house for yew, I'll slave for yew, anythin' – but yew must leave tha' trade."

"I can't Nance, not at the moment. I'm a wanted man, a price on my head. We can go to Holland, be married an' lie low for a while. We'll put it about that Cabern's dead, then I can start life afresh as someone else. Well, what d'you say?"

"Noo Rob, I cont just oop and goo. My parents need lookin' after now, an' Mistress Knoller's been wholly good ta me."

"Hard it is, Nance," his face darkened, "when a man's within sight of port to find himself blown seaward again." He took the lantern and placed it on the ground, clasping both her hands and kissing them. "Nance, ship with me now. A comfy berth awaits you an' a south-westerly beckons. We'll crowd on all sail for Holland an' be married in days."

"I cont not, Rob," she sobbed, tears welling in her eyes. At that moment, Jethro noticed a second man step out of the shadows and stride towards Cabern and Nance.

"I told you it was no good, Rob. Now grab her an' let's be orf."

Aghast, she recognised the voice as Rackhem's. Unable to hold back any longer, Jethro, the worse for drink, now lurched towards them. Cabern kept hold of Nance's hands still trying to entice her away while Rackhem seized her by the waist.

"Unhand her, Cabern!" yelled Jethro, rushing up. Cabern did so but only to throw a punch at Jethro's head making him reel backwards. He recovered and dived at Cabern and the pair fell to wrestling.

The fisherman Sorcy Solomon, meanwhile, had continued to walk along the path and was nearing the house when the affray began. By the light of the discarded lantern, he could see two men trying to drag away a young woman whilst a third intervened. That was enough for the old militiaman. He put down his basket and lantern, ran up behind Rackhem and pulled back his head in an arm lock as Nance prised herself free.

"Avast heavin! What rogues be yew tha' board strangers at night wi' out leave or notice?"

In the parlour, the revellers couldn't help but hear the commotion and staggered out of doors and across the bridge to investigate. By the light from the open doorway they could see Cabern, who by now had the better of Jethro, throwing him to the ground and kicking him several times as he tried to get up. Rackhem struggled to free himself from Solomon and elbowed him until his grip released. After several well aimed punches, Solomon too went down.

"It's over, Rob," shouted Rackhem. "Leave the wench. Let's go, or we'll be taken!"

Cabern turned to flee but Jethro dragged himself to his feet and stumbled after him as bemused and befuddled revellers, led by the Harvest Lord, also ran forward. Rackhem pulled a pistol from his belt and took deliberate aim at Jethro.

"I'll board you with a bow shot you little expected!"

He squeezed the trigger, the weapon bucked and Jethro was hit, sent reeling before slumping to his knees and pitching forward. Cabern reached the cart and pulled out a blunderbuss, turning to discharge it over the revellers' heads. There was a brilliant flash and a deafening report that rattled the farmhouse windows. It was a clear and simple message. The crowd halted and could only watch helplessly as Cabern and Rackhem mounted the cart, whipped the horse into a fast trot and disappeared into the night.

A terrified and bitterly distressed Nance knelt beside Jethro, cradling his head in her arms. He was carried inside and laid on a couch, where Nance and some of the other women tended to him for the rest of the night. Before dawn, a rider was despatched to Ipswich for Dr Abbett. Jethro had not been mortally wounded for the ball had lodged in his left shoulder near the skin and was soon removed. But pieces of wadding and clothing proved more difficult, and excruciatingly painful, to extract. The doctor's verdict was that time would heal the wound and the young man should recover fully.

Nance felt truly terrible and held herself responsible for everything. When he had treated the patient, Abbett took her aside and tried to find out what had occurred. He knew of Cabern's activities – who did not? – yet had never forgotten the little girl who had cared for her sister so devotedly and saved her mistress's life. Also, like many other men, he admired her and perhaps felt more.

In an age when everyone knew their place and there were few opportunities for pretence, George Abbett believed that, quite simply, either one was a gentleman or one was not. If not, then no amount of money or fine clothes would alter that. But if so, then nothing one did, even outside one's class, could change it either. Consequently, any woman and even a servant would find him to be not only a kind doctor but also, if necessary, a true friend. So when he had listened to everything she had to say, he realised there was no point in attempting the impossible and trying to turn the young woman's heart from her lover. Instead, he ought to offer her the benefit of his mature wisdom, softened with as much sincerity and understanding as he could muster.

He stood up and, as was his habit when the moment required some careful thought, produced an enamelled snuffbox engraved, tellingly, with an image of Leda being raped by the swan. In one elegant movement he opened it between thumb and forefinger, took a pinch, inhaled, and just as elegantly closed the box before taking out a dark silk handkerchief to dab away any remaining grains. He began to pace the room.

Cabern, he told Nance, was a product of his times. How could he alone stand condemned when so many others willingly accepted what he had to offer? Life was not always just – at least not in this world – and if he were caught there would be several among those watching him hang who should equally be accused. It made her shudder, sensing where this argument was leading.

And it was not only Cabern's fate that would bring grief for the innocent would suffer too, as indeed some already had. Nance couldn't help but think of her brothers; they may not have been so innocent, but they had been weak. Rob Cabern, the doctor continued, was an educated man but his associates were not and creatures like Rackhem and Moll were the underclass of society who lived by crime and played by different rules. Moreover, they were better at taking care of themselves than an honest soul like Nance, unpractised in villainy. One day, he predicted, she might well become involved, innocently and unwittingly, in matters she did not understand – and she would be the one to suffer.

"Put a distance between you," he advised, taking a seat opposite her and leaning forward with a kindly smile. "You love him and love is the noblest feeling one human being can have for another, for it means giving a part of yourself. It also means – and this is the hardest part – accepting that love may not be returned. Love him if you must, Nance, but ask yourself whether he really loves you. If he does, he will abandon his way of life that has caused so much suffering already, and nearly cost young Jethro his life. Keep a distance!"

She nodded her agreement, although she was in floods of tears by now. "One more thing, Nance," he went on, as he rose. "I told you once that if ever you needed a friend you had only to ask. I'm telling you again and I cannot make it plainer. In George Abbett you will never find a truer friend. And now, m'dear, I must be going."

She stood up and bobbed respectfully with a tearstained smile. But now, Nance's employers and fellow servants at the Abbeyfield Farm were set on blaming her for what had happened. Satisfied that Jethro was out of danger, she thought it prudent to resign rather than wait for dismissal and went to pack her few possessions. Finally, she went to Jethro to bid farewell, kneeling by the bed and holding his hand.

"Jethro, what can I say? I be ta blame fur all thus. Judge me yew must, thus only fittin' an' I'll not ask forgiveness." She began to sob. "But I want yew ta know, a man's not niver done what yew did fur me, an' it nearly cost yew yar life. I'll allus be in yar debt, Jethro. An' though I cont not marry yew, I think it a blessing for, where iver yew goo in the wide world, yew ont niver find soo worthless a wretch as me."

As she spoke, he prayed that were he indeed fated to die soon then please may it be now, whilst this poor and much-wronged creature, dearer than life itself, knelt beside him. He was still in too much pain to say much, and it was an effort just to stay awake and not give in to welcoming sleep. "Nance, I do not blame you. And I do not say I forgive you because there's nothing to forgive."

That day, she left Abbeyfield Farm and returned to live with her parents.

CHAPTER 7

BEGINNING WORK

John knew Sarah's mind. "You can't live Nance's life for her. She has free will too, just as you did, so please don't try. Besides, the living have troubles enough of their own without being frightened out of their wits by the dead, however well-meaning!"

"But I'm not d—"

"No more clumsy visits like that. Understood?" Sheepishly, she agreed.

"Good. You may well be able to help her, but subtly and unobtrusively. You may influence her for the better, but never try to force anything on her. Everything must be her decision. It is her will that must prevail, not yours. Do you understand?"

"Yes, I s'pose soo."

"Good. Now listen, the pool here in this garden is for you. I had it created especially. This is your portal to the earthly side of life, just as the one you saw in your meditations was to this world. You cultivated your gifts there, so you can use them all the better here. Whenever you feel that Nance needs your help, come and look into it. Try it now, over there where it's deeper."

Eagerly, she knelt on the scented moss and peered into the crystal-clear waters.

"There have been events in the family, sad events I'm afraid, since your earthly visit," John continued. "So make it your intention to see what has happened, rather than what might be to come. Concentrate your thoughts on Nance and the family."

As she looked, building up beneath the ripples and bubbles, she saw the image of a black-haired young woman, busily preparing what looked like bandages. The room was small with a low sloping ceiling, a solitary lattice window and a candlestick with a reflector. The only furniture was a bed, a chair and a washstand.

"Why, it's Nance – oh, dearest Nance."

"Can you see anyone else?"

"Yes… just a moment… There be a man lying on the bed wearing a nightshirt… he looks in pain. Ah, it be Cabern! I mought have known. He'll be the death o' har, one day har'ul swing for 'em." Tears moistened her cheeks.

"I'm afraid there's worse to come," said John, laying a fatherly hand on her shoulder. The waters misted over and then cleared again to reveal a moonlit scene with a man lying spread-eagled across a snow-covered path, his head at an awkward angle, eyes open and staring, hands rigid and black with cold.

"It be eawr Albert," said a shocked Sarah, "an' 'em be frawn ta dead! An' what's a-coomin' next?" The images shifted like scenes in a play to show Mark being shot and wounded while out poaching, staggering homeward and leaning against the cottage door. As it was opened, he collapsed. "Oh noo, not eawr Mark too?"

"I'm afraid so."

"But why didn't yew tell me?" she sobbed. "'Haps I could have helped 'um."

"There was nothing you could have done for either of them. These were the tragic consequences of their own actions. But don't worry, you can help them here. You'll see them both shortly." Again the waters cleared. "There's more to come but this is not so bad."

Now she could see her sister struggling with two men who were apparently trying to abduct her as a third intervened. "Why, tha' be

Jethro." She saw Cabern punch and wrestle him to the ground before fleeing, but not before another man fired at Jethro. "Nawthin's soo bad as not soo bad!" moaned Sarah. "Jethro be the one har's s'posed ta marry," she cried, seeing her sister cradling him in her arms. "Oh noo, John, don't say 'em be over har too now."

"Happily, no. He'll make a full recovery."

She continued staring anxiously, helplessly, but the watery stage merely reflected her own sad face now. Again she felt a hand on her shoulder and looked round for John, but it was Thomas beside her and his hand remained there comfortingly as she stood up. He was deeply touched by her far-seeing, tear-filled eyes and the misery in her features, and he took out a handkerchief to wipe the tears.

"We'll help your sister. And we'll find your brothers and help them too." He pressed his lips to her hand and would have withdrawn had she not held him and pulled him closer.

"Why do yew bother yarself wi' the loikes o' me?"

"Because…" – their lips almost met – "because Sarah, I think I can help you, and… and I think I love you."

Their feelings were mutual and both were at last acknowledging the innermost thrill of being beside the other, feelings that could never remain hidden. Sarah leaned forward and they kissed gently as a wave of tender emotion ran through both of them.

"I know we belong together, you and I. Our fates seem interwoven."

They kissed again, so naturally and lovingly that any onlooker would have thought them lovers who had always been together. He fingered her tear-moistened cheeks and brushed aside strands of clinging hair as they held one another in a long embrace. Her fears were now his and his love so uplifted her that from this moment he became her rock. From afar, John noticed the change in them and was satisfied that his hopes were taking root.

A while later, a happier though still troubled Sarah returned to her cottage for some quiet reflection and to tend once more her own garden. Yet no sooner had she knelt down beside a blossom to smell its fragrance than a familiar voice hailed her. As she turned, Mollie was already at her side.

"So you have a job already, Sarah."

"How dew yew know?" was the startled response.

"I just do. We all know one another's minds here. When one of us does or so much as thinks something, we all know. You're going to work with the gentleman, aren't you?"

"I s'pose soo."

"An' you'll be seeing lots of other people besides?"

"Soo it seems."

Mollie looked at her quizzically. "Well, aren't you going to get ready, you know, get new clothes and suchlike?" Sarah looked down at her simple robe and fingered it, tightening the cord.

"I s'pose this ul dew."

"What? You can't work with the gentleman looking like that, especially when meeting all those people."

"But Thomas niver said nawthin—"

"Well, men don't! You come with me, my girl," she said, taking her firmly by the arm and leading her inside her own cottage. She went to what looked like a tiny wardrobe that, when opened, surprisingly had space for dozens of clothes, row upon row. She selected a white ankle-length dress. As slim and elegant as a fluted column, it had a low neckline, high waist and long sleeves, puffed at the shoulders. "This should be just right for you, dear. It's the latest thing here and soon it'll become fashionable in the other place, just you wait and see. It's called the Grecian look."

"But I cont not poss—"

"Nonsense! I've plenty more just as pretty," she added, holding it up to Sarah. "Trouble is, I don't have a chance to wear them all."

"In't it kinda long?"

"No matter, I'll shorten it." Mollie held it up, shook it out firmly and measured again. "Perfect. It only needed an inch or so off. Oh, an' you'll need some shoes. I've plenty of those too. An' we'll have to do something with that hair."

"What's wrong wi' it?"

"It's a mess, dear." Mollie opened a box and took out brushes, pins, curling tongs and a tortoiseshell comb. "Sit down."

"I cont not trouble yew—"

"After all you did for me? If I turned you into a goddess I'd still be in your debt. An' I saw you with those children, the way you transformed them. I wanted to do something like that so now I'm being given a baby – it was stillborn, aborted I think – the baby I always wanted but couldn't have. My husband and I are going to stay together so we can raise it. Keep still, dear. Oh, you're so lucky for me!"

She began combing Sarah's hair, sweeping it up at the back, fastening it and curling the remaining locks so that they caressed her forehead and cheeks and cascaded over her shoulders.

"There you are," she said at last, holding up a mirror. "What do you think?"

"Is tha' me?" Sarah gasped. She viewed her reflection in stunned silence before finding her voice. "Niver mind noo goddess – yew've made a laday of me!"

"You are a lady, and a wonderful one too, that's helped many and will help many more. Only…"

"Only what?"

"Well, your speech, dear. You're a lady right enough but you sound like a scullery maid. Do as the rest of us do – think clearly about what you want to say, remember, everything's thought here – then speak just as clearly, softly and gently. It's much easier here than back there. Just listen to how your neighbours and I speak and try to copy us. Now, don't look so troubled – you'll soon get the idea, just like reading all that Greek you did."

"Yew's allus soo kind."

Mollie pressed a finger to her lips. "No, say 'You are always so kind.' Say it!"

"Dear Mollie, you are… always so kind."

"God bless you, dear," she said, giving Sarah a tender kiss on the cheek. "Now we both have our work to do. Run along!"

Meanwhile, the Auldfields, having lost their tied cottage just as Nance feared they would, had moved to a dilapidated one on Amberslea heath. Only the gifts from Cabern kept the family, with their dwindling fortunes, from the House of Industry's door. Old Zebedee, in declining health as well as prematurely aged, was dependent on Matty for the family's daily bread. Beth, who had led the weeding dames for many a year and toiled beneath many a harvest moon, was also ailing. Nothing had been heard from John, and Nance's reputation was so tainted by her association with Cabern that nobody wanted to employ her.

Jethro Merryridge had recovered from his wound and was back at his father's mill at Rudlesham. In time, as Dr Abbett predicted, he made a complete recovery, physically at least, for what remedy can heal a broken heart? His convalescence gave him ample time for reflection, though. Until now, his only ambition had been for the small world he knew, with Nance as the focus of all his hopes and endeavours. But if sharing his life with her was no longer possible, what was he to do – live as a bachelor labourer, a life that promised little? He knew there could never be another Nance.

Or should he seek something better in another land, perhaps the colonies? There were the sugar plantations in the West Indies... but they used slave labour. There was the East India Trading Company... but he was neither clerk nor soldier. There was Canada where, it was said, a man might farm as many acres as he could manage. And there was a new convict settlement in some faraway place called Botany Bay where, he had heard, a Government anxious to attract farmers to the new colony was offering a land grant to free settlers. Now there, as a countryman born and bred, was a place where he might prosper. On the other hand, would he want to spend the rest of his life with convicts? Would not Canada be a better choice? These thoughts continued to occupy his mind.

Wherever he might go eventually, he resolved to do as many a young man of his day was doing and seek his fortune in some far-off region of the empire. He would travel to London, make enquiries, and then embark on the first available ship. He told his family of his plans and his parents tearfully accepted his departure, raising as much as they could to enable him to book passage and support himself in a new land. Eventually, the sad day arrived. There remained just one more task, to bid farewell to Nance.

He found her tending the cottage vegetable patch and summoned up his courage to face his precious angel for the last time. She was loath to part from one who loved her so hopelessly and indeed had nearly given his life for her, and her emotions were so strong that in the world of thought they were felt by Sarah. In an instant, she was kneeling beside her pool, peering desperately into its enigmatic depths. The clouds cleared and a cottage garden came into view, then Nance and Jethro. Almost as though she were in their presence, she watched as they made their sad farewells.

"Where iver yew goo in the wide world," she told him, "my thoughts an' love goo with yew. I'll niver forget yew, and I pray one day us ul meet agen in Hivvin."

"Be it so, Nance. My heart will be with you always and I shall never love another. Wherever fortune leads me," he added, "to scorching deserts or wastes of ice and snow, or to the southern isles of the noble savage, my thoughts will be ever of you."

"If part we must, Jethro," she managed, her eyes brimming with desolate tears, "an' it dew grieve me deeply, more'n yew can iver know, then goo an' use a buttah fortune than yew could find with sich an unworthy wretch as me."

Sarah sobbed too and wrung her hands to see her sister failing to accept the man she knew instinctively was the one for her, letting destiny slip from her grasp. She watched as Nance let him take her hand and hold it gently to his cheek.

"I pray you will find the happiness and peace you deserve," he whispered, against all will. "Fare ye well."

She touched him with her lips and he prayed that the memory of this moment, of her moist lips and her fragrance, would remain with him all his days as freshly as the morning dew. Then he turned and dragged himself away reluctantly, pausing only for a final wave.

A little of the light in each of them was extinguished that day. As for Sarah, she withdrew from the pool, all the more fearful of what destiny had in store.

The seasons came and went for Nance with still no word from Cabern, though his gifts continued to arrive, the only evidence that he still loved her and would one day return to claim her hand. It was Matty who brought fresh news. The parish constable had told him that the body of a seaman, believed to be Cabern's, had been washed ashore at Bawdsey and was in the boathouse. To another it would have been devastating news, but Nance remembered their discussion about faking his death. She also had an intuitive feeling that somehow all was well. So it was that Matty drove her to Bawdsey by cart, not so much to confirm the worst as to receive reassurance that Cabern was still alive.

They enquired at an inn and were directed to an address where men of the Preventive Service could be contacted. The man who opened the door was none other than Garrow Merryridge, Jethro's brother, and he led them to the boathouse where the body was laid out. Needless to say, there was little good feeling between them. To him, she was Cabern's woman whom he blamed for his brother's wounding and decision to emigrate, whilst to Nance he was the one who had hunted her lover and come close to killing him.

Merryridge lifted a sailcloth to reveal a body in seaman's clothing. She stepped forward and gazed coolly at the partly decomposed face with a beard and pigtail like those sported by Cabern. There was even a scar on the side of the head where Cabern had been wounded.

"An engraved watch found on the body identifies him as Cabern," said Merryridge though, even as he spoke, a glance at her face told him the corpse was not his. She pretended to grieve and even managed a tear, but could not conceal an inner feeling of quiet, contented relief. The look in her eyes betrayed her to the officer better than any false statement made on oath.

"Believe me, Nance, I bore him no ill will," he said, showing some consideration on his brother's behalf. "And I've nothing against you. What's done's done." But it was clear to her that he had realised the plot.

"I understand how yew feel," said Nance. "I've allus hoped as how ul change. He weren't noo criminal when first I knew 'em. He's been led astray. I know he can make an honest livin' for us both. I pray soo."

"Then now's his opportunity," declared Garrow. "The body's decomposing an' there's only you to declare it's not his. Officially, I'll see that it is. Tell your friend to give up his trade and for my part I'll seek him no more. Do you understand? If I hear no more of Cabern the smuggler, I promise I'll not seek him out."

"Then I promise ta dew everythin' in my power ta make 'em mend his ways," replied a grateful Nance. He offered his hand and the bargain was sealed.

She returned home and the family struggled on, until the seasons brought another sad event to a family with more than its fair share of sorrow. Beth's health had worsened until she too took to her bed to await the Grim Reaper. The family gathered round while she mumbled her farewells and bewailed having to leave so devoted a husband and children. In a last attempt to remove her daughter from Cabern's influence, it was her dying wish that Nance go and keep house for her only living relative, her widowed Uncle Foster and his seven children.

When Sarah returned, appearing in a bluebell glade beside the lawn where Thomas was sitting, his first thought was that a nymph had somehow stepped out of an ancient wall painting or had escaped from the pages of Ovid. Even the birdsong in the overhanging leafy branches sounded like applause. In a moment he was at her side; he bowed, took her hand and kissed it then hesitated, as though unsure that it was really her.

"'Appen yew… I mean, don't you recognise your Sarah?" she whispered, offering her cheek for a kiss.

"Are you really… not some nymph in disguise, about to metamorphose into a tree or a stream? You look divine." Her hand encircled his waist in reassurance.

"Noo, yew… I mean, no, you silly boy. We all are divine, aren't we, even an old reprobate like you." She brushed his lips with hers and whispered something she had gleaned in his library. "An' this is what becoming a god really means, isn't it?"

They held one another close, locked in an all-consuming, beautiful embrace that threatened to bond their very souls. And who knows how long they would they have remained so, had they not noticed a man in rags, looking lost and wandering towards them from the avenue.

"Who the devil's that?" muttered a bewildered Thomas.

"Why, tha' be Ole Nick, the sexton from Amberslea," she mused, automatically lapsing into her old speech.

111

"Is the fellow half-witted or what?"

"Noo, 'em niver wanted fur nous. Happen he needs our help." She walked across the lawn towards him and beamed a welcome. "Woo, bor! How are yew diddlin', Nick?"

Nervous and embarrassed, the old man pulled the tattered cloth, which she could now see was a shroud, more tightly about himself. He looked around as though for some means of escape but with Thomas also approaching he was trapped.

"Dew yew know me?"

"'Appen I dew." She laughed. "Dewn't yew recognise poor Sarah?"

He was incredulous. "Law strike me blind!"

"Yew buried me, remember?"

"Why, soo I did." He blushed deeply in shame, remembering his old ways. "Oh Miss, I didn't mean wha' I said about collarin' the stiffens."

"What is he talking about?" Thomas growled, somewhat irritated that their sweet reunion had been rudely interrupted.

"But what am I doin' here? I wuz laid in t'earth ta rest."

Thomas was about to say something dismissive when Sarah nudged him, winked and indicated the open grave. He quickly sized up the situation and slipped into the part he was clearly obliged to play.

"And so you shall, old chap," he declared. "Over there, see, there's a grave freshly dug. Couldn't have done a better job yourself, eh? You may rest in there for as long as you like. Mind you," he added confidently and feeling more his old self, "it might be a trifle lonely with only the worms for company."

Nick considered the offer, looked at the pair, and slowly shook his head.

"I dunno. Must I really, sir?"

"No, not if you don't want to. Besides, I have a better idea. How would you like to be a hermit instead?" He pointed to the grotto. "Come, my good fellow, don't look so glum. You see that skull? Go on, pick it up. You may dwell here as the wise old hermit and, whenever somebody approaches, you just stand with it so, in deep contemplation."

"Why dew tha', sir?" Nick was even more thoroughly confused now.

112

"Well, because it's what hermits do – contemplate the mysteries of life and death." He pointed to a tattered robe and sandals. "See, there's even a hermit's costume that goes with the job. Surely it's preferable to that dirty old shroud? Think on't." He slapped the man's back and left him to think things over, but called back on a cheerier note. "I hear hermits are very fashionable in the other place just now, it's a sought-after job."

The bell tolled in St Margaret's ancient tower as Zebedee, Matty and Nance led the cortege from the cottage along the Amberslea road. As rain clouds lowered and they drew near the Old Rectory, a lone horseman rode up behind them from the direction of Ipswich, raising clouds of dust. Clad in sporting attire, a fowling-piece was slung over his shoulder. He approached and slowed his mount to a walking pace, removed his hat, held it to his chest and bowed respectfully. When he had passed he quickened the horse's pace and rode through the open rectory gates, hastily dismounting and dashing inside the house. A few minutes later the cortege neared the building and saw a figure in clerical attire hurrying away in the direction of the church; by the time they arrived, the visiting parson was standing in the south doorway, ready to begin the Office.

"'I am the resurrection and the life,' saith the Lord. 'He that belie-veth in me, though he were dead, yet shall he live.'"

The few mourners, including the Chenerys, took their places at the back of the church. Although Nance had attended all her young life, she had only a hazy idea of what religion was all about. Now, having lost nearly all her family, she looked wistfully at the chancel and wondered why no-one seemed to know the mysteries of life and death. As a psalm was sung and the Lesson from the First Epistle of St Paul to the Corinthians was recited in full, she busied herself with remembering all she could of her mother's life.

There followed a few kindly and well-chosen words from the parson, with a glance at his watch, on how devoted a parent her mother had been and how sadly she would be missed by all who had come to know and respect her. Had he the time, he added, much more could be said. Then the coffin was borne away to the far corner of the churchyard where three grassy mounds marked the final resting places of Beth's children. The sky darkened further and a steady fall of rain quickly turned the freshly-turned earth to sticky clay.

Unnoticed at first by Nance, a stranger had arrived late and now followed the mourners at a distance. Clad in a long dark cloak with a felt hat pulled well forward, he appeared to be in some distress. Unseen visitors were also present. Sarah, her other-worldly eyes now accustomed to witnessing earthly scenes, stood hand in hand with her mother and together they watched the coffin being lowered into the grave. Beth, not yet quite recovered from her last earthly ordeal, but all too aware of the family's sorrows, stood silent and bemused as though everything were unfolding in a dream.

"Man that is born of a woman," intoned the parson, "hath but a short time to live and is full of misery. He cometh up and is cut down like a flower…" Nance's tears flowed uncontrollably as she stepped forward to cast a handful of soil upon the coffin. When the parson, again consulting his watch, came to the words "…in sure and certain hope of the resurrection to eternal life…" she felt dizzy and had to be supported by Matty, staring fixedly at the coffin as the parson excused himself, bowed and departed.

The funeral over, the family started homeward. It was then that Nance again became aware of the stranger who was talking with the sexton, Old Nick's successor. He gave him some coins and the sexton appeared satisfied. Nance heard snatches of the conversation as they passed.

"Thus be a rum owd day fur a last farewell," said the stranger, pulling his cloak closer about him.

"Nay, lad. There're folks as say how rain be a good omen."

"How's tha', bor?"

"'Cos the rain washes the soul clean o' sin, afore it begins its jahney."

"Jahney ta where, tho'?"

"Ah, tha'd be telling! But one thing's fur sure, bor. One day all of us is a-gooin' ta find out!"

As the man turned away, Nance saw his face and was thunderstruck.

Though much altered in appearance, he was none other than her brother John. Where had he been? What had he done while he had been away?

A meal was hastily prepared of such morsels as could be found and before a smoky, crackling fire they were regaled with tales of derring-do and adventure. John had enlisted in the army and sailed for India to join the 33rd Regiment of Foot. Being a strong and healthy volunteer rather than a conscript, and having learned to read and write, he'd been seen as suitable for promotion, assisting the sergeant-major and being taught how to write reports and keep accounts. He also showed a flare for understanding native peoples and customs, even acquiring a smattering of local dialects. It was this more than anything, he thought, that brought him to the attention of General Charles Cornwallis.

Five years after his surrender at Yorktown in the American War of Independence, Cornwallis had been sent as Governor and Commander-in-Chief to India, where he was intent on breaking once and for all the power of a local ruler, Tippoo Sultan. He saw in young John an ideal person to mingle with the natives and gather information that would assist the British. Far into the night, John talked of spying missions undertaken in native guise, of sketching fortifications and making notes of armaments and troop movements. So successful had he been, and so trusted by the Governor, he was later sent on a mission to England with despatches for the government and granted leave to visit his family.

He had arrived at the cottage only to find it empty and his mother's funeral taking place. Not only that, but now he learned that his brothers Albert and Mark were dead too. It was indeed a strange world where a welcome change of fortune went hand in hand with such grief and suffering. Now the family was in direst poverty, yet he had to return to India.

One small but invaluable service he had managed to render was in paying the sexton for the burial, which the family could have ill afforded. It was a grateful Nance who went to sleep that night, resolved to plough a new furrow keeping house for her widowed uncle and looking after his children, as her mother had arranged. When John had departed next day, she shouldered her old scrip and set off to catch the wagon for Brandeston where her uncle lived, relieved that at least she was no longer another mouth to feed at home.

CHAPTER 8

REUNIONS

Sarah was smiling at the exchange between Thomas and Ole Nick but just then her attention was caught by a finely dressed man, walking tentatively up the avenue and frequently removing his hat to mop his brow. When he saw the mansion and garden he paused, looked about him, approached her and bowed respectfully.

"Pray tell me, good lady, if yonder be the way to London town," he said, indicating the avenue and doffing his hat. She curtsied.

"Happen yew—" she began, but checked herself. "I mean, you appear lost, sir."

"I am indeed. Truth is, I've been wandering for ages. I've no idea where I am but I must return to my London home."

"I'm afraid that will not be possible," said Thomas as he joined them. The man appeared more than a little angry.

"Why so, sir? Pray tell me, why I may not return to my own house?"

"Because London is on the other side of life, on the Earth," he continued patiently. "You've come over to our side now, the spirit world." Speaking again with someone of his former class was making him feel even more his old self. "And just as in Virgil, *Hic locus est partis ubi se via findit in ambus…* here is the place where the path divides in twain. Just keep right and yonder lies the way to Elysium."

"You speak in riddles, sir. To be in Elysium, I'd have to be dead."

"Yes, you are," Thomas replied bluntly.

"You're impertinent, sir!"

"Who, me sir?"

"Yes, you, sir. If I were dead, I'd be lying in my tomb awaiting resurrection."

"A tomb is of no use to anyone, I'm afraid."

"But I paid a fortune for it. It's made of the finest Portland stone and reworked Parian marble. Built to last too, for millennia if necessary."

Thomas appeared deep in thought and then remembered the new temple-like structure at the end of his garden. "Tell you what, I may have a solution to your particular difficulty."

"What, pray?"

"You see that mausoleum over there? It's one of the finest to survive from antiquity. I'll wager you saw nothing like that on the Grand Tour, eh? It's empty, and you're more than welcome to lie in there. You'll be unique to posterity and the envy of every schoolboy who ever construed a page of Greek."

"Hmm, excellent workmanship," observed the stranger, stepping over to examine the frieze. "But it's Hellenistic, definitely not Christian."

"It can be whatever you wish," said Thomas, trying hard not to laugh. "The statues are Nereids. They'll guard you well, but we can make them angels, if you wish, or saints even – how about St Peter?"

"Gadswounds, no, sir. I'm staunchly Protestant. None o' that Romish idolatry, if you don't mind."

"We'll settle for angels then."

"But there's no way in…"

"We'll soon find one." He called to Ole Nick, still dutifully gazing at the skull in his hands. "Hermit! Bring the ladder for the gentleman, so he can reach the burial chamber."

"You mock me, sir," retorted the man, even angrier. "I can't climb up and lie down in there. It must be pitch black inside and I couldn't see to move around, let alone get out."

"Well no, you can't get out, that's the point. You'll be safely interred until Judgment Day. Never mind, you'll grow accustomed to it, I'm sure. At least, after a century or two, it probably won't seem so bad. They say," he added sympathetically, "the first thousand years are the worst."

"Damn it, you mock me again!" He threw up his hands in a gesture of despair. "Oh, I suppose you're right. I must be snuffed out or I wouldn't be here. And I believed too, how I believed it was all going to be so different. I was so certain."

"The only certainty about belief is that it is seldom, if ever, quite true – that is, if there was any truth in it at all."

"But I so wanted to believe."

"Oh, don't worry, you're in good company. I wanted to as well, when what I should have wanted was to find out, to discover what's what. That is something entirely different. Belief, my friend, as I've found to my own cost, is a poor substitute for knowledge."

"Ah, there you have it, sir," the man conceded. "As Julius Caesar, no less, observed, 'Men are almost always ready to believe what they wish to believe.'"

"True, sir. And an atom of reality is surely preferable to a universe of belief. It's a hard lesson, friend, but one that once learned is, I assure you, never forgotten."

"Damnably hard! So what happens now?"

Sarah had been observing the exchange with amusement and not a little admiration for the manner in which Thomas dealt with the situation.

"You see over there, in the glade," Thomas continued addressing the man, "where the light penetrates the greenery ever more brightly?"

He peered, blinked several times and peered again. "It's so bright I can scarcely see. Wait, I can just make out a woman… Gads, why, it's my mother!"

"Go to her, sir. She's come to welcome you. Why do you hesitate? Go to her, she'll show you the way."

They watched the man cross the lawn dreamily as though in trance, enter the glade and melt into the woman's outstretched arms. Yet even as they turned back, their attention was distracted by angry shouting.

"You blaspheme, sir. I heard what you just said and I am a true believer." Another man had approached from the avenue, in coarse-cut clothing, clutching a Bible and sporting a patriarchal beard. "I thought I was in Heaven, but I see I'm amongst unbelievers. I must be in the Other Place by mistake."

"No," said Thomas, calmly, "there is no mistake. Heaven this is, nor is there any other place."

"No, no, this is some horrible dream. I was promised a bodily resurrection."

"And what do you inhabit now?"

"Well, er, a body of sorts, I s'pose. But everyone knows—"

"By everyone, you mean, presumably, everyone who knows no better than you do?"

"I mean everyone who believes as they're told to," he spluttered, "and, quite rightly, in the resurrection of the body."

Sarah eyed the man's dumbstruck expression, smiled and stepped forward to join in.

"A bodily resurrection, you say? What a painful thought that is. I mean, imagine being obliged to inhabit one's aged, broken or diseased body forever. It's enough to make one wish death really were the end of everything. Now, do I have a body, sir?"

"Yes, you do, Miss," he answered quietly, thinking it an uncommonly attractive and sound one. She couldn't help reading his thoughts.

"Do you think for a moment I'd want the old one back, the one that's buried in a churchyard? Or perhaps you'd rather see me in my old bones, with sickly decaying flesh wrapped in a winding-sheet... No? Then why wish that for yourself?"

"No, no... something's wrong here."

"Nothing's amiss," said Thomas. "We are simply telling you the truth."

"I'd sooner hear it from the Devil."

"Fine, go to him then, if you can find him. But if your friend won't tell you, will you come back and hear it from us?"

"I believe in the Devil," the man growled, jabbing a finger at Thomas, "and all this is pure evil. You insult me, sir! I was one of the few who truly believed." Crestfallen, he turned away and dragged his feet slowly back to the avenue. Sarah called after him.

"Never mind," she said gently. "You'll find a Temple of Healing a little further along the way." He hesitated. "Don't worry, they're expecting you." She stood smiling and waved as he continued walking, looked back anxiously once or twice before rounding a corner.

She sat awhile with Thomas to rest in the garden beneath a soft evening light, their fingers lightly entwined as they discussed the recent events. Suddenly, paradise was beginning to seem like hard work, however enjoyable. And before long, they were again interrupted, though by a friendly, familiar voice.

"I found these two wandering in the woods, completely lost," John said, standing a little way to the side with a bemused Albert and Mark on either arm. Overawed by the brightness of their surroundings, they did not at first recognise their sister, who now stood up and approached them with outstretched arms and huge hugs. Dumfounded, they looked at one another and again at Sarah.

"Yew boys look as though yew've seen a fetch."

"'Appen we have," gasped Albert. "Yew's dead!"

"So are yew, bor."

"What's yew a-doin' all dressed up, then?" he added.

"An' what be gooin' on?" chipped in Mark.

"Come along, yew sorft lollopin' ninnies. Yer big sis'ul have ta sort out t' both o' yew." She took each one's arm and marched them, still dreamy and confused, away up the avenue. As Thomas stood watching them, Ole Nick forsook his post by the grotto and ambled up again.

"I think, sir, yew be a-taakin the roise outta me. An' whir be Sarah a-gooin' wi' Bert an' Mark?"

"No, no my friend, I only wanted to help you. Sarah's taking her brothers to a place where they can rest and get used to this world. Why don't you join them – unless you'd rather stay and be a hermit?"

"Law bless yew, sir, I think I'll goo wi' 'em." He strode off.

As Thomas turned back he was astonished to see that the mausoleum had vanished and in its place was the forbidding entrance to a charnel house. John was standing beside it.

"I suppose that's for our next visitor's benefit? Who on Earth would want to dwell in there among piles of bones? Someone with no sense of humour, obviously."

"True, none whatever, but with less expensive tastes than your late friend – a Parian marble tomb indeed!" He grinned and then eyed Thomas squarely. "You're getting the hang of this work, just as I thought you would. But in future, please be a tad gentler, will you, and less patronising.

"Remember Sarah's kindness and concern when she found you. Be as much to these other less fortunate ones as she was to you. This is the way to enlighten the ignorant and correct the credulous and redirect the misguided. That's as much as I usually manage at this stage, anyway."

Thomas accepted the admonishment and bowed. "Where, then, is the next soul in need of help?"

"Oh, he's already inside. Thinks he's been interred along with his bones. Well, why do you hesitate? Go on, Thomas, in you go."

It was nightfall when the wagon trundled into Brandeston and set Nance down by the church. Guided by memories from childhood, she walked past its medieval tower, bathed in moonlight beneath a starry sky, left the churchyard behind and found the track, rendered almost invisible by overhanging trees that led down to the valley. Just before the chattering waters of the Deben, she turned left up another track and saw a light winking at a distance through the trees. She came to the well-tended though sparse garden of her uncle's cottage and as she drew nearer the window-glow from a roaring fire radiated a welcome. Her uncle embraced her as a daughter whilst the children crowded round to touch her hands, tug at her clothes and tell her their names.

A widower with seven children to bring up, he was a hard-working man. When he returned home, however, his daily work was left at the door with his boots and a father's duties took over. Yet when the children crowded round to welcome him, each with a kiss, all seemed well for another night at least. He considered himself blessed. Though middle-aged he was still a fine looking man and would have had little trouble finding a wife, had it not been for his undue modesty and shyness. When Nance arrived, therefore, she was a gift from Heaven to him, past hoping as he was for a companion to share his burden.

She began to run the house both as a mother and housekeeper and before too long had turned the little lath-and-plaster cottage from the previous century into a model family home. She managed frugally the limited resources available and saw to the children's education by making sure that they attended school. In turn she also benefited by asking the children each evening what they had learned, thereby adding to the rudiments of education she had received at Amberslea Hall. After a fashion, she even taught herself to read a little.

All might have continued in this pleasant way had not, a year or so later, a certain widow set her sights on Nance's uncle. His shyness didn't matter because she made all the approaches. Both liked the idea of a second marriage, he with a woman of some education and property who would be a mother to the children, and she with a respectable, hard-working husband. In no time at all they were wed. Very soon, though, she began to manage everything as she saw fit and, while Mr Foster paid the bills, it was Mrs Foster who wore the breeches.

Nance was treated not as a niece nor even a servant but as a slave, her new mistress finding fault with everything. Clothes were never washed properly, the house was filthy, the food appalling and the children left to run riot without discipline. Nance tried to bear her new burden uncomplainingly, if only for the children's sake; she also continued to question them and learn what they had learned as best she could.

That is until late one evening in the cramped and smoky scullery, where she spent most of her time, she heard a rapping on the outer door. Opening it cautiously a few inches while grasping a long-handled pan at her back, she enquired who the devil it might be at such an hour. She should not have been surprised by the familiar voice and beaming smile, for who else would come knocking at the back door after dark but Rob Cabern? Her heart was in her mouth and the old smouldering passion rekindled as the heartache of many seasons was forgotten in a moment, along with her present troubles. He stood there, the handsome bearded face with the dressed pigtail and smiling blue eyes. They embraced and kissed fondly but then, feeling again all she had suffered, she pushed him away with an angry look.

"Rob, I've not heard nothin' fur soo long."

"I've just returned from a long voyage, Nance. I went straight to the cottage to see you, but your Pa told me you were here."

She motioned silence with a finger and listened carefully to see if the mistress were about, then quietly closed the parlour door, brought a candle from the chimneypiece and placed it on the table. They sat down opposite one another.

"How are you, Nance?" he asked earnestly, and listened patiently to the list of sorrows and troubles that had afflicted the Auldfields. He even shed a tear at her mother's passing. At length he rose and took her in his arms. How could she remain angry for long with so tender and manly a lover? They hugged and kissed with a passion borne of their long estrangement until she was able to force out the words that had to be said.

"Rob, we cont goo on loike this. Yew must leave tha' trade."

"Nance, things will be better, I swear. I've a bit put by and soon I'll give it up for good. I'll marry you, Nance, and we'll have a cottage – no, a mansion of our own, just as we planned. And you'll never have to work again, leastways 'cept for us an' our children."

"D'yew really mean tha', Rob?" she almost sobbed.

"I would never lie to you. Diamond wants me to sail one last time—"

At these words, her bottled-up anger erupted and any temporary hope turned to bitterness and despair.

"Rob, dewn't yew not understand? Tha' thar Diamond's got yew on a leash. Cont yew not see? There'll allus be one last voyage."

"This time he means it. We shook hands on't. One more voyage, Nance, that's all, an' I'll have money enough to buy a small ship an' start an honest business of my own, tradin' along the coast between Harwich and London."

"Noo! Yew listen ta me, Rob Cabern. This time I be a-tellin' an' just yew be a-hearin'. Leave tha' man now an' dewn't dew nothin' more for 'em, not now, not niver. I talked with Garrow Merryridge a

124

while back. A body wuz washed ashore at Bawdsey with yar watch." Cabern nodded. "He wuz convinced it wuz yew. An' I wuz soo happy an' relieved it worn't, I let my feelin's show.

"But us agreed one thing. Yew dewn't dew noo more smugglin', an' he ont come haa'ter yew noo more. Cont yew not understand? Leave this trade fur good, an' officially yew're dead. Yew can taak another name. Us'ul make a fresh start together... as man an' wife." All the while her voice was growing louder and his eyes shifted from her fire-shot gaze to the floor. "Well, what d'yew say, Rob?"

"It's only the once, Nance," he pleaded. "Just this one voyage an' we'll have the money—"

"I've told yew afore, I dewn't want yar money!" she sobbed. "It's yew I want, Rob."

At that moment the scullery door flew open and in strode Mrs Foster. The sound of Nance's voice had risen until it penetrated beyond the parlour. Mrs Foster's plump cheeks were drained of colour, her eyes black with fury, and seeing Cabern only enraged her further.

"Entertainin' a sailor, an' in my hoom? Yew shameless whore! Oh, the disgrace of it."

"Please, Mrs Foster, it's not wha' yew think," pleaded Nance. "Me an' Rob are ta be wed!"

"Wedded to a scurvy rascal like this?" she gasped incredulously. She advanced on Cabern and waved her hand imperiously towards the door. "Begone this instant or I'll summon the Watch." He arose, took up his hat and tried to speak. "Leave my hoom!" she screamed. "An' niver let your poxy shadow darken my doorstep agen."

"'Haps I'd better go, Nance," he mumbled and stepped outside. Mrs Foster slammed the door and turned the key, then rounded on Nance as though to kill her with rage alone.

"As for yew, yew slut, yew bitch, yew harlot... how could yew do it ta me? I feed yew, I clothe yew, I pay yew good money – an' how do yew repay me? By bringing a poxy, scurvy sailor in ta my hoom."

Nance, seeing that all was lost, forgot any deference and turned on her mistress with barely controlled anger of her own.

"Yew'll not be troubled with me haa'ter tonight, not niver an' thus a promise. Yew accuse me wrongly an' condemn me unjustly. My relations with Cap'n Cabern are entirely proper. If I have any cause for regret it's this, tha' I live under yar roof."

With that she turned and left. A speechless Mrs Foster, her face purple, flailed her arms and vented her wrath on the nearest objects. Pewter was hurled to the floor, crockery smashed, and then the candlestick was knocked flying, leaving her in darkness. Nance flew up to the attic and into her room, slammed the door and pushed a chest against it. For a while she lay on the bed, thinking of Cabern, of how she might never see him again, of how cruel is fate and how wretched is life. Exhausted, she succumbed to sleep.

All the while, however, another had been present, one who understood and felt her pain keenly from afar. Sarah drew close to her beloved sister as though her ethereal limbs might physically enfold her, stroke away the hurt and somehow breathe fresh hope and vigour into her dejected and downcast spirit.

The sun often rises in circumstances like these as an unwelcome taskmaster, calling the long-suffering servant to arise and get to work again. When its earliest rays pierced the windowpane, they were as welcome to Nance as to a prisoner awaiting execution. Gloomy thoughts of the previous night came to mind, though with a little less intensity, but then more hopeful thoughts as she remembered snatches of a dream. She had travelled along a dark road but one where the way ahead appeared to brighten, and poor Sarah was somewhere nearby. But how could that be? Then a word came to mind, one that she thought she heard her sister speak. It was 'friend'. Yet how could there be a friend in all this when she had none?

Suddenly it became clear as she recalled the good doctor. What had he told her? "In George Abbett you will never find a truer friend." She arose, bundled up her few possessions and went down to the parlour where her embarrassed uncle waited. A smile and a kiss smoothed the way and all she felt it necessary to say was that she would not wish to come between him and Mrs Foster, nor would she wish to upset the children. Hopefully, they would soon forget her. As she was about to leave, her uncle pressed some coins into her hand.

She walked the first part of the journey before hailing a passing wagon bound for Ipswich. Wide-wheeled, drawn by eight horses and, as usual, smelly and overcrowded, it jolted and rumbled its way into Ipswich along the Woodbridge Road the following afternoon. Down to her last penny and in need of a wash and change of clothing, she realised the situation could not be more hopeless. She certainly could not return home and be another mouth to feed. On the other hand, how could she call on the doctor, in hopes of somehow finding employment, in her present state?

She had travelled the road in her dream but where was the light? There was nothing for it, she reasoned, but to visit the doctor and find out how true a friend he was. After all, the worst that could happen was that she would be turned out on her ear. A street pump near the Old Shambles provided water for a drink and a wash, whilst a shop window served as a mirror. She patted the dust from her clothes, wiped her boots with the hem of her skirt and set off for Orwell Place and the residence of the now eminent physician. How much had changed in her life in the years since she had ridden there on the carthorse. If only life could again be as uncomplicated as it appeared then.

She rang the bell. There was no need to worry about her appearance since the housekeeper admitted many visitors in a worse condition. As it happened the doctor was out, so a long wait in a comfortable chair at least gave her some rest. For the first time, she took up a newspaper and practised her newly acquired reading skills, trying to understand as many words as possible.

Eventually, in strode Dr Abbett in as happy a frame of mind as a man could be. His coat covered a well-proportioned chest and shoulders although, in middle age now, the creased, double-breasted waistcoat and tight-fitting breeches could not conceal a slight paunch. It was said that this 'gave a man a figure'. Cradled in his right arm was his beloved fowling-piece and under the left a bag bulging with wildfowl. For him, meeting Nance again was yet another pleasure in an already good day.

"I must apologise fur my appearance, sir," she began, but he would have nothing of it.

"Among friends, such an apology should neither be offered nor sought, m'dear. Now pray tell me your reason for coming and how you think I may be of service."

"Sir, I'm destitute," she began, struggling to retain a little pride. "I dewn't have noo money an' my family cont support me an' yew's the only friend I have in the world. I'm wholly desperate ta find a place in service."

"Then you have certainly done right in coming to me."

No sooner had he heard her sorry story than he ordered a meal for her and made arrangements for her to stay. Then he asked his housekeeper to take her in charge and assess her capabilities. She reported that Nance's work was excellent and she could do just about everything necessary, except write legibly and keep accounts, so the doctor set to writing a letter to a young lady of his acquaintance, Mrs Frances Turner, at Castlegreen.

Dear Mrs Turner,

I am happy to reply in the affirmative to your solicitous enquiry concerning a suitable person of experience and proven ability to work in the position of under-nurse and under-cook at Castlegreen. I have staying with me one Nancy Auldfield, who has been found willing and more than capable of undertaking all duties that would be required of her in the said position. She is experienced in household management and in the care of children.

She is honest and diligent and only left her previous employment, which was with her uncle's family, after a distressing personal experience that did not concern her duties. Consequently, I would recommend her for employment in the said position; and were there a vacancy in my establishment, would have no hesitation in employing her myself.

Your humble and obedient servant,

George Abbett

A favourable reply was received late the following afternoon. With an affectionate pat on her shoulder by the doctor, Nance set out at once for Castlegreen, wearing new clothes provided by him.

The Orwell

Castlegreen was an imposing private residence with a large garden behind a tree-shaded wall on the Orwell's lofty banks. It was the home of Jonathan Turner, Esq, a brewer and banker who owned the adjacent Castle Brewery. The river could be seen flowing in a semi-circular arc below the town, barely yards from the scores of houses that lined its banks. Earlier in the century the river had silted up and cargo ships bound for Ipswich had to unload onto lighters four miles downstream. Now, until dusk, the river's distinctive two-masted wherries could be seen, ferrying ships' passengers between Ipswich and Harwich.

That warm evening in May would be forever remembered by the Turner family and by Nance herself. As the sky began to redden with the approach of sunset and a welcoming breeze blew off the river, Nance approached Castlegreen and saw a lady beside two men who were sketching at easels in the garden. An old fisherman, strangely attired, moored a rickety sailboat by the landing-place below her and carried a basket of fish up the path to the house, pausing to chat to several children playing near the water.

The fisherman was Sorcy Solomon and the children were some of the dozen offspring of the house's owner. Seeing Solomon again filled Nance with foreboding, as she recalled their previous encounter at Abbyfield Farm. The lady was perhaps a year or two younger than Nance, but dressed in clothes the like of which Nance had never seen, a short-waisted white robe with a collar and a swept back, yellow over-skirt that brushed the ground. Two ostrich feathers adorned a yellow turban hat. This was Mrs Frances Turner, poet and botanist, and a patron to many an aspiring artist and writer.

The men were the portrait painter Daniel Gardner and his protégé, the young John Constable. Still working in his father's mill at East Bergholt, he had been introduced to the Turners by Gardner as a talented youngster intent on pursuing a career in art. Frances Turner's encouragement would lead to a lifelong friendship between them. Gardner, a distant relative of Frances, had turned to oils after making his name with family portraits in oil, gouache and pastel on canvas, which he glazed rather than varnishing. His latest pieces were celebrated for a curious rough texture, as though painted on towelling. Nance paused a little way off, hoping to avoid Solomon's eye as she listened to snatches of their conversation wafted on the breeze.

"I don't much care for portraits," the sharp-eyed young man was saying, his curly, bushy-brown hair combed forward in the neo-classical style.

"Not at forty guineas a time? That's what Gainsborough made," said Gardner, still sporting a head of thick brown hair and glancing at the other with dark, penetrating eyes.

"Am I, then, expected to turn a dowdy duchess into a goddess, or my noble lord's mistress into a lady to the manor born? I don't have that talent."

"Don't confound appearances with spirit, or the commonplace with art," replied Gardner, turning his attention to the fisherman and placing a fresh sheet of paper on his easel. "Beneath your dowdy duchess's breast beats a human heart. It may pine for a lover, but a necessary choice of husband has conferred on her the title of Lady. On the other hand, that mistress might be wholly virtuous except for lack of a wedding ring, and be a lady in every sense except that which society deems necessary. Don't you think both deserve some sympathy from the artist?"

His pencil was already filling in the outlines of the wizened old fisherman, watched closely by Frances, and highlighting his fantastic garb. At last he appeared satisfied and turned back to the sketches he had made of the children, then looked up in surprise as even more had come to surround the fisherman, wanting to know what his basket held.

"Now here's a ready subject," he began, "drawn from life. See how inquisitive they are. What title does it suggest to you?" Constable grinned knowingly.

"The Fisherman's Family."

"Indeed, the scene suggests loving children who have been eagerly awaiting their sire's return. Only if he were the sire, the chances are he'd shoo them away, sell their supper and get drunk on the proceeds."

At this point Frances, who had been peering intently over his shoulder, felt moved to comment.

"You have just remarked, Mr Gardner, on the need to distinguish between appearances and the reality behind them. You have an eye for a painting, but you don't know the half of the story behind what you just witnessed. As for the man himself, you are quite wrong. I tell you there is no kinder, more charitable soul than Master Solomon. For years he saved every penny to buy a new boat and, when at last he had the money, he lent it to someone he thought was in greater need. But the fellow was a rogue and simply absconded with it. So now Sorcy continues to ply his trade in that leaky old tub without a word of complaint – and with just as generous a heart as before. Can you paint that, Mr Gardner?"

He was silent for quite a while.

"By Heaven, I will try, Mrs Turner."

"Perhaps I should also try my hand at this," exclaimed Constable.

"Do so by all means," she replied, "but I think yours is an altogether different talent. Here in Suffolk we have some of the most beautiful countryside in England and in your sketches you make it come alive. Others have done this, notably Gainsborough, but they often romanticise it. However beautiful it is, the countryside is neither romantic nor idyllic if one has to labour there six and a half days out of seven." She paused and glanced across the river at the last of the day's wherries making its unhurried passage up river, as the shadows lengthened and dusk began to obscure the mildly flowing waters.

"And there is another consideration," she went on. "I have a horrid notion that all this is going to change within our lifetime. A generation from now, many of the labouring classes won't know what it is to awaken in the clear morning air and brush away the dew, or water their horses in a millstream, or snatch a brief rest at noontide in the shadow of an overspreading beech. No, for they will dwell amongst giant mills with screaming, devilish machinery going round the clock and foundries belching smoke and hellfire and mines tunnelled ever deeper into the bowels of the Earth. And people will live out their entire existence in the shadow of all this.

"Many of today's servants are exploited, it is true, yet at least they are free to breathe God's air and be content with simple pleasures. The industrial serf of tomorrow, however, will be spiritually bankrupt." She paused and then looked at the younger man. "Your paintings, Master Constable, could be a reminder of life as it was once lived and perhaps could be again."

"That's all well and good," observed Gardner, "but Constable has to eat now. Give the old fisherman a try, m'boy."

"Can't we do something to help the poor fellow?" asked Constable.

Mrs Turner shook her head sadly.

"He won't accept charity."

CHAPTER 9

RESCUE AND CAPTURE

How does the evening find you, Master Solomon?" Frances Turner enquired.

"Well enough, ma'am, if the demons let me be."

It was then that he recognised Nance, waiting timidly on the pathway, and remembered the warning he'd been given and the subsequent fight at Abbeyfield Farm. He could also see with his inner eye a numinous figure standing beside her as she hesitated, putting a hand on her shoulder as though to urge her forward.

"'Haps the demons be abroad after all!" he roared, holding out one of his charms and glaring at Nance and the spectre as though they were fiends from the Pit come to torment him. The ethereal form vanished leaving Nance bemused and frightened, dreading meeting him again anyway and now facing a clearly embarrassed Mrs Turner. The frequent appearance of the disturbed fisherman amongst the children and guests did not concern her since she considered him harmless. Frightening the wits out of a servant, however, was going too far.

"Master Solomon," she rounded on him, "I have found you an honest and fair trader and as such you are welcome, but I cannot permit you to frighten my guests or my servants. Your spells and mummeries are un-Christian and have no place amongst true believers here." He bowed his head and stood in sheepish silence as she turned to Nance and smiled pleasantly. "You must be Nancy Auldfield?"

"Yes, ma'am," she replied with a prompt curtsy. Frances had noticed the flash of recognition that passed between the two a moment earlier.

"Do you know one another?"

Nance was silent at first but as Solomon again started to become menacing she found her voice.

"He wuz wholly kind ta me once."

"I meant yew noo harm, Miss. I thought the demons wuz with yew."

"Really, Sorcy," said Frances, "you mustn't go around frightening honest, God-fearing people. Why don't you pray to the good Lord for deliverance like any Christian soul?"

"Happen the Lord'ul coom fur me when it's time," he muttered, taking up his basket and heading for the kitchen.

Frances was slightly plump yet handsome with a sculptured mouth, arched eyebrows and naturally pink cheeks. Her auburn hair curled over most of her forehead and her brown eyes were kindly and intelligent, occasionally visionary. Her composed smile was reassuring as she bade Nance follow her into the house and into the back parlour.

"Dr Abbett tells me you are experienced in domestic service. Is that correct?"

"Yes, ma'am. I wuz servant-of-all-work ta Mistress Knoller at Abbeyfield Farm, an' before that I helped Mistress Harvey. I've been a dairymaid an' have done agricultural work an' have just come from service at my Uncle Foster's where I looked haa'ter the cottage and his seven children."

"Is that the Mistress Harvey whose husband breeds horses?"

"Yes, ma'am. If it please yew, all will provide references."

"Good… yet your name sounds familiar in another respect," said Frances, searching her memory. "Yes, aren't you the Nancy Auldfield who once rode a carthorse to Ipswich?" Embarrassed, Nance admitted that she was. "It's certainly nothing to be shy about. From what I hear, you saved your mistress's life and at no small risk to yourself." Frances saw that Nance didn't want to speak further about it, and remembered that she had avoided horses ever since. "Don't worry, Nancy, I shan't require you to ride!"

She turned away and took a few paces to the window, meditating on a more difficult subject that came to her mind. "Everything is satisfactory," she went on, "except for one thing. Are you acquainted with one Captain Cabern?"

"Yes, ma'am," murmured Nance, resigned to the fact that the past had caught up with her yet again.

"There was a report that he'd drowned."

"Not quite, ma'am," said Nance, resolving to tell the truth.

"Then where is he at this moment?"

"At sea, probably, ma'am. I begged 'em not ta goo. He's noo criminal—"

"Really?"

"Well, sort of. I wants 'em ta... I pray as how he'll settle down. He can be an honest man, I know it."

"That's as may be," said Frances, "but while you are under my roof there is to be no communication with Captain Cabern or any of his followers, without my being informed and my permission given. Is that clearly understood?"

Nance nodded, still not daring to believe she would be offered a place.

"The wage for under-nurse and under-cook is three pounds and ten shillings per annum plus keep, with a daily allowance of tea and sugar and half a day's leave once a fortnight. There will be further opportunities for employment and you will be assessed according to your capabilities. Do you find this acceptable?"

"Yes, ma'am," an astonished and overjoyed Nance mouthed.

"When can you commence work?"

"When iver it please, my good lady."

Frances rang a bell and a maid entered. "This is Nancy Auldfield. She begins work tomorrow. Take her to the kitchen and find her something to eat." A delighted Nance, still not quite believing she had found a place in such a fine house, bobbed with the maid and followed her out.

As soon as Frances Turner had set eyes on Nance, she felt an instinctive sympathy for one whose life had been an obvious struggle. These were difficult times for a woman alone, as she herself could testify, and she had been more privileged than many. Born in London, her father moved the family to Ipswich whilst she was still young and employed private tutors to give her a literary education. She also had a natural flair for art but it was impossible for a single woman to pursue such a career.

The need for financial security led her to marry a man many years her senior. A permanent invalid, he survived only a further six months but left her with money, property and the coveted title of 'Mrs' in her twenties. Eventually she was introduced to the wealthy Jonathan Turner, twenty years her senior and a widower with twelve surviving children. They felt a genuine love for each other, though, and it was a marriage of practicality as well as for love. The children and the running of the house were left in her capable hands while he concentrated on building up his brewing business. As lady of the house, she also found time to pursue her literary and artistic ambitions and cultivate the friendship of men of the arts and sciences.

In the house, Frances expected everyone to attend to their duties in the proper place at the proper time and, from her first day in service, Nance was more than happy to oblige. She arose before the rest of the household was awake, emptied and cleaned the kitchen grate and built up the fire to boil water for the washstands. Then as under-cook, she began to prepare breakfast. By the time the family entered the back parlour, Nance had spread the table with bread, cheeses, cold meats and dishes piled with fruit. During the day, she polished every brass lock and door handle, scrubbed every floor meticulously and every kitchen utensil was scalded, scoured and returned to its proper place. In the nursery, she was no less competent and soon earned an increase in wages.

It was while supervising two of the boys on an outing to nearby Beggars' Green that Sarah again came to her mind. So strong was the feeling that her sister was present, she let the boys play by themselves and stood alone, trying to come to terms with this strange and inexplicable thought. How could someone dead these many years come to mind so vividly? There was no denying it, but no explaining either.

She was not sensitive enough to know, of course, but Sarah was indeed with her. Whilst at her own cottage, a feeling of fear and foreboding had overwhelmed her and Nance seemed to be the reason for it. In a trice she was kneeling beside the pool in Thomas's garden to stare into the water. Sure enough, there was her sister happily watching two of the Turner boys at play. What could be more innocent and normal? And yet… something was not as it should be.

Suddenly the scene was crowded with people of the spirit world, one of them distinctly calling Sarah by name. She felt compelled to think herself into the scene with such urgency that, instantly, she joined the others on the Green. The people from her world were looking anxiously at the boys and the wall behind them. One of them was an exceptionally beautiful woman with penetrating blue eyes, angelic features and honey-coloured locks that tumbled over her gown. With no introduction, she took Sarah's arm and pointed to the boys, young George and Frederick Turner who were wearing smart suits with wide white collars. They were playing bandy-wicket beside a wall that supported a property on which building repairs had recently been carried out.

"The wall is about to collapse," she said simply.

George bowled to Frederick who lashed out with his tiny bat, hitting the ball toward the wall. As it struck, it seemed to make more of a noise than a ball should. Intrigued, the boys began to hurl the ball directly at the wall, which made a hollow, rumbling sound.

"Good Heavens," cried Sarah, "you're right. We must do something."

"You're Nance's sister and I know how close you are. That's why I called you. Go to her and make her see what's happening. You might succeed where we cannot."

Sarah knew she must warn her sister and somehow impress her thoughts upon her. She succeeded, but with some desperation so that Nance was inexplicably filled with confusion, as though someone had seized and shaken her, followed by an inexplicable urge to end the boys' play at once and take them home. Feeling faint, she leaned against a tree.

"George, Frederick," she gasped, "I am unwell. Please take me home."

"But we've only just arrived," protested George, throwing the ball in the air and hitting it towards the wall with the bat. It struck with a hollow thud.

"Stop that, George," cried Frederick, seeing Nance steadying herself against the tree. "Can't you see Nance's ill? We must help her." The boys dutifully ran up and stood beside her.

"Please boys," she asked, "help me home. I feel faint."

They each took one of her hands and led her homeward, arriving back safely. She rested, recovered and thought no more about it. Meanwhile, the blue-eyed woman came to stand beside Sarah and, instinctively, they embraced one another.

"You've saved the boys, well done," she said.

"No, you did that. I heard the summons and I came but I didn't know what was wrong. I'm new to all this – you all seem so much more adept – and I didn't realise the danger. Who are you?"

"I am Nance's guide," smiled the woman. "I've watched over her since birth. My name is Teresa and I work with John so I know all about you and your pool and your gift for second sight. Your sister's special destiny in this life is to be instrumental in saving others. If what we have just witnessed is any indication, she will need all the help we can offer. I think we shall be seeing a deal more of each other."

The following morning Frances summoned Nance and enquired after her health.

"I'm quite recovered, thank you ma'am. I was with the boys and felt faint, that's all."

"You were at Beggars' Green, weren't you? Did you know that a wall collapsed there?"

"Why no, ma'am."

"It was yesterday afternoon. It must have happened very soon after you left so it was providential that you came away when you did."

A relieved, though puzzled, Nance bobbed and left. She could think of no explanation for what had occurred, but was grateful for the providential intervention, whatever it was. Had any harm come to the boys, she would have been the one at fault – and judged unworthy of the trust placed in her.

Cabern had returned from Brandeston to Walton on horseback and arranged with the ferryman to row him out to the *Kathy O* in the haven. When she hove to at dusk, he descended the steps from the mole to the ferryboat but then noticed a pinnace heading his way. Her oars brushed the water and pulled and feathered in unison. As she drew closer they were shipped naval fashion, leaving her to drift, and he was certain by her handling that she was a naval boat. He turned anxiously and started to climb back up the steps but there were men on shore advancing towards him. He retreated again only to see the oarsmen resume their stroke. The men on land reached the mole just as the pinnace came alongside.

Through a break in the clouds, the moon revealed a second ship further out, a cutter closing fast with the *Kathy O* while her half-dozen crewmen frantically made sail. Cabern, appearing as nonchalant as he could, went back up the steps and found himself face to face with a naval lieutenant.

"Are you Robert Cabern?"

"Ay, I'm Captain Cabern."

"Then Robert Cabern, I arrest you in the King's name."

The arrest had involved the co-operation of the Preventive Service and a press-gang. Its lieutenant delivered Cabern up to a waiting magistrate in Felixstowe, George Clarke, Esq. A number of documents could be seen by candlelight, arranged on the desk before the prisoner, the charges laid against him. These were for the attempted murder of Chief Officer Garrow Merryridge in the execution of his duty, and as an accessory to the attempted murder of the officer's brother, Jethro Merryridge, late of Abbeyfield Farm. There were also sworn statements from various witnesses that he was involved in smuggling. The Ferry House Inn had been raided and the Navy was even now in the act of seizing his ship. Clarke eyed Cabern with the relish that comes with an easy victory.

"There's enough here, Cabern, to have you tried and convicted several times over, though only once will be enough. You'll get the halter for this."

"You appear to have the advantage of me, sir."

"I have every advantage, Captain, and I'll have your poxy hide hung in chains for the birds to feed off—" He rose from the desk and began to pace unhurriedly and thoughtfully, before turning back to face Cabern. "—unless, that is, you are prepared to consider a reasonable alternative."

"What might that be, sir?" enquired Cabern calmly.

"The Navy needs men of your calibre. Confess your crimes and sign up for service aboard one of His Majesty's men-of-war, and I'll recommend a pardon for your offences. Otherwise, I'll have you remanded at Ipswich gaol this very night… and the matter will be out of my hands."

Cabern was determined to retain his dignity. It was well known that smugglers, because of their obvious skills, were especially valued by a Navy short of good men. It had even been declared in Parliament that smuggling was an excellent training ground for the fleet!

"Where do I sign?" he shrugged.

Clarke read out a written confession of all the offences alleged to have been committed and handed it to him to sign, pushing an inkwell containing a quill across the desk. The lieutenant then placed before him a paper stating his willingness to ship as a second-class volunteer and pointed to the space for a signature.

"Welcome aboard, Cap'n," he smirked, as his men took Cabern away.

The gratitude of the Turners for Nance's apparently providential rescue – and her exemplary domestic work – meant that she was soon appointed head maid with another increase in wages. A further opportunity for reward came when Frances noticed Nance prompting one of the boys during their daily lessons, when Master George confused James II with James I. It was something Nance had learned at Amberslea Hall. (The boy had been uncertain as to which century he was in.) Frances realised that Nance took a keen interest in the lessons and even used her limited reading ability to study on her own. From then on, she was invited to join the children for an hour during daily lessons. Frances also taught her handwriting and simple arithmetic.

Master Robert, the Turner's eldest son, had taken up the sport of stalking and shooting wildfowl on the Orwell by boat, with the encouragement of Dr Abbett and with a fanaticism second only to his mentor's. So frequently was he on the water, he became almost as well known as Sorcy Solomon and almost as reckless. Often, Nance was supposed to accompany him and she herself became an accomplished rower.

By mid-December, the weather had been unusually mild so one day Robert planned to slip away alone with his gun and spend the afternoon drifting on the river, sneaking up on wildfowl as they fed in the creek on the opposite bank near The Ostrich Inn downstream. He planned to return before the tide turned and in time for supper. He left the house unobserved except for young George, whom he swore to secrecy, and within minutes had cast off and was pulling for the main channel. But then the weather changed drastically with a sudden drop in temperature and an icy gale developing. The moon and stars were obscured by cloud and a south-westerly blew an increasingly menacing chill. As the clouds cleared, the ground hardened and puddles froze.

Jonathan Turner presided as usual at the head of the supper table, lit by the glow of a dozen candles, the roar and crackle of the log fire prevailing over the moaning of the rising storm outside. He was a chubby, jolly gentleman of forty-eight years with bushy hair that curled over his brow, and his figure was a good endorsement of the product he sold – fine ales brewed with water from the old monastery ponds at nearby Holywells. As he prepared to say grace, only now was Robert's absence noticed. No sooner had he enquired whether anyone knew where his son might be than he realised something was wrong. George, entrusted with the secret, had naturally told almost everyone so, as his father asked a second time, the others' eyes inevitably turned toward him.

"George, look me in the eye. Where is Robert?"

Fear gripped the boy as he weighed up the awful consequences of telling an untruth compared with remaining silent.

"He's gone to shoot wildfowl, sir. On the river."

"Oh dear, merciful Lord!" gasped his father, covering his face with his hands. "Out on the Orwell and on such a night. Mrs Turner, call the servants," he ordered, "and organise a search party. I will summon help from the brewery."

He hurried across to the French windows, flung them open against a howling gale and strode past the wind-bent trees to the brewery entrance. Below, crosswinds swept the waters, lashing them into breakers that pummelled the riverbanks. As he shielded his face from flying debris and crunched through frozen puddles, he mouthed a prayer yet was all but resigned to his son being beyond help.

When Nance heard the news she donned shawl, cloak and boots and tied a lantern to a pole. Snatching a spare candle, she dashed out of the house in search of her master and found him by the brewery, desperately soliciting help from the night watchmen.

"Go into town and rouse everyone you know," he was demanding. "Summon the Constable and the Watch – and bring torches!"

Nance approached and saw by the lantern's glow the face of a man already in despair.

"All's not lost, sir, for Master Robert be mighty resourceful. The tide's turned an' ul carry 'em downstream. An' the wind's coomin' off the water. He must have made it ta shore. We'll find him, sir, I'm sure. I'll goo with yew." George now approached timidly with his father's cloak.

"George, you stay with your mother while Nance and I proceed along the bank. Have someone follow us and see to it that they bring torches."

The pair began walking along the shore, further and further out as the tide receded. Near the bank, the mixture of sand and mud was as firm to tread as a beach but it becomes progressively softer and more treacherous towards the water. While Turner repeatedly called his son's name, Nance made wide sweeps with the lantern, straining the eye for any dark shape its gleam might reveal.

"It's hopeless," sobbed Turner, coming to a halt. "The boy is lost!"

Another power, however, was encouraging Nance apart from her own indomitable will, someone with spiritual vision who knew the boy was still alive. She urged her master not to give up and the pair continued walking until men from the brewery bearing flambeaux caught up with them near Downham Reach. All the while Nance's eyes roved across the bank and shallows. Strangely, in quieter moments, thoughts of Sarah were coming to her mind but she brushed them aside and concentrated on the search.

Sarah was indeed present, with Teresa, John and others. Seeking out Robert's spirit rather than his physical body, they quickly found him in the darkness. But how could they tell Nance when she was so dismissive of her sister's presence?

"Let's pool our energies with Nance's," said John, "and transform them into a light to guide her."

To Nance, a score of likely looking objects had appeared already, only to change shape in the flickering lantern's light and be revealed as broken branches, old netting or driftwood. Now, however, a strange unearthly glow further out caught her attention, hovering like a will-o'-the-wisp. She waved the lantern, squelching through the partially frozen slime towards it, and could make out a dark form that just might be a body. Then her boots began to sink and the mud held her fast.

"Over here!" she cried. "Bring a light, dew hurry!"

Two men wearing mud-splashers came to help her. The enigmatic Jack-o'-lantern had disappeared but in the pool of light thrown by their torches there could definitely be seen the form of a body, its head sideways in the mud. One man waded out until he reached it and recognised Robert. His companion then joined him and together they hauled the boy from the ooze, unconscious but alive, dragging him to firmer ground. A litter was swiftly fashioned from fallen branches and Robert was lifted onto it, whilst Nance threw her cloak over him. Then she announced her intention of running to the house to summon the doctor and prepare a warm room and hot bath. Run she did, barefoot, lifting her skirts and straining to see by the lantern's darting rays, back along the sand and through the mud to Castlegreen.

Frances herself had seen that everything necessary was ready and now Dr Abbett was summoned. Eventually, the boy was brought in, examined and lowered into the bath, then put to bed in front of a roaring fire. He recovered fully in due course and Nance, who had now been instrumental in saving the lives of three of the Turner's children, earned for herself a special place in the family's affections.

Whilst Diamond and others of his gang were still at large, Cabern had been taken under guard to Portsmouth with others of the *Kathy O*'s crew and rowed out to the seventy-four gun ship-of-the-line, *Brunswick*. She had been in dock for repairs and her captain, John Harvey, was using his 'best endeavours' to get the ship manned. Notices posted around the town invited every true patriot who loved liberty (and hated the French) to enter the service of His Majesty aboard a man-of-war of his choice. Better pay and conditions than those on merchantmen were promised, together with a bounty on joining and plenty of prize-money. Lieutenants, usually the most feared men aboard after the captain, advertised a rendezvous at a local tavern where prospective volunteers were plied with ale and regaled with tales of past glories and quick promotion.

Discipline was relaxed in port and watermen rowed the women of the town out to the ships, along with peddlers and their trinkets and illicit liquor, to entertain the crews. For the time being they were indulged with practically everything except, for fear of desertion, what they desired most, their liberty. Cabern smiled as he saw how everyone tried to convey the impression that life in the Navy was one long party.

Volunteers accounted for about half the crew. They comprised petty officers, mates, artisans and some able seamen, for whom life aboard was reasonably worthwhile. There were others escaping justice or domestic entanglements, and 'my Lord Mayor's men' – well-to-do youngsters, arrested for petty offences like drunkenness and affray, who did not wish their names read out in court. The remainder were pressed into service by gangs like that at the Ferry House Inn, who either boarded merchantmen before their crews could land or prowled the streets of ports and cities. They broke into taverns, brothels and even private houses, dragging sailors from their molls and husbands from their wives. Those who resisted or lacked stout enough friends to defend them, were cudgelled and dragged away in irons to awaken next morning aboard ship and be offered a stark choice: either to serve as an impressed crewman or ship as a volunteer. Legal appeals were seldom successful and most simply decided to make the best of it. The Foundlings Hospital also provided the ships' boys.

Cabern was taken with others down to the orlop deck, to be examined by the ship's surgeon as to their fitness for service, then it was off to the scuppers for washing and scrubbing with seawater. For the evening meal, the new recruits messed separately from the crew under the scrutiny of a marine with a loaded musket. Then they were directed where to sling their hammocks on the lower gun deck and left to themselves until lights out at 8 o'clock, while the crew enjoyed their final night of freedom. The ship's officers absenting themselves, drunks argued and squabbled then were obligingly lashed into hammocks or left to sleep where they had fallen. Cabern couldn't help but wonder how such an apparently unruly rabble could ever be the disciplined fighting force that was the envy of the world.

A few moments before eight bells, the boatswain's mates appeared at the fore and main hatchways and piped the long, shrill summons for all hands of the watch to turn out, followed by cries of "Ahoy there! All hands, larboard watch, on deck!" If this failed to produce the required response, men with hangovers or only half awake who had failed to turn out were promptly whipped with the 'starter', a long knotted cord, about the head and shoulders. Any still in their hammocks were cut down and then whipped. As eight bells was struck, they fell in and were dismissed to their stations. The work of restoring discipline in old hands, and instilling it in new ones, had begun.

Rob Cabern and his new comrades were left alone until after breakfast, which consisted of the usual burgoo. Then it was up to the main deck, to report to the First Lieutenant who examined each man as to his experience and suitability for duty. The finest mature seamen were chosen as the fo'c'sle or sheet-anchor men, whilst the younger able seamen became topmen, responsible for working all sail above the lower yards. Next in line were the after-guard composed of ordinary seamen and some landsmen, working the lower sails and serving a gun. The waisters, the worst of the seamen and the remainder of the landsmen, were employed in the ship's maintenance, and the idlers were the painters, polishers, cooks, butchers and odd job men.

Under the watchful scrutiny of the redoubtable Captain Harvey, a veteran of the Great Siege of Gibraltar, First Lieutenant Buller and seventeen-year-old Midshipman Andrews appraised the new recruits with the eyes of those cursed with the impossible task of moulding as motley a bunch of dolts, drifters and port scum ever assembled aboard one of His Majesty's ships into a disciplined crew. One by one each man stepped forward and stated his name and previous occupation, which was duly recorded in the muster book along with any distinguishing features (in case he should desert).

"Name?" demanded the midshipman.

"Cabern, sir, Robert. Merchant captain."

"Notorious smuggler, you mean," snapped the lieutenant. "We'll have no thieves in this ship, understood?"

"Ay, ay, sir."

"Because if it isn't, I'll have the skin off your back 'til only the bones show."

"I mean to do my duty, sir," Cabern replied, with what he trusted showed due respect.

"Boatswain, show this man to his duties in the tops."

As the lieutenant turned to the next man, Cabern felt a hefty kick in the rear that sent him sprawling. A boatswain's mate stood over him menacingly, armed with a starter, a foot on his neck.

"You'll not answer an officer back in my hearing again. Understood? Now up to the masthead and stay there, an' look lively!" Cabern leapt into the shrouds and began to climb. "Faster, you wooden-legg'd, crawlin' caterpillar! Move yourself, damn your eyes!"

He climbed as nimbly as he could until the deck lay far beneath. Enough of a seaman not to take the dishonourable way up through the lubber's hole, he was soon hanging almost horizontally as he climbed out over the futtocks before continuing up the shrouds to the top-gallant crosstrees. There he waited, never having been so high before, until he felt able to move around easily and do the work that was to come.

Below him the decks were soon crawling with waisters and others of the watch, pumping or sloshing water from buckets. Sand was liberally sprinkled and then the men knelt in rows for up to a couple of hours, scouring the planks with heavy holystones until they achieved the required whiteness. Brooms and buckets followed and when the dirty sand had been washed away, the task of cleaning was completed by beating the deck dry with long swabs of cloth – all under the watchful eye of a midshipman and the boatswain's mates.

Perhaps, thought Rob Cabern, being in the tops would not be such a hardship after all.

CHAPTER 10

THE GATHERING STORM

Early the following year, Jonathan Turner moved his family to the Norman House overlooking St Margaret's Green, a wide grassy expanse divided by a tree-lined avenue and at the edge of town. On one side of the Green, beyond the fish ponds, there was a view of the twelve church towers of Ipswich nestling in the dell with the Orwell in the background. Springs from the nearby Caldwell Hills supplied much of the town with water and flowed through it in washes.

Nance had now become housekeeper, though some of her time was still spent with the children, and she thought these days the happiest of her life. On one outing with the children she met the Fosters, visiting Ipswich on business. A much chastened and even penitent Mrs Foster poured out a sorry tale of how their circumstances were greatly reduced, having lost most of their property. How they would welcome her back – but Nance was not about to give up a rewarding and secure position that also gave her a sense of belonging. She commanded a certain respect, too, from every tradesman anxious to please the Turners, and even began to keep accounts.

All this while, nothing had been heard of Cabern. Although she still thought of him fondly and expected they would eventually marry, this silence caused her to think of him less; the devotional flame she carried in her heart began to burn less brightly. All who knew her, both on Earth and in another world, hoped that it might be extinguished altogether.

Frances Turner was becoming the doyenne of Ipswich society, both as the wife of one of the wealthier citizens and a patron of charities and the arts. Female emancipation was growing, with women like Frances enjoying a new independence. Accordingly, she also encouraged Nance to improve her literacy until she was able to read newspapers aloud to the servants. Frances broadened Nance's mind, too, by pointing out items of interest in other parts of the world and discussing them.

One topic that arose more than any other was the situation in France, especially the Revolution. Although the two countries were no strangers to war, past quarrels had been between their governments rather than their people. Englishmen travelled in France, even during wartime, and notable figures such as Montesquieu, Voltaire and Rousseau were happy to visit Britain. When the Revolution came, the English were at first complacent: after all, hadn't the French merely deposed a despotic monarch as the English themselves had done the previous century? As things progressed, however, it became alarmingly clear that the French concept of 'liberty for all' did not mean the same as it did to the English.

"The leaders of the Revolution," remarked Frances icily one day, "seek only to deprive others of power in order to acquire it for themselves. What should we think of government by an elite few who ignore the people's wishes, treat Parliament with contempt and manipulate men for their own ends?"

"I cont not reply ta tha', ma'am," said Nance. "But tha' Louis wuz our enemy. The way I see it, the sans-culottes did us a favour by gettin' rid of 'em."

"They have only deposed and murdered Louis XVI to enthrone and crown with oak leaves Citizen Robespierre the First! Now we face total war with the Republic."

When news of the Reign of Terror reached England, newspapers published long lists of Madame Guillotine's latest victims. The *Minutes of the Proceedings of the National Convention* were also published and made chilling reading.

"Just you listen to this!" cried Frances one day, jumping up from her chair and angrily waving the pamphlet she was reading, losing the place and then impatiently thumbing through to find it.

"Beg pardon, ma'am?" said Nance, lowering the ledger she was holding and coming to attention.

"Infamous wretches! Oh, where to begin? Women, apparently, are to be compelled to wear the cockade and have their dress regulated by law. Mirabeau's remains are to be removed from the Pantheon and Citizen Marat's transferred to it – atheists, heathens!" She took a few paces forward, found the place again and then waved it under her servant's nose. "And as for this… do you see what it says here?" Nance strained to focus on the trembling page. "Here," said Frances, pointing, "read for yourself. Not only have they shown a complete disregard for the sanctity of human life and a hatred of everything English… they now wish to destroy London."

A dutiful Nance began to read, her wavering voice hovering between righteous anger and incredulity.

"'The moment is arrived to thunder, with the rapidity of lightning, upon your natural enemy… Carthage thought as London does and the Romans destroyed it. Let London experience the same fate…' What happened to Carthage, ma'am?"

"The Romans saw to it that no-one would want to live there again. They slaughtered the population, burned the city and sowed the fields with salt." Both women fell silent in disbelief.

A hundred other tasks were accomplished while the decks were being scrubbed until the ship was ready for sailing. While topmen swarmed into the upper rigging and others manned the lower yards, unfurling and trimming the sails, others manned the main capstan to the hearty singing of a shanty, heaving away at the bars until the anchor was weighed. Cabern was assigned to a yard captain and took his place in line on the stirrup rope. He had worked plenty of rigging but never so high. When the sails were set, he watched with respect as some of the men hoisted themselves up and ran back along the yards like rope-walkers at a fair, even as the ship began to pitch and roll in open water.

There was something majestic, even almost spiritual, about the old fortress-hulled ships once they were under way, especially third-rates like *Brunswick* with its complement of six hundred and forty men. Once the yards were filled with acres of billowing canvas they resembled cumuli, whilst the towering hull left in its wake a glistening spray like a comet's tail.

Navy regulations required a ship's crew to be jacks-of-all-trades, from laying out on the yards, reefing and furling sail to washing and mending clothes, from mess cooking to learning the skills of small arms, the cutlass and the gun. Everything had to be right and midshipmen with a hierarchy of petty officers and mates ensured that it was.

Above these were the gentlemen of the quarterdeck and above them the captain, the sole lord and master of all whom none save a commissioned officer dared address and then only on ship's business. Each man was directly below someone but above another, and each group had another to despise. Even the idlers could bully the ship's boys. Officers could single out any man for some sleight, real or imagined, and make his life a misery – with no appeal. A midshipman, however young and inexperienced, could report a man to a lieutenant, who might report him to the captain and that would mean a flogging.

Midshipman Andrews had taken a particular dislike to Rob Cabern from the beginning and was particularly happy if he could inflict some humiliation on a new recruit learning the ropes. For instance, hammocks had to be lashed seven times, passed through a regulation hoop and stowed daily by eight bells.

"Seven times, Cabern," bawled the little tyrant, "not eight, damn you. Take it away." On wash day, it was, "Cabern, get those rags off the bloody rigging." He even made topman Cabern scrub the decks. "I said white, Cabern, you poxy vermin! That's blacker than when you bloody well started."

Then there was the food. Perhaps it was better than many ate on land but in practice it often consisted of two year-old salted beef or pork, or near putrid cheese in a stew. For dessert there was ship's biscuit, often containing maggots or weevils, perhaps with a helping of rancid butter. Cabern managed to exact some small revenge on Andrews, though, when he served his turn as mess cook. The midshipmen's rations were a little better and they in turn would 'borrow' food such as potatoes and onions from superior officers. As Cabern was often required to report to Master Andrews, but sometimes found no-one present, such delicacies found their way onto the trays of Cabern's messmates.

A midshipman's life, in truth, was far from easy since, until he had passed the examination for master's mate, he was effectively still at school. He had to stand watch, supervise the crew, check the stores and go to the tops when the sails were furled whilst also being the virtual slave of the first lieutenant. He had to present himself to the captain with his quadrant on the quarterdeck at noon, to work out the ship's position by the sun's altitude and dead reckoning. His berth on the orlop, below the waterline, reeked with stench from the ballast and bilges and was lit but dimly by tallow dips, not the best environment in which to study mathematics, navigation, astronomy, trigonometry and seamanship.

Yet Cabern could do all this and more. He could navigate by dead reckoning and at night with only the stars to guide him, sailing between rocks and sandbars. He could slip into a tiny cove or shallow creek, sail close to cliffs and be safely away on the ebb tide. He therefore bated the imp by merely hinting at nuggets of valuable information, which the other could hardly refuse. In this way, Master Andrews' academic abilities showed a marked improvement, as did the fortunes of Rob Cabern.

As time passed, he became more settled in life aboard and mastered all the tasks he was given. He had fired cannon before, mostly at revenue cutters, but in the Navy it meant loading, running out, sighting and firing a ship's gun within ninety seconds. He learned how to fire at a ship hundreds of yards away with the object of piercing its side, how to elevate the piece and fire in an arching trajectory so that the shot landed squarely on a sloping hull, creating showers of murderous splinters, and how to fire in order to slice rigging and snap masts. Such skills required split second timing, not to mention self-protection from the three tons of cannon as it recoiled, leapt and thundered back onto the deck.

By far the hardest duty, however, was in the tops. Not only were the topmen expected to race up the rigging and out along the yards to trim, reef and furl at speed, but sometimes to race one mast against another. It was not enough to have won the race, either, for all hands were expected to descend faster than they had climbed; to be the last man down was reckoned a disgrace. Depending on the captain's mood, punishment could vary from stopping one's grog to clapping in irons or even a flogging.

Grog time after meals was announced by a fifer playing a hornpipe, *The Ballad of Nancy Dawson*, and was usually the only pleasant part of the day. Grog consisted of four pints of beer or a pint of wine; if these ran out, half a pint of rum or brandy a day was allowed, mixed with often undrinkable water.

By year's end, Cabern had been appointed Captain of the Maintop. The speed with which the sails were worked was a compliment to the captain if the admiral noticed. And notice it he did. Richard Earl Howe, Vice-Admiral of England and Commander-in-Chief of the Channel Fleet was aboard the flagship, the first-rate *Queen Charlotte* in the Solent. Howe wanted his ship to be manned by the very best seamen and so Able Seaman Cabern exchanged the fighting-tops of the *Brusnwick* for those of the *Queen Charlotte*.

The French were now seen more and more as a mortal threat to the life and liberty of every British man and woman. The previous year had seen a poor harvest in France and, to stave off famine, the Committee of Public Safety had purchased large quantities of grain from America: a convoy of a hundred and thirty ships was sailing for France. Admiral Earl Howe's orders were to seek out the convoy and capture it, whilst the French Rear-Admiral Nielly was despatched with a squadron to reinforce the convoy. Further reinforcements lay in wait in Brest under Rear-Admiral Villaret de Joyeuse.

Howe commenced a sweep of the Atlantic near the English Channel, discovering nothing, then realised that the French had sailed from Brest. He received intelligence that the enemy were only a few leagues away and so gave orders to sail north-west. Cabern and his companions talked of the coming battle and verbally made their wills, although the talk was light-hearted as each expected to survive.

"You can have my watch," said one.

"An' you can have my old oak chest an' telescope," added another.

"What about me, lads?" asked a young woman, one of the few allowed on board, officially the wife of a petty officer. "Who'll have me?" Every man would have done except Cabern, whose eyes remained fixed on the table. "What about you, Rob?" asked Mary Dawkins, her cap resting atop a mop of provocative curls as she thrust out her chest, exposing her breasts above a low-cut orange gown.

"Bless you no, Mary," said Cabern. "I have a poll who is all the woman I could ever want."

"She must be very special. What's her name?"

"She's my Nance. I mean to take her to wife."

Mary fluttered her eyelids and put her head on one side. "Can't I keep you company for now, Rob?"

"Forget Cabern," said a messmate, "he's love-struck. Ship with me an' you can have half share of my prize money."

"Half?" she laughed. "Happen I'll have my own. Happen I'll serve a gun with powder tomorrow. We're sure to lick those Frenchies and then I'll be rich!"

"You can't do that!" said Cabern in alarm.

"Oh, can't I? With prize-money, I can be a lady!" With that she rose and went to find the captain's clerk, to ask that her name be added to the ship's muster.

Cabern turned in and tried to sleep since he was to stand the midnight watch. The Admiral decided to turn in as well and retired to his cabin; it would be the last time he did so for four days. Next morning, the enemy were discovered to windward and partially engaged before thick fog prevented the fleets from sighting each other.

The Sunday that would later be called 'The Glorious First of June' began with a cloudy sky and cool temperatures. Nance left young Harold Turner to play with his sisters in the Norman House grounds and went to the back parlour to supervise breakfast. The excited shouts of the children could be heard through the window as they romped around a steep-banked, deep pond overspread by a weeping willow. It reminded her of her own childhood, happy enough... and then Sarah came to mind again. If only she could believe that her poor sister was in a better place, but she was dead and that was that. Strangely, at times she did seem to feel her presence, as she did now, but how could that be? And she always seemed to come at times of crisis – but this was a quiet Sunday morning and what could possibly be amiss?

Sarah had, indeed, good reason for coming, again sensing danger. But this time she was followed by John, Teresa and several others, including of all people her mother Beth. Fully recovered from her last earthly ordeal, she now looked as young as her daughter and just as pretty.

"Sarah," said John, "there is about to be a great sea battle and hundreds, perhaps thousands, will pass violently and in distress before their time, including women and boys. We need you to help us. But don't be concerned for your sister, my friends here will watch over her along with her mother."

"They need you urgently, Sarah," said Beth, "and I can take care of my own."

"Of course, Ma. But that bad sailor-man's heading this way, the one that brought all the gifts."

"I know, m'dear. Now just you run along an' leave things to me."

She stationed herself in a corner of the kitchen as Sarah and the others departed, and watched as Nance busied herself giving instructions to the cook for breakfast and seeing that everything was ready. One of the girls then appeared at the tradesman's entrance and called to Nance that 'a strange man' wanted to see her.

"All right, where is he?" asked Nance, wondering who on Earth could be calling at that hour.

"He's with Master Harold."

That did not sound proper at all. Nance removed her apron and went into the garden to find Harold and his sisters standing near the pond and a middle-aged seaman talking to them. As he turned round she recognised the man who had left the bag of gifts at her family's cottage all those years before. It was the grizzled, tanned face and dark, unsmiling eyes of the man who had also helped bring about the family's ruin. Striding up, she placed herself between him and the children, asking what business he had with them.

"I seek the whereabouts of Rob Cabern, Miss," he replied. Her heart leapt but she managed to control her emotions.

"I've not heard nothin' these twelve months past."

"You've no word at all? No letter?"

"Nothin'," she said sullenly. He was unconvinced.

"If you do set eyes on 'em, say Jack Rackhem wants to see his old cap'n."

"I've already told yew, I've not heard nothin'." Nance was becoming annoyed. A hot temper had always smouldered in her, only held in check by a lifetime of servitude, but it was rising fast. "I've not heard nothin' so now get yew a-gooin'."

"Don't yer take that tone with me," snarled Rackhem, "not if yer knows what's good for yer, bitch!"

As he grabbed her sleeve, she slapped him with her free hand and dragged herself away but, enraged, he leaped forward and pushed her. She stumbled backward and fell against the boy, sending him toppling over the edge of the bank and rolling over and over, down into the murky waters of the pond.

"That'll teach yer," laughed Rackhem as he stalked away.

Harold thrashed about in the water, deep enough for him to drown. Nance's first impulse was to dash in after him but something checked her, as though a restraining hand had been laid on her shoulder. She told the girls to find Frances Turner and tell her what had happened, then raced to the nearby stable door.

"Jake, Jake!" she bawled, knowing the old coachman was inside preparing the carriage and pair for church. "Master Harold's drownin'!" she cried as the bemused elderly man emerged. "Fetch a long length of rope – an' find Jamie and tell 'em ta bring a ladder."

Back at the pond, the lad was starting to go under and she could not swim, so she grabbed one of the overhanging willow branches and swung herself from one to another until she was close to him, thanking providence that she had brothers who had encouraged her to do such things as a child. Grasping the last branch with both hands, she held it tightly as it bent under her weight and lowered herself into the water. Keeping hold of the branch with one hand and reaching out with the other, she managed to catch hold of the boy's collar and drag him towards her.

"There yew be, Master Harold," she said soothingly, "just yew hang on ta Nance." The water was numbingly cold and her saturated gown started to drag them under, the boy hanging around her neck, until she could only just keep her mouth above water. "Yew's gooin' ta be fine," she gasped. "Just keep a-hold."

Her mother Beth watched with increasing alarm. She had been so sure of coping alone, but now she wished her other daughter back to help. She knew that her Nance would never let go, even if it meant death for both of them. Teresa's thoughts came to her swiftly. "Your daughter's destiny is to save life. She can accomplish this task."

"But she could drown," Beth moaned.

"If there were no risk, if it were easy, there would be nothing to overcome, nothing to achieve and no lesson to be learned. We assure you this is not her time to pass."

"But my little one's drownin'…"

"Have the courage of your convictions. Go to her, inspire her, bear her up and remember that the greatest power of all is a mother's love."

It was Jamie the elderly gardener who appeared first, dragging the ladder.

"I dewn't see what use thus be," was all he could manage to utter, as he tottered to the bank's edge.

"Raise it an' let it drop through the tree!" called Nance.

"Are yew sure yew know what yew's a-dewin'?"

"Yes, Jamie! Now run out the bloody ladder!"

"Thus noo need ta taak on soo," he grumbled, his feelings hurt.

The water was up to Nance's nose and the terrified boy was trying to climb onto her head. For a moment, all seemed lost. Then she found within herself a strength she didn't know she had and with a huge effort managed to haul herself and the boy inches farther up the branch. She found her voice again.

"Where's the ladder?"

Jamie held it up and let it fall against the tree, then guided it as it slipped through the drooping branches and came to rest just above Nance's head. She grabbed it and let go of the branch. It fell into the water and she went under with the boy clinging to her; but it floated, they surfaced and she managed to keep hold.

"Catch the ladder, Master Harold," she coaxed. "Goo on." The boy held it. "Yew hang on and dewn't yew be a-lettin' goo," she told him, leaving him and grasping the branch once more. "Pull, Jamie, pull! Bend yar back!"

The man tugged the ladder but it scarcely moved. By this time, Frances Turner was arriving and she scrambled down the bank to help. Between them, they heaved back the ladder with the boy on the end until it was high enough up the bank for her to climb down and help him to safety.

Jake finally arrived with the rope and performed rather better than the gardener. Nance managed to catch it, letting go of the tree with her remaining hand and holding her breath as she went under. Jake tugged and heaved, she surfaced and was towed safely to the bank. She emerged from the water with her tresses wreathed in sedge and her chest heaving over a clinging gown, as though stepping out of a painting of *Thetis Rising from the Deep*. Clambering shivering up the bank, she walked with as much dignity as she could muster back to the house.

A relieved Beth took her leave, glad to have been of some little help and prouder than ever of her daughter.

Out in the Atlantic, 140 leagues west of Ushant and half a degree north, no-one including Cabern had had much sleep for days. Since the French fleet had been sighted and battle joined, Admiral Richard Earl Howe had not left the quarterdeck of the *Queen Charlotte*, ordering meals to be brought to him and snatching sleep in a chair. Aged sixty-nine, suffering from gout and wearing an ordinary seaman's jacket and trousers, Black Dick – as he was affectionately known on account of his swarthy complexion – had the weather on his side. Yet, described by Walpole as 'undaunted as a rock and as silent', he was seldom seen to smile.

For two days, thick fog prevented the fleets from sighting each other, but by Sunday morning it had almost cleared and a bright, early sun soon played on the crests of a moderate swell under a brisk south-easterly. A cry of "Sail-ho!" alerted Howe to the presence of twenty-six enemy ships to leeward.

"I think we shall have the fight today," an officer remarked. "Black Dick has been smiling."

At the same moment, aboard the French *Sans Pareil*, an English prisoner, Captain Troubridge, was being taunted by her officers. Seeing the British apparently in no hurry to engage, one lowered his telescope.

"There will be no fighting today," he observed. "Your admiral will not venture down."

"Wait a little," said Troubridge, holding the proffered glass to his eye, "English sailors never like to fight with empty stomachs. I see the signal flying for all hands to breakfast. Take my word for it, they will pay you a visit soon."

Sure enough, at 8.15 a.m. Howe ordered his flag captain, Sir Roger Curtis, to hoist Signal 13 to 'Prepare for battle' followed by 36 for 'Each ship to steer for and engage her opponent'. And from the quarterdeck of each of the twenty-five British ships came the order, 'Clear for action'. Immediately, Cabern and his topmen raced up the shrouds with hammocks to screen the dead-eyes and lanyards. They hung the yards with chains, crowded on sail and prepared their muskets and volley-guns in the fighting-tops, whilst the fo'c's'le men stretched netting above the deck as protection from falling debris.

Mary Dawkins, who had volunteered as a powder monkey, donned a borrowed jacket and trousers and reported to the ship's copper-lined magazine. She exchanged shoes for felt slippers, picked up a leather powder keg and joined the ship's boys to collect a cartridge for the first broadside. Far below him, Cabern saw the fire engine being assembled on the poop and hoses run out, whilst buckets of water and swabs were placed around the ship to lessen the risk of fire.

"Hands to quarters!" ordered Curtis.

"Hands to quarters, Boatswain."

"Drummer-beat to quarters!"

The boy began a steady double drum roll as the lower sails and hammocks in the nettings were drenched with water and the decks sprinkled with sand. On the gun decks, each gun captain was issued with a powder horn and tube from the gunner's stores and prepared his match, a cotton wick soaked in lye, leaving it burning over a basin of water. His crew, up to a dozen for a thirty-two pounder, cleared tackles and breechings, made ready the sponges, wadding and rope rings containing the round shot, and placed one bucket of seawater and one of fresh beside each cannon. Heavy, dimly-gleaming battle lanterns were lashed between the guns.

Most of the marines and infantry fell in on deck, the remainder being stationed below ready to shoot any man disobeying orders. In the cockpit, the surgeon's loblolly boys drew a sail-cloth over an operating table and spread canvas on the deck for the wounded. Rum, laudanum and water were brought and buckets placed nearby for amputated limbs. Candles were in position and battle lanterns swung from the overhead beams.

Mary and the other powder monkeys began delivering their cartridges to the guns, each battery under the command of a lieutenant. The gunners stripped to the waist, to keep wounds clean and to keep cool in the coming intense heat, before binding their heads tightly with neckerchiefs to protect the eardrums.

Every man was now in position, waiting for battle to commence. Most were tense yet spirited, not because they liked fighting but because they looked forward to the chance of prize-money and a rousing spell in port. Also, discipline was relaxed during a battle – except for the marines – and even officers donned old clothes and mixed with the men to cheer them on.

From his vantage point, Cabern could see the British closing the gap with the French who were still sailing north-westward and barely a league away. Howe intended his ships to sail on a diagonal bearing and go abeam of the French on their weather-side, then pass at right angles through the line and engage to leeward. To that end, Curtis signalled for 'Breaking the enemy's line at all points'. The ships' crews cheered each other and sang *Rule Britannia* as the distance between the fleets narrowed.

The leading French ship *Trajan* then opened fire on the British at long range and *Caesar* returned it, but her rigging was damaged. *Bellerophon*, the second in line carrying Rear-Admiral Paisley, and the third, *Leviathan*, were still hampered by damage inflicted in earlier battles but they engaged the opposing *Éole* and *America* to windward. The remainder of the fleet kept their gun ports closed, with the gunners permitted to lie by their guns, a risky manoeuvre; but in previous actions Howe had not rated French gunnery too highly and thought it worth the gamble.

From the quarterdeck of his flagship *Montagne*, Admiral Louis Villaret de Joyeuse, the handsome forty-four year-old commander of the French fleet, watched the *Queen Charlotte* bearing down on him. His orders, from Robespierre in person, had been to locate the grain convoy and escort it safely into port (or lose his head). But now that Howe had found him, he guessed the grain convoy was not far away and he had no choice but to fight.

Citizen Jean-Bon Saint-André stood at his side. The minister for the Navy – and the man most responsible for the adoption of the Tricolore as the national flag – Saint-André had presided over the reconstruction of a diminished fleet that until recently had been the equal of the British. Revolutionary zeal, however, seemed more important than experienced seamanship, and ships often put to sea in a state of disrepair and poorly provisioned. Yet by the time the *Queen Charlotte* drew near to *Montagne*, she had received several broadsides and a number of crewmen were dead. The first lieutenant bowed respectfully to Howe.

"My lord, an Englishman can't bear to receive blows without returning them and we must fire."

"Then fire, lads, and be damned!" snapped Howe.

Seven ships up the line, Cabern watched the seventy-four gun *Defence* scudding and closing fast with the French. Going hard-a-starboard at the last moment, she was the first to break the line, passing between *Mucius* and *Tourville* and firing broadsides as she went.

"Look at *Defence*," exclaimed Howe. "See how nobly she goes into action." Howe's lieutenant held back from giving the order for the

Queen Charlotte to fire, grudgingly admitting that the old warrior might be right in his determination to show the sans-culottes the old English way of fighting, not to fire before he could see the whites of their eyes.

CHAPTER 11

BLUE ISLAND

James Bowen, the sailing master of the *Queen Charlotte*, piloted her into battle and she drew closer to *Montagne*. At first, Howe doubted there was enough room to pass between the hundred and twenty-gun flagship and the eighty-gun *Jacobin* astern, but was determined to force a way through.

"Starboard the helm," ordered Howe, moments later.

"My Lord," replied an anxious Bowen, "you'll be foul of the French."

"What is that to you, sir? Starboard!"

"Damn my eyes," Bowen muttered, "if you don't care then nor do I. But we'll be near enough to singe our whiskers."

In the tops, Cabern and his men were laying out on the yards, ready to trim sail when the ship completed her manoeuvre, going hard about and hauling to the wind. On the gun decks, the lieutenants signalled for port lids to be opened and the cannon run out. Each gun captain pushed a priming-tube through the touch-hole until it pierced the cartridge, then laid a trail of powder from the horn in the channel leading to it. Picking up the smouldering matches, they awaited the order to fire whilst the crew retreated to safety.

The lieutenants waved their hands to signal the first broadsides. As the ship passed between the *Montagne's* stern and *Jacobin's* bow, each gunner in turn applied the match. Long plumes of smoke were followed by flashes and a funnel of flame, a barrel's length, roared from the mouth of each cannon. They leapt, recoiled, crashed onto the deck and came to rest. True to his word, Bowen had steered the *Queen Charlotte* so close to *Montagne* that her main and mizzen shrouds brushed the French ensign and her jib-boom brushed *Jacobin's* mizzen shrouds. Her bow carronades, the 'ship smashers', shattered *Jacobin's* bow and blew an enormous hole in *Montagne's* stern. As she swept past, further devastating firepower was unleashed: round shot demolished her cabins and swept the gun decks with an explosion of splinters and glass slivers, maiming and blinding the gunners and killing some three hundred. On the quarterdeck, a wounded Saint-André retired below.

As soon as each cannon had come to rest, reloading began. The worm was pushed down the barrel and rotated to remove any bits of smouldering charge, then a wet sponge was thrust in to cool the chamber. A ladle deposited the cartridge whilst the first wad of rope yarn was rammed home, followed by round shot and a second wad. Within ninety seconds, each gun was again run out and primed.

Further up the line, Cabern could see *Defence* encircled by three French ships, having suffered heavy damage. Her despairing lieutenant, seeing *Republican*, the three-decker that had shot away her main mast, bearing down on him, dashed up to the quarterdeck and addressed Captain Gambier.

"Damn my eyes, sir, but here is a whole mountain coming upon us. What shall we do?"

"How dare you come to me with an oath in your mouth, sir? Go down and encourage your men to stand to their guns as brave British seamen."

Invincible, however, came to their rescue and, as she passed, her captain, Thomas Pakenham, called out to Gambier.

"I see you are pretty well mauled. Never mind, Jimmy – whom the Lord loveth he also chasteneth!"

Royal George, *Queen*, *Majestic* and *Valiant* all managed to break the line, but the French closed ranks, seeing their intention. Yet doing so made it impossible for them to recover. *Brunswick* also attempted a breakthrough but became entangled with the *Vengeur du Peuple*, her starboard anchor fouling the French fore-chains and locking the ships together. Her master wanted to cut her free.

"No," Captain Harvey observed, "as we've got her, we'll keep her."

The *Queen Charlotte* now went about after making her pass and luffed up to engage *Montagne* to leeward, but became entangled with *Jacobin* and found herself caught between the two. Howe ordered broadside after broadside. The entire ship shuddered, groaned and heaved, her rigging shaking as she rocked in the water. On the lower gun decks, the cannon were leaping so high that they were nearly hitting the overhead beams. The three ships soon became completely engulfed in dense clouds of billowing smoke.

All the while, Mary and the other powder-monkeys raced along decks and gangways to keep pace with the firing, holding the kegs containing the powder cartridges tightly under their jackets to protect them from sparks. The British gunners were firing twice as fast as the French, and cheered wildly after each broadside. They aimed round shot at the hulls, intent on wreaking maximum havoc within, and swept the decks with grapeshot, whilst the French fired higher up and cut the rigging with chain and bar shot. Marines and soldiers picked off topmen with muskets, and they in turn raked the decks with muskets and seven-barrelled volley-guns.

After some fifteen minutes of this carnage, a horrified Cabern saw that the fore-topmast had been shot away and the remains of the fore-royal and fore-topgallant were fouling the rigging and other sails, dragging the ship to starboard. The foretop's captain had been cut in two, others had been knocked off the rigging and those who remained, nervous and confused, were taking little decisive action. He nominated a man to replace him and took the quickest way down which was by rope.

Cabern leapt onto the shrouds and descended until he saw a small chance to leap into the netting. Surely no sane man would contemplate such a thing… but then, a man-o'-war in the heat of battle was hardly the place for sane acts. He launched himself into space, time standing still as his mind filled with thoughts of past misdeeds, a wasted life and of Nance smiling at him with dewy black eyes. He wanted to cry out to her but the net hurtled up to meet him and he thudded into it, almost hitting the deck. He was still alive and, mercifully, unhurt.

Rolling across the net, he reached the fore shrouds and began to race up them to the astonishment of all who watched. As others stood by, dazed or paralysed with fear, he reached the foretop and seized an axe with a broad grin as the crippled vessel floundered and pitched in the swell.

"Steady, lads, steady! For England and old King George!" he cried as loudly as he could, attacking the broken rigging and hacking away until the ropes were severed and the broken mast almost freed. Chain-shot shredded the sails and musket balls whistled around him. In that living Hell, his attitude and actions, risking his life for his shipmates, inspired them. Now others recovered their courage and took up his cry, joining in with renewed vigour until between them they had cut loose the topmast and sent it hurtling into the sea. More crewmen rushed up from below, too, and dragged away the remnants of the damaged sails. No sooner had they freed the ship, however, than chain shot again sliced the rigging and the main topmast snapped at the very place where Cabern would have been standing.

Through his telescope, Howe watched as Cabern encouraged and cheered on his men, wielding his axe like a modern day Hercules. The maintop was soon cut away and once more the ship was freed. Howe turned to his sailing master.

"Mr Bowen, isn't that our smuggler friend?"

"Yes, my Lord. He's just cut away the foretop as well."

"Damn the fellow. Should have been an officer. And do stop calling me 'my Lord' – don't y'know I am Black Dick in the fleet?"

As the battle raged, a rescue had already begun with spirits from a higher world descending to gather up the fallen. Most of the deceased were found in the ships, either still instinctively at their posts or wandering the decks in a dreamy daze. They all seemed to sense that something was amiss but didn't quite know what, and wondered why every man jack looked straight through them as though they didn't exist. Out on the waters there were scores more, their bodies heaved over the side, either hanging there or draped over broken yards and other debris. Hundreds upon hundreds of bemused, unhappy and anxious souls.

A strange bark now hove into view. It showed no identification, was unarmed and was invisible except to her intended passengers. It glided silently on an even keel, no bow-wash dividing the waves, no foam trailing in her wake and no sail was lowered. She hove to frequently so that her crew could help those adrift on the waters into smaller towed boats. Then she rendezvoused with one ship after another, her British and French officers stepping aboard and ordering their compatriots to muster by the ship's rail and prepare to board the enigmatic vessel. Welcoming outstretched hands helped them aboard with assurances that they were all homeward bound. Whether British or French, each had suffered and inflicted suffering; now they reclined side by side, their duty done. The ships' companies left behind still took no notice.

Sarah herself was on the *Queen Charlotte*, scouting the orlop for dying ship's boys and for a particular woman she had been told would be with them. A glum Rob Cabern walked past her, apparently unscathed except for a bandage. Then she saw the woman, Mary Dawkins, standing alone and dreamlike beside her body as it was hoisted onto a seaman's back to be heaved overboard.

"Come along, my dear," said Sarah, gently taking her hand. "You've been snuffed out and I've come to take you home." As she was led away, barely sensible, her ethereal form passed right through a seaman; startled, he felt a sudden chill and shivered.

"Blimey, someone just walked over me grave!"

The women ascended the gangway to the main deck and came to the rail. To Mary, everything seemed dark and misty and, as Sarah effortlessly helped her across to a ship's raft, she saw her own body tumble into the waves. The raft was now crowded with the fallen and Sarah waited until Mary could feel the timbers beneath her feet.

She resumed her work searching for more boys and found one holding his head with both hands, surprised to find it in place after being severed by a cannonball. Another, newly disembodied, was darting about playfully, delighted to be able to get up to all kinds of mischief without being seen. She took the pair to the raft and, when she could find no more boys, turned to searching the orlop again. A hand on her shoulder heralded the welcoming, uplifting presence of John beside her.

"Come along, Sarah. Your work here is done."

"No, please… I can't leave all these brave lads. Some of them are in a terrible state – such suffering. How can men do this to each other?"

"You're as stubborn and headstrong as your sister! Very well, stay a while with my blessing. But I warn you, you're not used to this work and the strain will be great. It will necessitate a long, long period of rest."

Within twenty minutes of the *Queen Charlotte* breaking the line, the battle had been virtually won, although firing continued into the afternoon. *Montagne*, her stern and quarter almost demolished but with rigging mainly intact, crowded off accompanied by most of the other French ships. Villaret attempted to form a new line but the British broadsides proved too strong and it was abandoned. Nine French ships were by now totally dismasted.

The *Queen*, carrying Admiral Alan Gardner, engaged no less than eleven ships in a series of encounters, during which her captain, John Hutt, was mortally wounded. *Marlborough* was the last to break the line, then *Bellerophon* and *Royal George* took on and fought off two ships apiece. At one point *Bellerophon* passed beneath the stern of *Terrible*, a three-decker. On the quarterdeck, Midshipman Mathew Flinders noticed a battery of cannon primed for action but unmanned whilst their crews trimmed the sails. He seized a burning wick and fired each in turn into the Frenchman's stern. Rear-Admiral Paisley, who had given the general order to fire as fast as possible, came up and grabbed him, shaking him by the collar.

"How dare you do this, youngster, without my orders?" he demanded.

"Sir, I just thought it a fine chance to have a good shot at 'em."
As Paisley strode angrily away, a ball from a French broadside took off
one of his legs and he was carried below.

The hottest duel of all was between Captain Harvey of the
Brunswick, Cabern's old ship, and Captain Jean-François Renaudin
of *Vengeur du Peuple*, both seventy-fours. Locked together, the ships
swung against each other and *Brunswick*'s lower-deck port lids became
jammed against the Frenchman's side. Harvey ordered a broadside
to be fired right through them, which was returned by *Vengeur*. The
flames from the cannon turned the lower gun deck into a furnace, with
smoke everywhere and visibility reduced almost to zero. The starboard
port lids were opened in an effort to clear it, whilst *Vengeur* delivered
another broadside and another, followed by wild cheering. Blinded
by smoke, with only the glow of battle lanterns and burning matches
visible, the British gunners somehow reloaded with double shot and
returned the broadside and the cheers. *Achille* approached, her captain eager to capture *Brunswick* and ordering his crew to the rail and
shrouds, ready to board her. But the British were ready and waiting
with a broadside of grape shot, scattering the enemy crew. Captain
Harvey himself sustained multiple injuries, first from a musket ball
that took off his right hand, then from a heavy splinter lodged in the
back of the head and, finally, from round shot that smashed his right
elbow. These wounds proved fatal.

The slaughter on both sides was horrific, with hundreds wounded
or killed. Throughout the fleet, men lay huddled in rows by the score
on the orlop, many with extensive burns, internal injuries or broken
limbs. They waited to be examined in strict rotation by the surgeon and
his assistants, but many bled to death before they could be examined.
The surgeon only had a few seconds to make his diagnosis, to decide
whether to save a limb or amputate. If the latter, then the patient was
given a shot of rum and a gag, and held down while the surgeon did
his awful work.

Still the battle between *Brunswick* and *Vengeur* raged with broad-
sides fired at a distance of a few feet, shot ripping through one side of
Brunswick's hull and penetrating the other. Eventually, Captain Henry
Harvey in the *Ramillie* sailed to the aid of his brother and poured

broadsides into *Vengeur* until she was cut adrift and had lost all her masts. Renaudin, with at least half his crew dead or wounded, reluctantly agreed to surrender but could not strike his colours because they had all been shot away, so he held up English ones instead. Renaudin and his young son, amongst others, were taken prisoner.

Left to themselves, the crew of *Vengeur* rigged up a makeshift sail on a mast-stump and attempted to escape, but were prevented. Now listing heavily and shipping torrents of water, its crewmen wave the Tricolore from the bows and sang *Vive la République* as she sank with some three hundred and twenty souls. The badly damaged *Brunswick* dropped astern and sailed for England with more than a hundred wounded.

From high up on the broken masthead, Cabern could see *Marlborough* still entangled with *Impétueux*, then *Mucius* appeared through the smoke and collided with both. The three ships exchanged fire for some time, all taking heavy casualties. Aboard the *Marlborough*, the wounded and indisposed captain was heard to speak of surrender, whereupon Lieutenant John Monckton took command.

"I'll be damned if she should ever surrender," he cried, and nailed her colours to the broken mainmast. Immediately, shot smashed a hen coup in one of the boats and out fluttered a cockerel that perched above the colours, clapped its wings and crowed. The crew took this as a favourable omen and fought on with fresh heart, crippling both opponents.

After some four hours, all firing had ceased and Cabern saw four of the dismasted French ships being taken in tow by their frigates. Their surviving thirteen ships of the battle-line withdrew and the British secured the remaining six as prizes. Exhausted crews set to work repairing the damage, erecting jury-masts, replacing yards and hoisting new sail, almost as energetically as though they had not been in a terrible battle. By now Howe, blackened with soot, was exhausted and he retired to his cabin, relinquishing command to Curtis. He concluded that the ships were too badly damaged and the crews too fatigued for a pursuit and instead organised a rescue of *Vengeur's* crew. 'You today, us tomorrow' was his philosophy.

The British lost almost three hundred killed and nine hundred wounded, whilst the French lost some seven thousand. It was written in British history as a complete victory yet Villaret himself was quietly satisfied. For the loss of "half a dozen rotten old hulks", the honour of France had been upheld, the grain convoy saved and with it his own head.

Before he left Sarah to her work, John reflected for a moment on the horror of what they were witnessing.

"Every time men settle their differences by slaughtering one another, we have to pick up the pieces. Sometimes I wonder why we should. Then every now and then someone like you comes along and I know why." He smiled, gave her an affectionate squeeze and was gone.

As the roar of cannon ceased and a kind of peace reigned, broken only by the roll of muster drums and barked orders, Sarah resumed searching the orlop and then the gun decks, wincing in the dense and oppressive atmosphere at the stench of newly-spilled blood. Passing over mangled corpses, she shuddered at these broken temples of the spirit cast aside like broken toys. Even the subtle elements of her world reeked with the emanations of suffering. Trying to move around was like treading the Orwell's mudflats again, every sinking step an effort, whilst the thickening ether created near impenetrable barriers.

For those she had come to rescue, it was like being trapped in blanket fog, seeing nothing and not knowing where to turn, an unfolding nightmare with no apparent end. Yet once she had located a man, her smile, gentle touch and invitation were usually all that were needed for him to accompany her willingly. She took them all to the raft. There, a grim and ashen-faced Mary Dawkins stood looking around at her fellow travellers. Just what was happening? She seemed to be in possession of all her faculties… but had seen herself hoisted up like a sack of potatoes and dumped over the ship's side. She must be dead – yet how could she be if, in some unfathomable way, she was still alive?

British and French sat side by side, victor and vanquished, adrift on a fatal flood that might as well be Acheron. Most realised that in some way they were still alive but had left behind wives or sweethearts, sons or daughters, and the loss of those they would never see again hung heavily on them. Some had lost treasured possessions forever. Some were apprehensive, others resigned and even a few seemed content. But where all are suffering, there is no wish for retribution; those who had been deadly enemies were now becoming comrades in a different way of life.

A group of Frenchmen made room for Mary beside Lieutenant Buller and others from the Brunswick, and she knelt down listening in silence as one or two relaxed a little and began to engage in banter. As for Buller, he too could not comprehend the situation, of somehow being in the world and yet no longer of it. Lacking much French, he tried to talk to a French lieutenant. "Excusez-moi, ou est... ici, Frenchie?"

"Je ne comprends pas."

Someone with a slightly better grasp of the language joined in.

"Pardon, monsieur. Ou sommes-nous?"

"Ici," the lieutenant shrugged, "is your fay-moss Davy Jones' lockeur. Why ask me, Engleesh? Et ego in Arcadia."

Buller noticed a British ship passing to leeward and jumped up, pulling off his jacket and waving it frantically. "Ahoy there, ahoy!" he yelled, but the ship continued on her way, none of the crew taking any notice of him. The Frenchman shook his head and smiled coldly.

"They cannot see us, mon ami. We 'ave tried already."

One of his compatriots now felt in his pockets and jumped up angrily, pointing an accusing finger at Buller.

"Merde, je n'ai pas d'argent. On m'a volé!"

"Don't look at me," objected Buller, hastily pulled out his pocket linings. "I have no money either – pas d'argent."

Mary too became alarmed and suddenly found her voice.

"You mean we ain't gonna get our bleedin' money?"

"Somehow," said Buller wistfully, "I don't think that matters now."

Downcast, Mary sank back on her heels, her face revealing more graphically than words that the loss of money troubled her more than the loss of her life. Other seamen, at last finding something amusing, began to grin and exchange knowing glances to which she muttered a few oaths in return, the mildest being "Goddamn!" but this only produced more amusement. Eventually she came to her senses, lifted her worldly-wise head, shrugged and managed a wry smile.

"So it was all for bleedin' nothin'!"

An embarrassed Buller looked away but the apologetic French lieutenant gallantly took her hand and kissed it.

"Pardonnez-moi, madame."

Before long, a second ship appeared to leeward sailing, unbelievably, directly into the wind and on a collision course with the one that Buller had hailed. Nearer and nearer she drew, her sails limp, yet bearing down rapidly on the other's lee with neither crew taking evasive action nor even seeming to notice. The raft's company watched incredulously as she passed right through the British ship, her bowsprit, hull and rigging emerging unscathed. A freed Spanish black slave, Pedro, pointed excitedly at it.

"Mira hombres," he gasped, "es el barco fantasma!"

"What are you jabbering about?" Buller snapped impatiently.

"Is true, is true! The legend, sir!" he sighed tearfully and crossed himself. "We call her 'el barco de las almas perdidas'. She come to rescue lost souls. We safe now!"

The ship approached the raft bow-on, loomed overhead and hove to, surprisingly stable in the heavy swell. Rope ladders were lowered and officers ordered their respective countrymen aboard. Cautiously, taking his time, Buller obeyed the summons.

"I hope you're right, Pedro. Anyway, we have no option but to board her. Follow me, Dawkins."

"Oh, no sir, not me!"

"Do as you're told, woman! That's an order."

"Ay, sir." Meekly, she climbed a ladder after Buller, followed by Pedro and the trio were the last to clamber on deck.

"Welcome aboard, Mr Buller," said the captain, extending a hand. The lieutenant was faced with a salty-white bearded figure with reddish leathern skin and twinkling yet all-commanding eyes, a veritable grand old man of the sea.

"How do you know my name, sir?"

"You're on our muster and you're the last officer to board." He turned to his crew. "That's everybody accounted for, at least for the present. Set a course for Blue Island. And as for you, my lad," he added, reading Pedro's mind and laying a reassuring hand on his shoulder, "you can rest easy. There are no lost souls here, only shipmates bound for Blue Island an' as comfy a berth as a man could want."

Pedro was astonished. Never had he been addressed in so friendly a manner by an officer, let alone a ship's captain. And come to think of it, this seemed to be a quintessentially English captain whose word was law yet had a hearty welcome for all, even the French. On top of that, there were Frenchmen among the gentlemen of the quarterdeck... The newcomers mingled with the thousands aboard already and wondered how, curiously, there always appeared to be room for yet more.

Sarah heard the captain's order from afar and was the last to board, making straight for Mary who was cowering beneath sailcloth and kneeling beside her.

"I've neglected you, but I meant what I said. I'm taking you home."

Mary's sobbing eyes stared uncomprehendingly from a still ashen face as Sarah held her closely, brushing aside tangled hair and dabbing her tears. There came a thankful acknowledgment of her rescuer – then a look of horror. "I probably look as bad as I feel," cried Mary, "but what the bloody Hell's happened to you? You were so pretty... now you look like you belong in a bleedin' charnel house."

"I don't feel so good either, Mary," she murmured, hastily covering her face. "But don't worry. I'll see you safe ashore, at least as far as the harbour. Blue Island is a land of peace and rest at the world's end for those who pass suddenly an' in distress – an' you can stay as long as you like. You can sleep there too, the sleep of ages, a sleep such as you never had before. Then when you're ready, I'll take you to your new home, or rather the one you left long ago. You don't remember now, but you will in time."

"But why are we aboard ship?"

"Because there are so many of you. I'm new to this work but they tell me that with fallen soldiers after a battle, for example, they can round them up and march them through a portal to the spirit world. With sailors it's more difficult, being scattered over the deep and beneath, so they use a ship. Besides, what could be more reassuring for distressed mariners than a rescue ship?" They felt their ship beginning to move. "See, we are underway already. It won't be long now."

Instead of sailing, however, they felt her rising.

176

"Nous allons au paradis," murmured some voices.

"If we're going to Heaven," said Buller, "I suggest we start praying."

"Oui, prions," agreed the French lieutenant, fingering a rosary, kneeling and crossing himself. He began a solemn and heartfelt *Ave Maria* and other voices joined him in a ragged chorus. Buller now wished he had kept silent.

"Popish nonsense," he muttered to his countrymen. "Let's hope this Blue Island has a berth for God-fearing Protestants."

In no time, the world of sea and ships, the floating debris of battle and the still drifting clouds of black smoke, lay far beneath. Although there was little sensation of movement, they travelled at enormous speed through a dark pall of mist before spotting a distant light, like a harbour beacon, growing ever brighter. Then they were in daylight and once more upon waters, entering a cerulean lagoon beneath a sunless yet bright sky, puffed with silvery-white clouds. The ship's idle sails caught the tangy breeze, billowed and carried her along effortlessly, the deck scarcely listing as the bows rose and dipped in the sounding swell and trailed sparkling foam astern.

Sarah helped Mary to the rail and pointed out the coastline as they approached. Ahead lay a craggy natural harbour with lush greenery beyond it, dwarfed by a sheer, marble-white headland. Here and there fissures and narrow ledges supported trees, their braided roots seemingly growing in air, their branches hugging the rock face. Overhead, above the verdant slopes could be glimpsed rolling acres of green and turquoise woodland, bathed in the soft sapphirine light. At the ship's approach, seabirds took off languidly from the water to cleave the air and wheel aloft, some winging over the headland while others came to perch on spray-washed rocks. An all-pervading, conscious presence breathed peace in all the new spirits' hearts. Sarah, herself lost in wonder, nevertheless had to leave now.

"I must go, Mary."

"No, please stay with me."

"I can't. You said how dreadful I look. I need to rest and I don't want others to see me like this. But do come and visit me in my cottage, just as soon as you feel ready."

"Where do you live, then – I won't know how to find you."

"Ah, don't worry about that. Just think of Sarah Auldfield and I'll come and fetch you. Then we'll have a good old talk, woman to woman." As she gave Mary a parting kiss she noticed the French lieutenant taking more than a passing interest in her. "Pardon me, monsieur, would you—?"

"Bien sur, madame," he said, understanding perfectly what was required and offering Mary his hand. "I will protect you with my life."

"But you just friggin' lost it!" she pointed out.

"Then what do you call this?" he retorted, indicating the harbour and shore with a sweep of the other arm. Among all the new arrivals, he seemed to have adjusted the fastest, the most philosophically. "Is this not life? And you – can you take my arm and question matters if you are dead?" She nodded agreement, though her tears still flowed. "Who knows," he continued, "perhaps after all this is what Voltaire called the best of all possible worlds where tout est au mieux – all really is for the best!"

"'Ere, you're all right, Frenchie," she chuckled, wiping her tears and giving him a peck on the cheek before resting her head on his shoulder.

"My name is Jean," he said. "And you are?"

"Mary."

"Bien, Marie, whatever fate has in store for us, we will face it together."

They entered harbour and docked at what appeared, reassuringly, to be a sort of naval depot. Neat white buildings stood beside a stone quay and sailboats rode at anchor in the quiet waters. The ship's passengers disembarked and were welcomed ashore by other officers.

"Where's the lovely lady?" asked an English sailor. "The one who rescued us poor Tars – carried us, waded through blood she did."

Even as they looked for her in vain, all were ushered inside one of the buildings where they found dormitories furnished with hammocks and bunks as though on board ship, but with plenty of room and, as they would gladly discover, no ship's bell to summon them and no watches to stand. Through the open windows wafted a healing balm from nearby woodlands, watered by purling brooks beneath a bluish ether. Nearby, as they would discover, others like them also lived, more numerous than the forest's falling leaves in autumn.

Those who had awoken that morning prepared for battle now lay down to rest in peace, their labours in the other world done, before preparing themselves for a new if uncertain beginning in the labours of this new world. Whether friend or foe, young or old, of high status or low, all were equal now.

CHAPTER 12

A HERO'S RETURN

Bemused and somewhat lonely, Thomas paced the terrace for a while and then went down to the lawn, surveying the dazzling flowerbeds where everything he saw reminded him of Sarah. He came to her little pool, knelt down and peered into its enigmatic depths, but saw only his own reflection. What strange power did she possess that transformed it into a scrying-glass? How he missed her! Then, even as he gazed, a second watery face appeared – not so much a lovely nymph as an ugly death-mask. He turned to look at her aghast. Her eyes gaped, her matted tresses tumbled over a skeletal brow and a tattered gown hung like a winding-sheet.

"Where in the world of Heaven have you been?" he gasped.

"I haven't," she mumbled, "I've been to a Hell on Earth." She swayed as though struggling to find the strength to stand, then looked down at herself. "My gown!" she shrieked. "It's ruined! Mollie gave me this."

He couldn't help smiling at her greater concern for the dress than for herself.

"I don't think you need to worry about that too much. In this world your clothes become a part of you so, as you recover, so will your dress. Remember how down-at-heel I looked when first you saw me?" She nodded meekly. He stood up now to catch her by the waist, pull her closer and hold her tightly. As her head fell back, his kiss breathed all the love and strength his spirit could muster into her corpse-like form. Gradually, strength and feeling returned to her emaciated limbs, some colour to her pasty cheeks and even a spark or two twinkled in her dark, sunken eyes. They remained joined in mind and spirit until she was more her old self.

"Just what have you been doing?"

"The English and French were at each other's throats again. There was a huge sea battle – hundreds, no thousands, have come over." Her eyes roamed an imaginary sea as though the battle with all its horrors were still being waged. "I helped where I could."

"But surely that's a job for the higher guides, the seasoned warriors?"

"Yes, I was only supposed to help the boys and a woman. But when I saw all those brave lads suffering so, I just couldn't leave them. John warned me but I had to stay and help… yet I could not have found the strength without the thought of returning to you."

"Well, next time I shall come with you." They stood rooted to the spot, his generous heart invigorating hers with its fiery energy, bound together as one.

Far away, all Great Britain erupted in an outpouring of rejoicing and national pride. The fleet returned to Spithead with over two thousand prisoners and the six prizes in tow. The Georgian victory anthem *See the Conquering Hero Comes* played Admiral Richard Earl Howe and his officers ashore in Portsmouth harbour. From there, Sir Roger Curtis set off for the Admiralty in London, bearing Howe's despatches.

The Prime Minister, Lord Chatham, went straight to the King's Theatre in the Haymarket, the home of Italian opera, where a performance was in progress. At his bidding, the theatre manager strode out past surprised performers in mid-song to the centre of the wide, crescent-shaped stage as the strains of the orchestra died away. Almost encircled by five tiers of boxes and dwarfed by the huge proscenium arch, he announced, in ringing tones audible in every part of the auditorium, the victory.

There was a stunned silence followed by gasps of delight and a storm of thunderous applause that could be heard across the street. Gentlemen and ladies alike in the boxes stood and applauded, bowed, waved, embraced and offered up prayers of thankfulness. The band played *Rule Britannia* and the soprano Maricelli sang *God Save the King*. The principal soprano, Brigida Banti, was spotted sitting in a box having newly arrived from the continent, and was prevailed upon to sing the national anthem.

The Duke of Clarence ordered his carriage to Covent Garden where another performance was halted and the audience informed, reacting with the same intensity, and similar scenes were played out in New Drury Lane. Footmen shouted the news to passers-by and within hours the streets were filled with boisterous revellers, banging on doors and waking every household to demand that a lighted candle be placed in every window. The street lights, two and four-branched oil lamps in glass spheres that normally spluttered out after eleven o'clock, were kept burning all night serviced by an army of greasy lamplighters with fish-blubber oil tins, sparking flambeaux and rickety ladders. Even the roads leading out to villages up to seven miles away were illuminated. As news spread throughout the kingdom, bonfires were lit and church bells pealed.

The King proclaimed the day of battle 'The Glorious First of June' and presented Howe with a diamond-hilted sword, also signifying his intention of bestowing upon him the Order of the Garter. Gold chains were presented to the admirals and a gold medal, depicting Britannia wielding a trident and riding a sea-horse, was presented to some of the officers for outstanding devotion to duty. Sheridan wrote a musical spectacle and Howe was painted at the height of battle, wreathed in smoke and standing motionless on deck in full dress uniform with drawn sword.

Within days, news of the victory reached the provinces and the Ipswich Journal carried reports of the battle. In the Turners' parlour overlooking St Margaret's Green, the talk was of nothing else and the excitement of even the servants could not be contained. Frances called them together.

"I see we shall have no work from any of you until the latest intelligence is known," she began, conscious of the fact that it was the first time in her capacity as lady of the house she had felt obliged to say such a thing. "Nancy, pray be seated and be so good as to enlighten us."

"Very good, ma'am." Taking the newspaper from the silver salver on a side table, she seated herself and, in a halting voice, put into practice her improved reading skills, describing the admiral's deep gratitude for the "resolution, spirit and perseverance" of the *Queen Charlotte's* officers and seamen.

"Thank you, Nancy," said Frances, rising from her chair. "Now let us bow our heads in grateful prayer to Almighty God for His deliverance and for the victory that He has been pleased to grant." She then dismissed them to their duties but, the following day and for days after, the morning reading was repeated as every edition brought with it some fresh excitement, until she began to despair of the household returning to normality again. Nothing, however, could have prepared her for the disturbance caused by the account, reprinted from the London Gazette, published two days after the royal family's visit to the *Queen Charlotte*.

Earl Howe, it seems, had not identified all those who deserved special praise but the King himself had been conversing with the humbler seamen themselves to learn about the actions they had taken part in.

"They in turn," read Nance, "pointed to one of their number who, they declared, had taken a prominent and decisive part at a critical stage of the battle. It was Able Seaman Cabern—" She gasped and a crimson flush came to her cheeks. Surely it could not be her Robert?

"Read on, read on!" chorused the servants.

"It was Able Seaman Cabern, they affirmed, who, casting aside all thoughts of self-preservation and intent only on devotion to duty, had almost single-handedly saved his ship from further harm, after her main-top and fore-top masts had been shot away by enemy action. Upon being commended by His Majesty and being asked if he intended to remain in the service, Cabern modestly replied that his only concern at present was for the welfare of his intended, a Miss Auldfield residing in the county of Suffolk who, he believed, did not even know he was in the Navy... It's him, it's him!" she shrieked, throwing up her arms and staring wildly.

"It is he," Frances corrected her. "We do not forget the grammar we have so carefully learned just because we are the recipient of news, however surprising."

"Noo, my good lady, forgive me," she said, adding excitedly, "it's he, it's he, it's—"

"Nancy, that will do. Kindly compose yourself and run along and attend to your duties."

"Yes, ma'am, beg pardon, ma'am." She dropped a clumsy curtsy before, scarcely able to control her limbs, turning to stumble towards the door and dashing upstairs to her room.

Frances dismissed the servants and sat alone for some moments to reflect quietly on this news that had winged its way into her household like an ill-omened owl that, far from saluting the dawn, merely signalled a coming storm. How war changes everything! A man who had shown scant regard for his country's laws and would gladly risk life and limb for gold, had turned patriot and become a hero. And it was surely only a matter of time before he came knocking at the door with his prize money, promising the world. Her hapless servant was already besotted, so what would she not do now for the hero of all Suffolk?

It was just possible, of course, that he was a changed man. And if he could put half the daring and enterprise into an honest venture that he had into villainy, he would surely prosper. But be that as it may, Frances wanted some evidence first. The uneducated commonly believed that good deeds can cancel out bad ones but, if that were so, people would literally get away with murder…

Frances felt it was time to acquaint Nance with a few home truths, however unpalatable, and made her way upstairs to her room. She began by pointing out that Nance's behaviour had been quite out of keeping with her position.

"I dew beg pardon, ma'am. I wuz wholly buffled, it wuz such a shock." Her moist eyes looked imploringly at her mistress.

"Of course, it was. I do understand and I have not come to scold you. I come as a friend and one very much in your debt. Although I cannot hope to repay it in full, I can at least pay some of the interest owed."

"Yew've been wholly kind ta me, ma'am, far more than yar poor servant deserves."

185

"What I have to say now concerns another, Master Cabern. Now, I have neither seen nor met the man but, like everyone else, I hear things. Whatever one is now, it is the past on which one is judged – it is the only thing on which anyone can be judged, so that we may be certain of them.

"He has rendered a noble, courageous and selfless service for king and country. If he has the necessary will and strength of character, he can change his life for the better and put his old ways behind him for good. No man could have a finer opportunity and I pray that he will take it and walk in the ways of the Lord rather than of men." She would have liked to leave it there, but felt compelled for her servant's sake to continue. "Men like him do not realise the harm they do. They are dismissive of honest working folk – and I am thinking of your family here. They lead them on and thereby bring about their disgrace and ruin."

"I know yew dewn't approve of 'em, ma'am."

"What I have heard, I admit, is hearsay. But the consequences of some of his actions are evident and cannot be gainsaid. Why, I have heard you, as honest and upright a woman as can be, called a smuggler's mistress! I know that is a wicked lie, yet unsubstantiated remarks like that are only made if people believe them. I am sensible of the fact you have not had the advantages in life some have. Had providence decreed otherwise and reversed our roles, I too, unsuitable for the hand of Mr Turner, might be impressed by a man like Cabern."

"Law bliss yew, now my good laday be a-jestin! Yew's noo servant and I'm noo laday."

"But we are both, I trust, good Christian women." She said this deliberately, having been shocked to discover that Nance cared little for religion, despite her outward show of conformity. Indeed, everything she did was for the purpose of pleasing people, rather than duty to God. "Allow me to make a suggestion, Nancy, that I think will prove beneficial for both our sakes."

"Let my good laday be a-tellin', an' I be a-hearin'."

"Give Rob Cabern a chance to improve his prospects by all means, but not at your expense. Keep your distance and accept nothing more from him, as your family did. Inform him that if he wishes to take you to wife, he must first provide a permanent home, a reasonable income and evidence of honest employment. This is now well within his capacity. If he has any true feelings for you, he will jump at the chance. And if you are ever in doubt, pray to the good Lord for guidance and place the matter in His hands. What do you say?"

Nance felt a little dazed for no-one had talked to her on that level before. Moreover, the requirement for a man to do all that had never occurred to her either. Marriage for the lower orders was merely a matter of exchanging vows before the parson. Given what Frances Turner had said, she could hardly disagree.

However, accepting advice was one thing but putting Cabern out of her mind was nigh on impossible. If anything, the enticing prospect of a home in advance and security only served to enhance her desire for some kind of idyllic existence that would last forever. She began to daydream about her future residence, becoming ever grander as time passed, with servants and fine food, presided over by Captain and Mrs Cabern. As she went about her daily tasks, her mind was increasingly elsewhere, imagining 'Captain and Mrs Cabern will be At Home' or 'Captain and Mrs Cabern require their carriage' and so on. And late in the evening, mindful that several Ipswich men had been in the naval engagement, instead of going to bed she began to slip out without permission to visit taverns frequented by seamen, seeking news of Cabern. Consequently, she didn't get to bed until the early hours and arose still sleepy in the morning.

As the weeks passed with no news, her obsession only strengthened until she was thinking of Cabern constantly and dreaming of him in what little sleep she could manage. Dreams of Sarah also came, but they were unwelcome. Sarah always seemed opposed to her, just as she had been in life, warning her about associating with Cabern. She was still a prophet of doom!

True, when she had felt Sarah's presence in the past it had proved opportune, but what on Earth could be wrong now, what possible danger could there be? If Sarah did still live somehow and was trying to warn her, what was the warning about? Surely there was nothing to be concerned about, now that Cabern was a changed man – and a hero to boot.

Her eyes were often vacant and her mind unable to focus on her tasks. When immersed in thoughts of him – sensual, arousing and full of hope – her heart's embers smouldered and ignited again. Unsurprisingly, her work suffered and Mrs Turner was obliged to make her feelings known. Worse still, seamen began to call at the house with pretended news of Cabern in the hope of cadging food and ale – and household items went missing. Frances was on the point of issuing a final warning.

Nance crossed her heart, hoped to die and promised to pay full attention to her duties from now on and to entertain no more strangers...

In her downy bed at the cottage, Sarah slept again the sleep of ages. With Mollie watching over her and Thomas at hand, little by little her strength returned and her spirits revived. Yet even as she slept, her sisterly fears instinctively led her to revisit Earth and she repeatedly found herself in Nance's garret room. There she found her sister either pacing the room, hunched deep in thought or fallen exhausted across the bed. Clearly, something was wrong. She wanted to stay and find out what it was, but she was not strong enough and inevitably found herself slipping back to her own world.

As soon as she felt her old self again, she went to Thomas' garden and the scrying pool where she knelt and focused her mind on Nance, staring fixedly at the images unfolding before her. There was a street scene but so dark that she could barely discern any detail. The street lamps had gone out so it had to be near midnight or later. Then a hooded woman came into view, her cloak wrapped closely about her. She seemed to be visiting all the taverns, entering one and emerging moments later, then entering and leaving another. Intrigued, Sarah thought herself further into the scene and found herself standing in a puddled and muddy Carr Street, just as the mysterious figure paused before the door of The Salutation Inn. Now she knew it was Nance before she even saw her face – but what was she doing here at this hour since she never drank anything stronger than small beer let alone frequented taverns? Sarah followed her into the murky, candlelit parlour.

Stoke Bridge, Ipswich

Nance approached a far corner and asked several carousing seamen if they had any news of Cabern, pausing before one man in particular with his hat pulled down over his forehead. He seemed to be taking an interest in her, too, even as he banged the table with his tankard and muttered a string of oaths. Apprehensively, Sarah saw him raise the hat and Nance recognise, too late, the cracked, brown face and calculating eyes of Mad Jack Rackhem. Unwilling to face him, she turned to the others as though appealing to their better natures, but they also stared coldly back, every eye upon her.

Sarah felt her sister's dark terror as she backed away towards the door, grasped the handle to wrench it open and bolted outside, splashing through the puddles in the direction of Upper Orwell Street. The pavement was deserted with only candles flickering in a few windows to light the way. She bounded along, pursued by steps that sounded ever closer, but her legs lacked their usual vigour and weakened until she could barely stumble. Vice-like arms grabbed her from behind and hoisted her off her feet.

"Gotcha, me hearty," cried a gruff voice. In an instant she was surrounded, several men thrusting their faces close to hers. "Where's Cabern?" Rackhem demanded. "Is he back yet?"

"I dewn't know."

"'Appen you do."

"I dewn't know nothin'. Would I be axin' ivery Tar in town if I did?"

"Well, 'appen you don't," he conceded, still holding her roughly by the arm. "But I want to know as soon as he's back. Understand?"

"Let goo of me!" she cried indignantly, struggling to free herself.

Rackhem, the worse for rum, thrust a hand over her mouth to quieten her but, finding his fingers against her lips, she bit them. "Bitch!" he snarled, slapping her face hard.

Like a cornered beast, she opened her mouth and howled, her cries echoing down the street and rousing the elderly night-watchman, dozing in his watch-box. Taking up a lantern and cudgel, he stepped out and walked towards the commotion in the darkness guided by the screams and oaths.

"Who goes there?" he demanded. "Who disturbs the King's peace?"

The quick-tempered Rackhem was beside himself with rage. "I've 'ad it up to 'ere with you, you soddin' bitch."

She continued to struggle. By now several windows had been flung open, heads were thrust out and angry voices demanded to know who was disturbing the peace. The watchman tottered toward the group, holding up his lantern.

"Halt!" he cried. "In the name of the law, halt!"

"Cap'n," shouted one of the crew, "for Gawd's sake leave her be or we'll be taken. I don't want to swing for no bloody woman. Leave her be! What good is she to us?"

"All right, blast your eyes!" conceded Rackhem, turning back to Nance. "'Ere's something to remember us by!"

He punched her squarely on the jaw. She reeled from the blow, banged her head on the wall behind, slumped against it and collapsed. Rackhem and his men made off whilst several tradesmen in nightshirts and hastily-donned breeches ventured out of doors, a lantern in one hand and a sword or pistol in the other. At first they could see nothing but the ranging light of their lanterns soon fell upon the prostrate form of Nance, face down and unconscious in a pool of water.

Sarah had watched the assault helplessly, as had Teresa who had instinctively and speedily joined her, and both knelt tearfully at Nance's side, thankful at least to see her still alive.

"Oh Nance, dearest Nance," sobbed Sarah. "I knew something like this would happen. I did try to warn you. Oh, dear Lord," she prayed, "please save my sister from further harm, for I cannot."

The watchman raised the hue and cry and organised search parties, whilst the parish constable was roused from bed. Two householders remained with Nance and one bent down to examine her.

"Why, it's Mrs Turner's housekeeper," he said, raising her shoulders and cradling her head. "Damn me, if she didn't near drown. Her nose was fair under water." Soon several women and their servants joined their menfolk.

"Carry the poor woman inside," ordered one. "Just look at the state she's in. Quickly, bring her into our house and fetch the doctor!"

As Nance was carried inside, still unconscious, a servant was sent to nearby Orwell Place where the good Dr Abbett lost no time in getting dressed and throwing a cloak about his shoulders. Within ten minutes of being summoned, he was beside Nance as she began to revive. Seeing all the peering faces, the terror she had just experienced returned, but then she recognised the kindly eyes of her old friend.

"Don't fret m'dear. You're among friends now."

The constable arrived at last, bearing his elaborately decorated staff of office. Initially annoyed at having his sleep disturbed, he was as shocked as everyone else by so vicious an assault. As soon as Nance had recovered sufficiently, he leaned over her.

"Did you recognise the villain, Miss?"

"Oh yes," she said icily, "it was Jack Rackhem."

Sarah and Teresa stayed with her throughout the night. The following day, Frances sent her carriage to bring Nance back to the Norman House where she was carried up to her room. Mr Turner immediately offered a reward and a handbill was posted throughout the town:

WANTED
TWENTY POUNDS REWARD
is offered by J. Turner, Esq. of the Castle Brewery, Ipswich,
for information leading to the apprehension of Jack Rackhem,
also known as 'Mad Jack', sea captain and notorious smuggler,
for a most dastardly Assault upon, and Attempted Murder of,
a Female Person.
Signed: T. Otis, Esq. and E. Riches, Esq.,
Justices of the Peace.

Nance spent a few days recovering before being well enough, on Frances' instructions, to be conveyed home for convalescence. Her place would be kept open until her return and Frances spared her the scolding she thought she richly deserved, thinking she had suffered enough.

But what Nance discovered on her return to the family cottage was even more sorrow. Her father was by now an invalid and Matty was doing casual labour nearby so that he could look after him. This was burdensome so he had decided on the only solution he could think of. One evening, he had taken his father's arm and walked with him, a few steps at a time, through the village, past the church and along the carriageway leading to the Seven Hills. Taking a track to the right, they had passed the Poorhouse with its cracked windowpanes, leaky thatch and crumbling lath and plaster walls. Further on they reached the Workhouse, screened discreetly by trees.

A crimson sun hung low in the sky as they paused outside, this their last journey together coming to its inevitable end. For the old man whose life's journey was drawing to a close anyway, it was a poignant moment. The former village statesman, master ploughman and proud father could no longer support himself, much less the family, so now he would have to rely on the charity of strangers. He had settled himself on a grassy knoll, rested his chin in his hands and gazed thoughtfully in the direction of Amberslea.

"My owd Pa rested here when I wuz a young'n, taakin' 'em ta the Workhouse," he said quietly after a while, as he savoured the last moments of freedom, resignation paving the way for the final steps. Matty had listened tearfully and remembered his father's love, his many sacrifices and acknowledged, belatedly, the duty owed by a son. He laid a tender hand on his father's shoulder. "Haps it's time us got a-gooin'."

"It is tha', Pa," declared Matty with a change of heart. "Us be a-gooin' hoom." They retraced their slow steps back to the cottage.

When Nance found out she was determined that, no matter what, they would stay together even if she had to work all hours and keep house as well. Considering the best cure for ill-health was to be up and about, she soon took over the running of the household once more, enjoying being home again and beginning to think less of Castlegreen and Norman House. In her old familiar surroundings and with the passing of time, her passion for Cabern might also have abated had not a letter from him been redirected from the Norman House to the cottage.

> *Queen Charlotte, Portsmouth, 28th of October.*
> *My dearest Nancy,*
> *I hoped by now to secure my discharge and join you at Amberslea and present you with my prize money, but it is not to be. I am bound to serve for another two years and cannot obtain leave, as repairs are completed and we sail to rejoin the fleet.*
> *You are ever in my thoughts and I will sustain myself throughout two further years of exile with making plans for our future together.*
> *I love you more than you can ever know. You are all the world to me; and the day cannot arrive too quickly when I will kneel and beg you to become my wife.*
> *Your most ever loving and devoted servant, friend and future husband, Robert*

Inevitably, the intensity of her passion increased for a while and the letter could scarcely have been more precious had it been written by King George himself. But at least she could rest easy in the knowledge that he was safe for the present and could also reconcile herself to not seeing him for two years.

Once her woman's touch had brought order to the little cottage and everything was back in its proper place, with anything broken either mended or thrown out, she began to seek employment. With Matty in local work, she intended to return to Castlegreen but had forgotten to inform the Turners of her intentions, and eventually the position was filled. It proved hard to find local employment since her reputation as a servant, at one time impeccable, still suffered from her association with Cabern.

Even agricultural work, except for daily hiring, was becoming more rare. It was now past Michaelmas, the time of year when there was least to do on the land. Traditionally, farmers would have hired for the year. There were in-servants for the domestic and light agricultural work, and skilled workers who lived in tied cottages and enjoyed some security. Extra labour would only be employed for haymaking and harvest, but now there were more casual jobs than permanent ones and more workers seeking them.

All the family frustrations and disappointments were sensed by Sarah whenever she thought of her sister, whether tending her own garden, or helping Thomas, or wandering as a free spirit among the parklands and wild retreats that dominated her region. Consequently, she visited the old cottage more frequently, usually finding her father in his old rocking chair by the fireside, watching Nance busy herself with her chores.

"Yew've not found work, Nance?"

"Summat ul turn up, Pa," she shrugged. "Summat allus does."

"Why dewn't yew ask the Harveys, or the Knollers?"

"I have."

"And—"

"It's not like it wuz, Pa. Times are a-changin'. Time wuz they paid us same money year after year. Now they say, 'cause of the war, prices goo up an' down an' what they pay one year haps they won't pay the next. Then, the lean harvests o' late mean they dewn't want soo many workers. Blas more, now there's more folk livin' than afore, an' less work, it means they want yew when they want yew, fur the least pay, or they dewn't want yew at all."

Sarah watched her father's gaze shift between the flames curling around the crackling log and the phantasmagoria on the smutty hearth.

Names from the past came to mind. What about this one and that, an' old so-and-so, he suggested: yeomen farmers, who laboured in the fields with their workers, ate at the same table and sometimes needed extra hands.

"Not now, Pa. Those good souls aren't around noo more. Others have bought 'um out, almost all of 'um. The gen'leman farmer, he dewn't work in the fields. He stays in the parlour an' gives orders – who stays, who goes. He has plenty work, but there's plenty more as wants it. Why hire for the year when he can hire by the day, or even the hour? An' happen it rain, why hire at all?"

"There's still the harvest," the old man suggested, reminiscing. "Everyone's needed fur tha'. Tha' wuz the crownin' glory o' the year."

"There'll always be harvest but even tha's not what it wuz. Us used to complain 'bout getting up next day ta goo ta work, but then us had work ta goo ta. Not now. It's not family an' loyal servants noo more," she added sourly, "it's just business, a bargain struck atwixt farmer an' headman for bringin' in the harvest." She continued with her work while her father contemplated sadly how his world was changing.

Nance had to accept the lowest form of domestic work which was charring. She would rise while it was still dark and make her way to a prospective employer's home, ring the tradesman's bell and wait until, eventually, a maid deigned to open it. Then it would be scrubbing floors, scalding pewter, boiling clothes and linen and polishing endless piles of silver, all without a break and all for at most eight pence per day. She'd return home, usually in the dark, to cook for her father and brother. If there was no work, she kept house.

"I wanted better fur yew, Nance," confessed Zebedee. "This world was made fur gentry. It's them as owns the land an' them as charges us fur the privilege o' workin' it. Blas more, if they's a mind ta, they can see us dewn't work at all."

"What do yew suggest, Pa?"

"The way I see it," he chuckled, "us has ta becoom gentry. Then the land be ours an' us can pay ourselves fur workin' it."

"Fine chance us has of becoomin' gentry."

A fine chance indeed, yet how different things might have been had she chosen Jethro. He would have given her a decent home and a lot more besides, perhaps children.

Some two years later a seaman, unusually well-dressed, presented himself at the tradesman's entrance of the Norman House on the Green and asked to see Nance. The servants refused him entrance but he persisted, ringing the bell at the front door which brought Frances herself to face him. By his lack of deference, which to her mind bordered on insolence, she guessed he was Robert Cabern – a hero, yes, but also an associate of Jack Rackhem, wanted for many crimes including the assault on her former servant.

"Nancy Auldfield," she said sharply, "has not been in service here for two years. She's probably with her family. Good day."

The door was promptly closed. Taken aback but still determined to return to Nance, he set out for her father's cottage. Before he left Ipswich, though, he noticed a weathered Wanted poster for Rackhem. Making his way across country, he came to the cottage where Zebedee drew back the bolt and leaned on the doorpost, weary with ill-health and stooping with age.

"What brings yew ta Amberslea?" muttered Zeberdee.

"I come to ask for your daughter's hand, Mr Auldfield," announced a confident Cabern.

"Tha' be in the expectancy she has a mind fur yew."

It had not occurred to Cabern that she might not be of a mind. Surely that could never be.

"Though I be unworthy of her, I know she do love me and I mean to make her happy. I have my liberty pass and prize-money, forty golden guineas. And as God's my witness, I swear I'll make her a true and loyal husband. Why, as soon as my feet touched land I set a course for here."

"Prize gowd, yew say?" Zebedee almost sneered, unimpressed. "Will gowd bring back my boy Albert ta me, or Mark, or my dear Beth as died o' grief? An' my darter's good name, nay, the whole fam'ly as once wuz? Will it bring back John, who went off a-seekin' his fortune, haa'ter havin' his head stuffed wi' nonsense from the loikes o' yew? Can gowd recall the departed spirit or quicken the dead? Tha' be a rare kind o' gowd yew got, Master Cabern."

"I cannot undo what was done in times agon, Mr Auldfield," said Cabern, bowing his head and appearing remorseful. "And of much of it, I had no knowledge, believe me. Now please, will you tell me where Nance is?"

"Why, where she is ivery day, workin', tha' is when she can get work. Bonen har fingers, brusen har knees an' worken all the hours the good Lawd sends. An' tha's not takin' account o' the bruises an' cracked skull she got from Rackhem." He shook his head and added ruefully, "Soo tired she be o' late, an' still hard a-worken of a night 'ere, she ont goo ta bed without I maak har."

"What's this, Jack Rackhem hit her, you say?"

"Yar owd first mate, as wuz soo obligin' ta Bert an' Mark. Dollop't har good an' proper 'ee did, 'em an' tha' thar crew o' his, rogues an' pirates ivery one. Left har fur dead. Yew keep bad company, Master Cabern."

"As Heaven be my witness, I knew nothing—"

"Soo Nance dewn't want ta see yew noo more. Now be off wi' yew an' dewn't yew coom a-knocken here noo more, not niver."

"But Mr Zeb—"

"Begone afore, owd as I am, I give yew the thrashin' o' yar life!" growled Zebedee. Summoning up his remaining strength, cursing and breathing hatred, he raised his weak arm, lurched forward and landed a feeble fist on the other's shoulder.

"Avast boardin', old man," muttered a dejected Cabern, stepping back. "I'll not stay."

He turned, shouldered his scrip and plodded away with a heavy heart. After all he had gone through, it seemed he had even lost Nance, the guiding star of his destiny and the object of his every dream. So, Rackhem was responsible. Even though he had once owed him his life, the man had deceived him more than once so he shouldn't be surprised that a faithless friend had become a ruthless enemy.

Rackhem must have been looking for him and had lashed out at Nance when she crossed his path. Well, if Rackhem wanted to see him, he would oblige. If he could avenge Nance and offer her Rackhem's head, it might atone somewhat and, who knows, give him another chance. The difficulty was where to find him, elusive as he was. Some of their old crew must surely know, so he decided to make for the coast, beginning at Felixstowe where he knew that one or two of them lived then, if necessary, all the way up to Lowestoft.

CHAPTER 13

THE HIGHER LIFE

As the seasons passed, the torch that Nance carried for Cabern still burned though less brightly. Her father had said nothing about his visit and no-one else had seen him, for he was sticking to his old habit of avoiding people, treading the lonely heath or woodland path instead. Moreover, now that he was stalking Rackhem, he travelled at night and visited in disguise the inns frequented by seamen.

A chance encounter in an Ipswich street reunited Nance with her former mistress, Mrs Turner. Neither of them, for different reasons, mentioned Cabern and Frances assumed that common sense had prevailed. She also immediately saw through Nance's pretence of having regular employment. Whilst there was no shortage of servants nowadays and others aspired to the position of housekeeper, only Nance had truly fulfilled it. Would she like her old place back? It was all Nance could do to restrain herself from falling at her saviour's feet.

She returned to the Green in late winter, in charge of all the domestics again, and Frances had no cause to regret her impromptu decision. The house was managed impeccably, the children loved having their old nurse back and the servants were happy to see their duties apportioned fairly. As for Nance, regular wages meant that she could pay a woman to keep house for her father.

One day as she sat in the pantry, poring over the accounts, she heard a commotion outside on the Green. She shrugged and returned to the ledger but through an open window came more shouts and the shrieks of women and children. She put down her quill, jumped up and ran to the front parlour window where a face appeared, looking in at her, that of a young woman. She seemed to be speaking – at least, Nance understood an inner voice to say, "Come quickly!" She dashed back and out through the servants' entrance but saw nobody at the front of the house. Thoughts of Sarah came to mind – was it really she who was at the window? Yes, the face did resemble her but surely it could not have been Sarah. Who, then, and why?

The shouting on the Green persisted, and near the fish ponds she could see people milling about and darting in all directions. Then she saw the cause – a rogue bull was running loose and threatening everyone, mostly women and children. One or two stumbled and fell but they were saved each time by the bull's indecision; every time it lowered its horns to gore a prostrate form, its attention was distracted by someone fleeing in a different direction. Nance slipped off her patterns, lifted her skirts and raced across the Green where a solitary boy stood helplessly in the bull's path. This time it halted before him, snorted and pawed the ground, then charged and knocked him over. It gored him slightly, turned and lowered its head to gore again.

Nance dashed up and placed herself between the bull and the boy. Its response was to toss her. She managed to grab the horns but the bull made light of her, lifting her up and heaving her over its head. She kept hold of the horns for as long as she could and her momentum brought her legs over her head and down so that she landed on her feet. The animal turned to attack again but was now facing a more formidable adversary. Her old hot temper flared, and the indignity of going 'arse upards' over the bull released her from any fear. Her black eyes shot fire and her clenched fists were raised as if to punch the beast into submission as she advanced upon it. Bemused at first, then enraged, dripping saliva and snorting, it pawed the earth and lowered its head to charge.

A frightened Sarah watched helplessly and frightened – hers had been the face at the window – but in a trice Teresa was at her side to reassure her. "Help is at hand!"

"What do you mean? How can we possibly stop a charging bull?"

"We can't, but others can. You see those three men running up?" she indicated with a hand. "For them, wrestling is a sport and casting a bull is even better. I've hurried them along."

Sure enough the men, seeing what was happening, dashed to Nance's aid. One of them, well known for his sporting prowess, took the charge head-on but managed to seize the horns and lift his legs as he was carried backwards. Another younger man threw his arms round the neck and swung his weight under it, their combined strength stopping the beast in its tracks, so that the third could trip the bull's leg and throw it to the ground. Nance turned her attention to the boy, who was barely conscious. After satisfying herself that no bones were broken, she helped him up, lifted him over her shoulder and carried him back to the house.

The gathered crowd raised a cheer and the men threw their hats into the air. Nance was unsure how to respond and just carried on walking, feeling embarrassed at being the object of attention. A closed door behind her was never so welcome. It turned out that the lad lived a few doors away on the Green and was a relative of one of Mr Turner's employees.

When not feeling obliged to watch over her impulsive and sometimes misguided sister, and when not with Thomas, Sarah stayed at her cottage and often received visitors, strangers attracted from afar by the welcoming aura of the garden she so carefully tended. One day, she noticed John at the wicket gate, admiring the blossoms, in particular the lofty sunflowers, geraniums and hollyhocks that overhung the pathway and concealed much of the cottage walls. She greeted him at the doorway, framed by clusters of sweet-scented roses.

Entering the cottage and treading the stone floor, he noticed with approval the simple pine chairs, chest and dresser, the depending crockery-rack and rustic (if somewhat redundant) chimneypiece where a fragrant bouquet fanned out like a sunburst. This was a thought-form consciously projected by Sarah from the flowers outside. Shafts of energetic light filtered through the window-lattice, tingeing the white walls with pallets of cream and gold and diffusing a soft radiance across the beamed ceiling. The atmosphere in here was charged and concentrated the awareness, focusing the mind and expanding it to a heightened consciousness.

"Just like my home," murmured John, noting how everything blended in an harmonious whole. He motioned her to be seated and told her how happy he was with her progress and the work she was doing with Thomas. "I thought," he went on, "you might like to accompany me on a little journey."

"I would be honoured, John."

"It would be easier if you were asleep. Just relax and close your eyes." As she sat down, his hand lightly touched her forehead. She relaxed further and slipped into a trance. He then took her by the hand and coaxed her out of the chair. "Come with me – that's it, just walk this way – and now open your eyes."

Astounded, she realised they were no longer in the cottage. They had passed through a portal of some kind into an unfolding mystical landscape, the colours brighter, more vivid and translucent even than in the world she had just left. Although no sun hung in the gold-threaded, azure sky, everywhere was radiant with light. In front of her she saw several tree-arched, mossy avenues, but meandering and artfully rising and falling, now further apart, now closer together. They traversed rolling acres of variegated, velvety lawn, neither grazed nor scythed, between shimmering and exquisitely proportioned buildings. These seemed to be made of a kind of marble or crystal, more window than wall. Around them swept borders glimmering with oases of gem-like flowers, carefully harmonised by size and colour so, like the parkland, they too appeared minutely managed to the last stem and petal.

As for John, she saw that his robe was no longer drab and monk-like but golden brown and apparently woven in threads of light. He held her gently with his left hand and touched the crown of her head with the right. Her vision expanded until she became aware of the very roots of every tree, shrub and flower, drawing up energy like pulsating light into every leaf and blossom, which in turn radiated a unique prismatic halo. Every trunk and stem, every blade of grass even, was contributing something personal to the evolving whole by its individual, inimitable existence. Gradually, the enhanced vision of incomparable beauty faded…

At her feet, the scene was reflected in a glassy rivulet, fed by a bubbling spring from a leafy grotto, its droplets resonating in harmony as they splashed. John touched her head again and she experienced an expansion of sound far beyond the normal senses. From the arboreal avenues, the woodlands and borders, she could now hear ethereal voices as though of a choir, singing by turns, or solo, or counterpoint, or in concert, all blending in a vast symphony. Like a cathedral organ, every voice was at once individual yet inextricably part of the harmonious whole.

With a third touch, her consciousness opened even further beyond mind and spirit, until Sarah Auldfield became boundless and encompassing everything – a rolling wave within an ocean of consciousness, in union with the Source of all potential, of all knowledge and wisdom.

How long this divine communion lasted she couldn't tell – the idea was meaningless – but by degrees it contracted until she became her former self, standing once more in the landscape of unrivalled beauty. Curiously, the feeling arose that she had experienced something like this before, albeit in a very dim and distant past. She turned quizzically to John.

"Your soul memory is true," he said. "You did indeed experience something of the sort in our Father's House, which you and I left aeons ago as particles of consciousness – and where we shall return as fully realised beings one day. You have evolved sufficiently to remember something of what it was like. Perhaps you can appreciate, too, that however wonderful this experience is only a small part of our potential for infinite consciousness."

His words, though not fully understood, resounded in her deepest being and she continued to gaze around in silent rapture, whilst shielding her eyes from the brilliant light. Again, John responded to her thought.

"No, you aren't used to it. If – when – you are ready to come and live here, a new body will be necessary, one finer and subtler. It will be like the butterfly emerging from the chrysalis. Some call it the second death." He paused for a while as though considering his next words carefully. "It's natural that all this seems strangely familiar to you because this is your home. What Thomas now thinks of as the real world is only an intermediate state. This is the real one or, rather, the first of several. It was from here that you set out with a mission for your latest earthly journey. I know you don't believe that you fulfilled it—"

"I failed to prevent the ruin of my family."

"—yet you did your very best and that's as much as can be asked of anyone. Besides, some of the results of your efforts have yet to be seen. The experience that others have gained there has already been of great benefit, and will prove to be even more so later. And anyway, it doesn't end here for there are higher worlds, infinitely more beautiful yet formless."

As they neared one of the crystalline buildings, its interior could be seen, bathed in the lighter colours of the spectrum. People in pastel robes woven of gossamer threads like John's were entering or leaving. Fair or dark, of every skin colour, all seemed serene and busily engaged in some purposeful undertaking. A group of children saw the pair and in the blink of an eye stood beside them. Although somehow altered, Sarah recognised them at once as being from among the children she had met and played with at her cottage.

"Hello, Sarah," cried one. "Have you come to be with us?"

"I'm not sure," she replied, glancing towards John, "but it's so wonderful to see you again." She knelt down and hugged them all, remarking how much they had changed since their last meeting.

"This," explained John, "is where the little ones who pass before their time grow up. They learn their lessons and reach adulthood just as they would have done on Earth, except that their tuition is, I think, rather better."

"But they still have no parents?"

"On the contrary, new ones are found for them, often from among those who would have liked to have children but could not." She understood from his manner that he was suggesting this as a possibility for her. The children chattered excitedly and told her all about their new school; this time, before they parted, it was Sarah who had to promise to visit them.

For Nance, now settled in her old job as housekeeper at the Norman House, life was again relatively happy. Her father was being looked after and on her afternoon off she had only a relatively short walk to visit him. Even her passion for Cabern had cooled somewhat, although hope remained that he would eventually return and propose marriage. Things might have continued in this contented vein had she not read a newspaper account of a battle between smugglers and the Preventive Service.

North of Bawdsey was Shingle Street, a stretch of beach bordered by Oxley Marshes and Bowan's Creek, with three sizable islands and several smaller ones offshore. It was a wilderness of shingle and wild flora partially shielded from view by the islands, and with the River Ore and Orford Haven to the north it was ideal for smuggling. One day, Garrow Merryridge was tipped off that local men were to land contraband there that night so he and six dragoons gathered before sunset near the track leading to the marshes. They concealed themselves within the sea beet, the kale and the colourful wild flowers and waited.

The pale half-moon beamed softly upon the gently pounding surf, vanishing intermittently and leaving a mantle of blackness. Merryridge didn't even see the smugglers' boats until a bluish flame from a sawn-off pistol signalled their approach. A lantern waved from the marshes in reply, then the moon reappeared briefly to reveal dark forms wading from the boats onto the beach. The light faded and darkness returned. Merryridge put a whistle to his lips that mimicked the cry of a seagull, the signal for his men to prepare for action.

As the smugglers began tramping up the shingle, his men levelled their weapons and listened carefully for them to reach a predetermined point that would give a clear field of fire. Anxious moments followed as they waited for the moon to reappear. They heard footsteps pass them and halt, then the thuds of heavy objects dropped on shingle before the footsteps tramped back to the boat. Overhead, a cloud floated away and a wan light shone down. A dozen or more forms could be distinguished heading back to the water, a little ahead of where Merryridge and the dragoons lay concealed. He again blew a seagull's cry followed by two more, which were followed by the clicks of flintlocks being cocked. Merryridge stood up, a pistol in each hand.

"Halt in the King's name!" he commanded.

The surprised smugglers grabbed their weapons, fired a shot or two and scattered. A number of flashes stabbed the darkness and the cracks of discharges resounded along the beach. Three or four men were seen to stagger and fall but others returned fire and decided to make a fight of it, realising too late that they faced soldiers alongside the riding officer. Each dragoon drew his sword and advanced to confront them.

"Halt, in the King's name!" repeated Merryridge, rushing up and drawing his cutlass, lunging at the first smuggler to confront him. Plunged into darkness, scarcely able to see, they thrust and slashed wildly. Merryridge's men shouted their own names as arranged and whoever did not reply was attacked. A few smugglers made a dash for the marshes whilst others were cut badly, run through or clubbed to the ground. By the time Merryridge and the dragoons answered only to one another, the distant crunching of boots on shingle had grown fainter.

"Let's see what the haul is," said Merryridge.

A tinder-pistol and touch-paper were produced and, in a hollow scooped from the stones, a candle was lit and placed in a lantern. Taking this, Merryridge advanced on each of the fallen as his men stood by, swords at the ready. Of the first seven he examined, two were dead and five wounded. At the eighth, the jumping flame revealed the unmistakable face of Mad Jack Rackhem.

"Where's Cabern?" was all Merryridge asked.

"Where you'll never find him," Rackhem gasped.

"Where's that, sirrah?" demanded Merryridge. "What happened?"

"Dead… drowned dead." An exhalation and a smile betrayed quiet satisfaction before the eyes gaped and became vacant, the head slipped sideways and the body relaxed in death.

Nance read the newspaper account and, at the end, Cabern's name. Her stomach hardened, her heart thumped and her face crumpled into a pitiable mask of despair as a piercing wail rising from her inner-most being resounded throughout the house. She wanted only to die. Frances found her prostrate on the parlour floor and ordered her to be carried up to her room.

Dr Abbett could do nothing, neither could the tearful sympathy of fellow servants nor even the compassionate words of her mistress. There is, she reminded Nance gently, no death.

"We must necessarily fall asleep in this transitory life," she added, "or else how may Jesus raise us up to eternal life? Put your trust in the Lord and be guided by His Holy Spirit."

Nance's submissive eyes, red with weeping, told Frances that her mind might wish to agree but her heart pined irrevocably for Cabern. The best course of action, Frances reasoned, was to send her back to her family, resigning herself a second time to losing an excellent servant. Before Nance left, however, she overheard a conversation between two maids in an adjoining room.

"If only," said one, "we hadn't sent him away."

What had she just heard? Nance shook off her lethargy and rose from her bed, stumbled into their room and confronted them, demanding to know what they meant. They had no option but to tell her about their orders not to admit any seamen; they had guessed it was Cabern who had called by his persistence in ringing the bell until the mistress herself sent him on his way.

The shattering news thrust Nance back into her twilight exi' tence, hovering between oblivion and the pain of life. So, half-ali' she was conveyed back to the family cottage and into the fe' arms of her father. Even he had not realised her depth of feelin' Cabern. Aware that his actions had probably contributed to i' to hide his guilty look, the old man averted his gaze. He c' inwardly whether or not telling the truth might ease her pa' what, or make it worse.

John took Sarah by the hand and led her along one o'   t
leafy avenues, pausing now and then to point out var'   n.

"Here are the Halls of Learning and the Grand Universal Library. All the knowledge that the peoples of Earth ever discovered, and more besides, is held within its walls. Over there is the Academy of the Performing Arts and beyond is a palace of galleries containing the finest painting, sculpture and craftwork ever executed by human hands. It is here that the philosophers, artists and scientists of the future come to study and practise. The knowledge and skills they learn, and the ideas they develop, they take with them on their return to Earth. Your century – the Age of Enlightenment, I think they are calling it – has indeed produced much that is innovative and beautiful."

She halted for a while and tried to take in everything with a wondering, still blinking eye.

"I cannot begin to describe the beauty of this place."

"No-one can, for we are not looking at representations of beauty here, this is beauty itself."

"What do you mean?"

"The physical beauty of the familiar world you lived in is finite, passing and fragmentary. By its very nature it is subject to birth and growth towards possible perfection, but then all too soon there is decline and decay. Moreover, what appears beautiful to one person might be less so to another, although everyone has some idea of what beauty is or it could not be recognised. In the intermediate world, where you met Thomas, the differences are less pronounced but it is only here that we experience the idea of beauty in its lasting fullness.

"For example, it is the same with justice. Everyone in the other place has some idea of what justice is or there could be no such thing. But it is often partial or biased, and one person's idea of justice may be another's injustice. In the intermediate world, such wrongs are righted and there is some compensation, so that everyone sooner or later arrives at an understanding of what justice is. Those planes, however, are still only a pale reflection of this one where justice and the idea of justice are not different – here there is no longer any argument about it, for here is simply justice and nothing else."

His words rang true somewhere in the depths of Sarah's mind, ough they were hard to grasp fully. And all the while there was one ıtter that her thoughts kept coming back to.

"So what about love? Surely it is the most powerful of all feelings yet it is my sister's love that has caused so much trouble for our family."

John sensed the touch of pain returning to her and took both hands, looking into her eyes with compassion.

"What mortals call love is almost always conditional or selfish, a love that expects something in return. Your dear Nance's so-called love is more in the nature of obsession or infatuation. It is a kind of love, yes, but misplaced."

"Everybody thinks so, but just you try telling her!"

"Precisely. But how may she come to understand what love is until she has learned to recognise, by lengthy and painful experience, what it is not?"

"It will be a hard lesson, then. But her intentions are good even if she makes mistakes."

"Have you not heard the old adage that the path to Hell – or, should I say, self-inflicted suffering – is paved with good intentions? Take, for instance, my love for you. There is nothing I would not do for you that is appropriate and within my power. But real love does not extend to condoning wrongdoing, however well-intentioned.

"Here, we learn to love everyone without conditions because all is love. Not to do so would mean being out of love, which is…" he shrugged, "not possible here."

They left the avenue and trod a pathway between cultivated parkland and an expanse of wilder natural beauty. Seemingly innumerable woodlands, plains and hills unfolded before a never-ending horizon. Every few paces revealed a different view, taking the eye from one to another, so that a narrow pathway emerging from a secluded grove became an avenue to a tree-ringed lake, or mossy banks became a poppy meadow, overhung by a shaggy, tree-clinging cliff. Sarah breathed in the peace of it all until, inevitably, more questions arose.

"I think I understand something of what you have been saying. But there is something else that puzzles me deeply."

"Your question is not simple and wise men have never been able to answer it satisfactorily – although ignorant men never stop trying. You are wondering just who is the Father?"

"You always know my mind. Yes, is the Father the same as God?"

"The Father is not a name we like to use here because it is all too easily misunderstood. The Earth's deities with their human characteristics have very little to do with the Being I can only describe as beyond anything we could ever imagine. Who or what could not only have created all this—" he waved an arm to indicate their surroundings, "—but also fully lives and breathes in it all?

"I can only say that God is love, even though here in the real world we still cannot say precisely what love is, only what it is not.

"It is like I was saying earlier… In the familiar world, beauty and justice and so on are limited – one may be beautiful but unloving, while another may be loving but unjust. Here in this world, everything is interrelated. We can recognise qualities such as love but we cannot say precisely what they are, only what they are not. Well, if all these qualities are interrelated and nothing exists independently of them, then some Being must know exactly what each one is and how it is fully dependent upon others. Try to imagine a Being that can encompass all this." He paused for a while, realising how difficult these thoughts were to absorb, then tried again.

"Think of the worlds you already know about and try to imagine those you do not. Then imagine all the other subtler worlds that are to be found occupying the very same space, just as the spirit world you arrived in is interwoven with the Earth. All these worlds throughout the universe, indeed the universes, are in some sort of relationship with every other one.

"How did it all come about, what Mind could possibly have conceived and initiated everything, if indeed there ever was a beginning? It is only possible to say what this Mind, this Father, the One or the Absolute is not. So I just say that God is love."

Whenever they seemed to arrive at one destination, something new and unexpected caught the eye. Beyond a wooded lake a rocky pathway led to a towering silvery waterfall and numerous hills dotted with dwellings. More distant still curved the bay of a foam-specked ocean, the tumbling surf overlooked by blanched cliffs. The light was still too dazzling for Sarah's already strained eyes. John pointed to a tiny cottage on top of a rocky promontory.

"That is where I live."

She gazed towards it without seeing, the light becoming too overpowering.

"John," she said, shielding her eyes with an open hand, "why is it so bright here?" He took her hand and stroked it so that she felt soothed by a warmth that infused her whole being.

"Because, as I told you, this is a world of unconditional love. And unconditional love is blind. Love is like light, it penetrates and permeates every living thing.

"In the earthly world, men and women are able to filter out light and love to some degree, even block them entirely. But here there is no escaping either, for love and light are one and the same and one cannot possibly exist without the other."

Merryridge meanwhile, was not content to leave the last word to a criminal like Rackhem. Accordingly, he set out on Cabern's trail once more, surprising several of his old crewmen lying low in safe cottages along the coast and learning that Cabern had indeed returned a while ago, not to rejoin his old shipmates but with the intention of wreaking vengeance on Rackhem for assaulting Nance.

Cabern had stayed at the Ferry House Inn and let it be known that he was willing to do free trade again, which had been enough to bring Rackhem to the inn one evening. His only motive all along in trying to trace Cabern had been to renew their successful partnership, with himself and Diamond in the background. But the pair had very different agendas and soon fell to quarrelling with threats turning to blows until both had to be restrained. They left, witnesses said, each with a cutlass and the avowed intention of killing the other and were last seen walking across Langer Marshes.

Later that night, two of Cabern's old crewmen were walking back with a lantern to their bolthole on the other side of the marshes and heard repeated groans. They went to investigate and found Cabern up to his neck in a bog, bearing the cuts and bruises of a fierce struggle. Rackhem had won, he told them, and had dumped him there assuming him dead. Now Merryridge understood what Rackhem had meant by 'drowned dead'.

So Cabern was alive after all. He did not seem to have been involved in further smuggling so was it possible he intended to pursue an honest living? Merryridge thought he ought to tell Nance the news, if only for his brother's sake.

Back at the cottage, the old man was settling down and preparing to tell Nance how he too had turned away Cabern. He gazed fearfully at the floor by his feet. She was already suspicious that he was hiding something.

"Is there summat yew want ta tell me, Pa?" she prompted. "Coom on, just yew be a-tellin', an' I be a-hearin'."

Another moment and he would have confessed but he was saved for the present by a knock at the door. She arose and opened it to Merryridge.

"Might I have a word, Nance… in private?" She stepped outside. "I think yew should know that Cabern's alive. I've ascertained the fact myself."

Incredulous and lost for a moment in jumbled thoughts, she struggled to comprehend. She wanted to believe but didn't dare to because it would be too painful if untrue.

"Are yew wholly sure?" she began cautiously. "Yew swear it?"

"I do. Rackhem thought him dead, as was reported, but he's not. I've just met the men who pulled him alive from the bog where Rackhem dumped him. I know how devastated you were… how you wanted to marry…" His voice trailed off as he saw the same expression of relief on her face as when he had shown her the body washed ashore at Bawdsey. He told her everything he knew but couldn't help warning her that Cabern might still be up to his old tricks. And he reminded her of his promise that he wished the man no harm – unless the law were broken again.

CHAPTER 14

DESTINY

Sarah's mind was elsewhere as thoughts of her old life intruded on the ethereal beauty of this higher world.

"Men like Rackhem and Cabern… how do they fare when they come to this place, if they come at all?"

"They will come eventually, for this is their home too, but not for a long, long while. They would be like birds with fishtails or elephants with wings – that is, even if they could stand the light which even you cannot for long. No, they will inhabit the darker places on the lower plane. The light cannot penetrate to them because they shun it."

"But I still don't really understand why it cannot reach them."

"As I described before," John explained patiently, "light and love are one and the same, and that the one cannot exist without the other. Men like these don't love anybody, not even themselves."

"So where are their guides – they do have guides, I suppose? What are they doing?"

"Of course they do, as does everyone. But if they remain deaf and blind to their guides' every prompting, ignoring everything spiritual and seeking only material things, not caring whom they hurt along the way... what are their guides to do? They can only stand aside and wait.

"All men have free will. Buried deep within Rackhem's selfish, corrupted material shell – like some ancient sea-creature encrusted with barnacles – the true self does indeed shine, for even he is divine. But it is his choice. No, when they pass from the Earth these men will inhabit the places they have chosen for themselves, just as Thomas had when you first found him."

"Why would anyone choose such a hellish existence?"

"Why indeed, if only they knew better. But they do not and must therefore learn."

"And I thought Hell did not exist."

"It doesn't. You found Thomas in the very conditions he created for himself but let me assure you, there are far worse places to be found in that forest and beyond. Rackhem and those of similar ilk must live there until they learn what they should have learned earlier, and unburden themselves of the many debts they have incurred.

"Cabern, though, is different from the others. He could change if he truly wants to. In the naval action, he showed great courage and a readiness to lay down his life for others – although he was only doing for the right reasons what he had previously done for the wrong ones. He hasn't yet chosen the better path because he lacks the wisdom to weigh the results of his actions. Still, there will be opportunities for him to make a new beginning. It won't be easy, and Providence will place obstacles in his path to test whether he is serious."

"Do you think he is?"

"It is not for me to judge him."

Sarah's eyes were weary with the light and her heart aching with feelings from the past. It was time for them to return. She took one more long look around as John took her arm and gently touched the crown of her head. When she opened her eyes again, as though awaking from the deepest sleep, she found herself sitting in a chair in her cottage. For a while she felt so serene that no thoughts intruded. Eventually, she returned to her former self to see John sitting patiently nearby.

"How would you like to live and work there, Sarah, with the children?"

She felt humbled and, for a moment, full of joy at the prospect, and was about to accept when thoughts of Nance and Thomas returned. She shook her head sadly.

"No, I'm sorry... Forgive me, but I just know that something terrible is going to happen to my sister and I have to be near her. And Thomas has been... well, I love him."

John smiled warmly.

"I thought you might say that before I asked, but you always have a choice. In any case, I didn't mean for you to leave here right now, just that this is your future if you want it. Remember, you have eternity before you and what you think of as long periods of time will pass before you are even aware of it."

"So it really doesn't matter, then, if I stay as I am for a while?"

"Many delay their progress, or so it seems. Indeed I have, in order to be of service to others. After all, it is the highest aspiration of humanity to put another's interests before one's own. You will lose nothing by it. As for your sister, though, I'm afraid she must follow the path she is creating for herself in her own way and, yes, there will come a time soon when all appears lost. But the worst will not happen."

"Will I still be able to help her?"

"Yes. And Thomas will also be there for her just as you were for him. It was I who guided your steps through the forest, and I did so because I knew that Thomas could help you. First of all, though, he needed someone to help him and only you could do that because you are more on his level of awareness. Remember, I was there with you both at one point and he didn't even see me. How could I help him when he didn't even know I was there?"

She was silent for a moment, absorbing all these thoughts and feeling a little fearful because of what he had said about her sister.

"What of Nance, then?"

"She will have to endure suffering and there will be many ordeals to undergo, but things will not be as bad as they seem at first. And the opportunity will still be there for her to find true love and make a success of her life." As though anticipating her next question, he added, "No, even I cannot fathom exactly how it will come about."

The conversation with Garrow Merryridge brought back memories for Nance of Jethro. If Cabern had not come along, she would gladly have married him and her life would have been entirely different.

"Did yew iver hear from Jethro?" she asked him.

He had often thought about how to answer this question, should she ask. His brother had made a new life for himself on the other side of the world and Garrow saw no purpose in awakening old passions. If she knew where he was she might try to contact him but then, she being clearly still besotted with Cabern, the sorry cycle of love and rejection would begin again. Far better, he reasoned, to lie.

"I've heard nothing since he left England," he mumbled convincingly, with a sad shake of the head.

"Well, if yew iver should…"

"You'll be the first to know, Nance. Fare ye well for the present."

She stepped forward and grasped his hand before he turned away, then re-entered the cottage where Zebedee beheld a rather different daughter from moments earlier.

"Now Pa, I think yew have summat ta tell me."

He tried to speak, but the words were punctuated by sighs and protestations of woe. When he'd finished his confession at last, her eyes drizzled tears that spotted her apron as she repeated what Merryridge had just told her.

"I dewn't reckon as how me an' Rob ul iver get a-gooin' together – summat allus coomes betwixt us. Well, 'least he's alive, an' thus a mercy an' a comfort." She fell silent.

"Aren't yew a-gooin' ta scold me, then?"

"Haps I should," she said with a wry smile, "but why? It ont dew me noo good if I dew. Yew know what's best fur me. Soo does everyone."

It was now May and a warmer sun was coaxing into bloom the laburnum beside the flowering hawthorn. The woodpecker and cuckoo were heard and swifts glided over the heath where the cowherd, resting at noon beneath a leafy beech, was lulled to sleep by the murmur of bees.

Nance's health was recovering and she harvested the first new potatoes in her tiny garden. She would not be eating them, though, as they would fetch between 7d and 9d per pound at market, and a basketful earned as much as a week's charring. She brought the basket indoors, but noticed a pair of crossed knives on the kitchen table – an ill omen. Superstitiously, she straightened the knives but knocked another off the table so that it fell into her basket and stuck in a potato; she recognised this as a second sign of bad luck. Something, for sure, was about to happen… Returning to the garden she noticed a seaman walking down the lane from the direction of the Felixstowe Road. He trod the rutted surface uncomfortably in light shoes, flicking a neckerchief at insects hovering around his moist brow, then he paused at the wicket gate, removed his hat and bowed politely.

"Would this be where lives a Miss Auldfield?"

"It is. I'm Miss Auldfield."

"I comes on hurgent business an' must speak wiv yer," he blurted out, clearly relieved. She was immediately suspicious. In her world, strangers did not call on single women unannounced and, moreover, this man's accent was harsh, abrasive and, to her ears, intimidating.

"What about?"

"It's Cap'n Cabern, Miss."

The name was, as usual, enough to unsteady her and the stranger did not fail to notice.

"Haps yew'd best coom inside then."

"No, Miss," he replied, aware that she didn't live alone. "With respect, Miss, I'd rather us talk somewhere more private, like." Still irritated, he again flicked at an insect and appeared even more uncomfortable when a magpie alighted on an overhanging bough and perched there, as if on purpose to watch and listen.

"Talk then. There's none can hear us," she said, leaning over the gate and dropping her voice. "What about Cabern?"

"'Ee's in trouble, Miss. 'Ee's down in London an' needs yer 'elp."

"In Lunnon!" she gasped, but quickly lowered her voice. "How can I help 'em thar?"

"'Ee's been happrehended and fined – quite hunjustly, for somefing wot 'ee never done – an' 'cause 'ee can't cough up the readies, 'ee's in gaol for debt."

"Gramercy! An' wha' be the fine?"

"Twen'y powns, Miss."

Twenty was more than a year's wages! What could she possibly do? Her mind started to swim and the familiar leaden feeling rose in the pit of the stomach. She was still suspicious but had to learn more.

"Law help me! An' how am I ta raise twenty pounds? Women round here dewn't earn tha' in a year, nor two."

"There is a way, Miss," said the man confidentially. "First, might I hintroduce meself. Foxby's the name, Truand Faithful Foxby. I'se an old shipmate o' the Cap'n's. Like I says, 'ee's in 'ot wa'er. This here's the letter wot 'ee wrote me in London." He produced a piece of folded parchment and handed it to her.

> *The Fleet Prison, London.*
> *Dear Foxby,*
> *The Excise has seized a quantity of honestly acquired spirits I*
> *had in store. I protested my innocence, but was arrested and*
> *fined £20. I cannot pay and so am imprisoned for debt.*
> *As my old and trusted lieutenant, please deliver the enclosed*
> *letter to Miss Nancy Auldfield at her cottage in Amberslea,*
> *Suffolk.*
> *Your old friend and captain,*
> *Robert Cabern*

Nance read the letter carefully and thought she recognised the handwriting as Cabern's. Foxby then handed her a second letter.

> *My dearest Nance,*
> *I am fallen on hard times and must humbly beg of you your*
> *assistance, as there is no one else I can turn to. All my prize*
> *money went on an honest business venture, but I was arrested*
> *on a trumped up charge and ordered to pay a fine of £20,*
> *which, if I cannot, I will stay in gaol. Worse still, I have not*
> *the means to pay for food and a bed, so will be reliant on*
> *charity or starve, if not first eaten by rats.*
> *As I have always promised, it is my firm intention to make you*
> *my wife; and to that end I have been in London on business to*

*make enough money to buy a property and ask for your hand.
This will I still do, if I can but raise £20.*

*The bearer of this letter, my good friend Mr Foxby, is an old
and trusted shipmate. Please be guided by him and God
willing, we will soon be husband and wife.*

Your ever loving friend and husband-to-be,

Robert

Nance was quite overcome, both by the shock of the situation and by the old heat of passion rekindled by the words 'husband and wife' – a passion that overrides intuition and banishes common sense. She felt dizzy and only the gate prevented her falling in a faint at the man's feet. As she slumped over it, she saw a grass-snake emerging from the picket fence, slithering between them and disappearing beneath a bush.

"There, there, don't take on so, Miss. I knows of a way to 'elp." The preliminaries over, Foxby's voice took on a coarser tone. Despite nature's warnings, she didn't seem to notice this, nor his fawning and patronising manner. "As I said, Cabern's an old chum, like, an' there's a way. But yer must do your share if we're to 'elp 'im."

Her nervous sable eyes, already oozing tears, looked blank.

"How in the world am I ta get twenty pounds?"

"Can you ride an 'orse, Miss?"

The entire world seemed to stand still for a moment. Hearts skipped beats, the wind ceased to breathe, the bees to hum, the birds to chatter, and the magpie above cocked its head and looked directly at Nance with piercing eyes as though destiny itself hung on her answer.

"I used ta. Happen I can dew soo agen."

"Then yer can save Cabern," he declared confidently, well aware of her skill on horseback decades before. "I knows of an 'orse, see. An old 'ack in a field. It don't do nofink, an' no-one troubles 'bout it. But it's worf twenny quid easy."

"How ul this help me?"

"If yer was to borrow it like, yer could ride to Colchester an' sell it."

"But it must belong to sumun?"

"Oh, someone feeds it, but hotherwise it don't do nofink. It wouldn't 'ardly be missed. Now like I says, if yer was to borrow—"

"Yew mean prig it?"

"Lor' no, Miss. It hain't stealin', just borrowin'. Cabern'll pay for it when he gets out. Twenny quid's small beer to 'im. 'Ee can make an 'undred times that on one deal. 'Ee'll pay the owner free times wot it's worf. Cabern hain't no fief. Would a respectable laidy like yerself love a fief?"

"But I cont just taak it."

"Nofink could be heasier. Like I says, no-one watches it, an' it's in a field all alone. Now, if yer was to ride to Colchester an' sell it, yer could catch the London coach – I'll cough up the fare – an' yer'd 'ave the twenny quid to free Cabern." He scrutinised her carefully and caught the gleam in her eye as she contemplated the possibility, then pressed home the deal. "I even 'as a spare saddle an' bridle an' a sailor's jacket an' trousers. Dressed in 'em, none'd even know yer was a woman. So if yer was seen, none'd know, see. Now, wot d'yer say – is yer game?"

Piercing squeals shattered the peace of the countryside as a hovering barn owl mounted the air, a writhing mouse in its claws. Managing to free itself, the mouse fell into long grass… but was again seized by the owl, this time firmly, and borne aloft.

Far away in another dimension yet separated only by a heartbeat, Sarah collected Mary Dawkins from the Blue Island and welcomed her to the cottage. Though largely recovered, Mary remained a little shaky and apprehensive. Sarah gave her an affectionate hug.

"May I offer you a cup of China tea?"

"Why yes, how kind. D'you still drink tea here?"

"Yes, er, when I have company." She hung a kettle on a hake in the chimneypiece behind the floral display, then seated herself opposite Mary. "Now, while we wait for it to boil, tell me—"

"But… you haven't lit a fire."

"I don't have to," laughed Sarah. "Oh, you'll soon see, everything's done by thought here. I meant to ask, are you from London?"

"Yes, how d'yer guess?"

"Oh, I met a few Londoners when I was on Earth. I'm a Suffolk girl myself but I got on with them well enough, that is, when I could understand what they were saying." The kettle's lid rattled and steam rose from the spout so she filled a teapot and waited for it to draw. "Weak or strong?" she asked a still surprised Mary, pouring out a cup and adding milk. "And sugar?"

Mary stirred her tea, sipped and winced. "Blimey, it's certainly hot!" She sat back for a moment, lost in thought. "I never believed in all this, I mean, an afterlife an' all."

"Don't worry," Sarah smiled, "you'll soon discover that we have no need of beliefs here, any more than we do of fire. Either we know a thing or we don't, and if we don't, we can find out."

"Pity the great an' the good can't do that on Earth, instead of settlin' their differences by orderin' the rest of us to bash the bleedin' daylights out of each other… like what we just done. It'd save everyone a whole lotta trouble."

"Can't or won't – the great an' the good, that is?"

Mary sipped her tea. "This here's bloody good stuff. Never tasted nothin' as good. Ain't you gonna drink yours?"

"I'll just think it a bit cooler… there." She all but drained the cup then instinctively, as in her earthly days, took it in her left hand and swung it in a circle three times from left to right. She upturned it over the saucer and waited until the last of the liquid had drained, and laughed as she realised what she had done. "I used to read the tea leaves. Old habits die hard, I suppose, even here! Still, no harm in looking." There, on the side of the cup and overlapping the bottom circle, she could see the unmistakable tail and hindquarters of a mouse putting its head into something.

"Well," said Mary, "what can you see?"

"This doesn't make sense. It's a mouse putting its head into… what, a hole? No, by Heaven, it's a noose! And on the other side is a black cat urging it on." She put the cup down sharply on the table and, despite herself, a tear came to her eye. "This isn't my fortune, Mary, oh, dear Lord no, it's for Nance!"

"Who's Nance?"

"My wayward sister. Something awful's about to happen to her, I just know it. Excuse me, will you? I must go an' look for myself."

"I'll come with you."

"No, Mary, this doesn't concern you."

"It bloody well does. You've been so blinkin' decent to me. If your sister's in trouble, perhaps I can help."

"Oh, very well," a distraught Sarah conceded, "here, take my hand."

In an instant, a startled Mary found herself standing in Thomas' garden. Even more surprising, she saw Sarah drop to her knees and gaze into a pond. Although flustered, Sarah saw the dark image of her sister eventually come into view. Nance's appearance, nervous fidgeting and wild gaze betrayed desperation and instability of mind. Also appearing in the water now was a distinctly sly character who, she divined, was encouraging her sister to break the law, supposedly to help Cabern. She was horrified.

"For pity's sake, Nance," she shouted as though standing next to her, "have nothing to do with that man. It's all lies!"

Few indeed are the inhabitants of Earth who are sensitive enough to be aware of the spirit's advice, even though it may be just a whisper away. Nance did not hear her. Sarah would have to try and influence her later when her mind was more receptive, and for the moment she could only watch and listen. An equally horrified Teresa now joined them by the pool.

"Where be the hoss?" mumbled Nance, beginning to consider the possibility of going through with it.

"Why, it's in a field be'ind the 'owses on St Margaret's Green."

Sarah guessed that somehow the hack in the field was not the horse he had in mind. No, he was thinking of one far more valuable. Oh, Lord, no – she realised it was one of the Turners' carriage horses! But all her sister was thinking about was an opportunity to meet Cabern. How could she be so naïve as even to contemplate such a foolish thing? Sarah thought herself into the picture followed by Teresa and both vanished before an astonished Mary, who was wondering why such a fuss was being made over something seen in a garden pond.

"No, Nance, no!" cried Sarah as she now stood beside her sister, but her voiceless words registered not so much as a glimmer of recognition.

"Of course," continued Foxby, "us'll have to wait for a moonlit night. There's too much cloud at present. Two or free days an' 'appen the weather'll clear."

Nance's mind was a whirlpool with but one objective and Foxby knew it. In just two or three days, she was thinking, she could be with Cabern.

"The hoss be a-runnen' free yew say?"

"Free and fancy. Just frow a saddle on 'im an' then orf yer goes to Colchester, then on to London and Rob."

"Haps sumun'ul see me?"

"At two in the morning? An' what if they do? You'll be in Colchester afore first light. Just a Jack Tar ridin' an 'ack, a common enough sight. Just sell 'im an' you've got twenny powns. Then there'll be catchin' the mail-coach, an' when yer gets to London – why, there's more Tars there than any port in the kingdom. Who's to know you from 'undreds of others?"

"Where'ul I see yew then?"

"I'm to be found of a hevening at The Salutation. Just yer wait for the moon an' a clear night an' meet me there."

With his prey hooked and no reason to prolong the conversation, he removed his hat, bowed respectfully and strode away up the lane. She was left leaning on the gate, gazing vaguely at the ground, her mind a world away.

"I sent her every bad omen I could think of," Teresa said glumly, "and she ignored the lot. That's why I sent for you – you saw my message in the tea? What can either of us do?"

"She believes in those superstitions too."

"That's the trouble with beliefs, they're so malleable. They can be modified or set aside or, in this case, ignored entirely."

Helplessly, they watched Nance who appeared at once hopeful and apprehensive – at one moment bold, at another fearful – dragging her feet back to the cottage and sinking into a chair opposite her father. The situation being as grim as it could be, Sarah's only consolation was that the mental trauma was making her sister ill and sure enough the tension soon brought on vomiting and a fever. There would be no going to London for a week or so and, after that, the next moon was a fortnight away. Perhaps there was time to dissuade her.

Mary, left alone by the pool, was further astonished to be greeted with a polite bow from a handsomely-dressed Thomas.

"I must apologise for my friend," he began with a smile. "She can be here one moment and literally gone the next, like a jack-in-the-box."

"I'm sure it doesn't matter none, sir."

"Oh, but it does, m'dear. I'm afraid manners aren't Sarah's strongest point. Permit me to introduce myself. I'm Thomas."

"And I'm Mary Dawkins, sir... er, m'lord."

"It's just Thomas, we have no use for titles here. Now, while we await her return, allow me to show you the garden." A bemused Mary took his offered arm and together they walked between the flowerbeds and beneath the overhanging leafy boughs of his ever-growing personal Eden. "Well, how does my little estate find you?"

"I'm not sure, Thomas, it ain't nothing like what I'm used to. I'm a London girl m'self – streets and houses, like – that's before I went to sea."

"How came a woman to board a man-o'-war?"

"My old man's a boatswain's mate an' I had the chance to sail with him, so I went. I thought it'd be a change from the city fog but I soon found it weren't. When the fight came, I signed on as crew to qualify for prize money." She shuddered at the still recent memory. "My God, if there's an 'ell it can't be no worse than a gun deck in battle. Explosions, showers of splinters, severed limbs an' blood everywhere – an' you can be blown to bits any second. I was hit something awful an' me heart just gave out. Then I saw meself – yes, me, it were weird – bein' slung overboard. That's when Sarah rescued me an' put me on a raft."

"All that's in the past, m'dear," he said soothingly. "Why not stay here awhile, as our guest, until you're stronger?"

"I dunno, sir, I mean, Thomas. I ain't used to all this. Like I said, I'm a sailor's woman an' truth is I were happier on that Blue Island with the other sailors, especially Jean. He's a lovely French lieutenant who helped me an' looked after me a treat. An' we can live just like we did aboard ship, only please ourselves, if you see what I mean."

Sarah and Teresa reappeared with a tearful explanation, and Thomas understood immediately the wickedness of what was afoot and the tragedy it would inevitably lead to. He knew even better than Sarah what the law did to horse thieves, and the public's attitude toward them. Yet Teresa had to admit that, no matter how grave the circumstances, none of them could lead Nance if she would not follow. They must stand aside while events took their course and the inevitable happened.

The one lucky star that Teresa could see in Nance's otherwise murky firmament was that in some strange way – and even she could not fathom how – Nance's soul seemed to be following a definite destiny, heedless of the suffering it might cause herself. There was a love in her heart, a very great one, though curiously not for Cabern despite all appearances. She could only guess that in some strange way Nance's soul was seeking a reunion with Jethro Merryridge whom, she felt sure, Nance would have married had there been no Cabern. Yet how such a thing could possibly come about, she couldn't say; only a far higher authority would know that.

As for Nance's sufferings, she could only simply remind Sarah that life is eternal; and that what threatened to be a lifetime of misery would, in reality, be over in a trice. And whatever might befall her, she felt sure that Nance would eventually find the love that her soul so desperately sought.

"Try and understand this," she added soothingly. "Once a chain of events is set in motion, it must necessarily run its course and there is little we can do. That is the law." She glanced at the pool, picked up a pebble and tossed it in. "Once the stone has been cast there is no way of preventing those ripples from spreading out. It's all part of life's school.

"It is also a matter of choice. In the physical body, thought precedes the action – you think and then you choose whether or not to put the thought into action. Either way you must live with the consequences. In our world, of course, we only have to think and the thought is already in action. That's why it's important to learn how to have good thoughts! But the moment your sister mounts that horse, the stone will be cast and there is nothing we can do to prevent the ripples.

"The higher laws, though, are also merciful. And in Nance's case we may eventually be able to lessen some of the consequences." She glanced at Thomas who had remained attentively at her side. "As for you, Thomas, I feel you will have a very special task to perform, sooner or later. Indeed, everything will depend upon you."

When she had left a somewhat shocked Sarah and Thomas, they noticed Mary sitting alone on a bench, trying hard to come to comprehend what was going on. Apologetically, Sarah hurried over to her but Mary simply smiled and took her hand in hers.

"Summat terrible's about to happen to your sister, ain't it? Do you want to tell me 'bout it?"

"Yes, my new friend," said Sarah, "I think I would." She sat beside Mary and poured out the long, sorry tale.

CHAPTER 15

NIGHT RIDE TO LONDON

Nance's fever lasted a week and her convalescence the better part of another, so she was in no condition for the dangerous undertaking on which her heart and mind were firmly set. When she did recover, there was no moon and then the weather was unsettled and overcast. Finally the moon reappeared, however, and neither her sister's anxiety nor even an angel's command could have dissuaded her from riding to her lover's rescue.

On a fateful May evening when the sky was clear and the waxing moon bright enough to light the way, she made excuses to her father, walking to Ipswich and into The Salutation. Sarah and Teresa watched Nance enter the parlour and, sure enough, seated there in a far corner enjoying his supper was Foxby. He bade her join him and they chatted earnestly, their faces averted from the other patrons. Having finished eating, he was the first to leave, followed a few moments later by Nance as though they were going their separate ways. She followed him through the streets to his lodgings, where he left her to don the cream and black striped trousers, light-blue waistcoat and short dark jacket of a seaman. She greased and combed her wavy hair straight like a man's and tied the ends in a pigtail. Then she pulled a seaman's hat well over her forehead. With her tallish build, lithe gait and now masculine appearance, surely nobody would suspect her not to be a man.

Sometime after one o'clock, the two Tars, one of them carrying a large scrip, reached the Green. They passed the Turners' mansion, came to the meadow beyond and saw the hack in the long grass. It neighed as they approached, turned and cantered away. And despite a number of attempts made to capture it, at every approach of the shadowy, unknown humans it bolted. Foxby the horse thief had guessed this would happen and Nance should have known it too. At length Foxby suggested that they abandon the nag and look for another: nearby was the Turners' stable and he suggested they look in there.

"Thus be the carriage hosses," she objected. "I durstn't."

All the while, Sarah and Teresa were following their every move and Sarah had only to glance at her sister to see that, despite her efforts, her mind was set on the hare-brained venture.

"Is there nothing we can do for her?" she sobbed.

"Sadly no, my dear," said Teresa, taking her hand to console her. "She has free will and we cannot interfere."

"There's no 'arm in just lookin'," urged Foxby meanwhile, pretending sympathy. "Let's just see what they 'as."

He led the way through the paddock to the stable doors, picked the lock easily and prised them open. Nance was now truly fearful that they would be caught, especially as Jake the coachman slept in his quarters above them. In the moonlit interior she could see a horse she knew well standing in its stall. It grew restless, neighed and pawed the ground, so she went over to it and held a hand under its nose to sniff then stroked it.

"Good boy, Chaser, good boy," she said gently as she had done many times.

"He knows yer!" whispered Foxby, feigning surprise. "Just fink, on 'im yer could forget about Colchester an' ride all the way to London town."

"I told yew, I durst not taak a carriage hoss," she gasped. "Tha'd be wholly priggin'."

He put a cautionary finger to his lips and whispered, "It hain't priggin', Miss. Like I says, it's just a loan. Cabern'll pay ten times wot its worf – an' this one's an 'undred guineas easy. Now what d'yer say? If yer game, we could 'ave Rob freed by tomorrow night."

Tomorrow! She began to consider the idea of 'borrowing' the horse, much as the maiden might pray, 'Lord, keep me chaste, but just this once.'

"Yus, Cabern'll be a free man," he encouraged and suddenly she could imagine herself walking proudly on his arm through the gaol gates. "Yer can even be married in gaol. Did yer know that?" She did not. "If yer won't do it for yerself, then do it for Rob's sake."

"Yes, fur Rob," she mumbled, her old impetuosity coming through, "my future husband. I must save 'em!"

He took out a piece of paper and showed it to her.

"Ride straight to London and sell the 'oss, then go to St Giles parish – heveryone knows it – and find this haddress. Ask for Gen'l'man Jim. 'Ee's another old pal o' me an' Rob's. 'Ee knows the ropes, see. Show 'im the money an' 'ee'll arrange everyfink – pay the fine an' get Rob out. 'Ee'll be a free man by tomorro' night."

By now Sarah was sobbing uncontrollably and even Teresa had lost her usual tranquillity.

"It's all lies," she snapped angrily, "except that Jim is Foxby's pal. But he'll rob her blind. And another thing – Cabern's not even in gaol. I've checked, he's in Suffolk."

To their dismay, though, they realised that all Nance was thinking about was freeing him and marriage. While she stroked Chaser's head, Foxby entered the stall and took from the scrip a saddle and bridle. At his bidding, she strewed straw from the stall along the floor and into the yard, to muffle the clatter of hooves when the horse was walked out. In no time, being an old hand at this, Foxby had it saddled, out in the yard and on the Green.

"For pity's sake, no!" cried Sarah as her sister took the reins in her hand and prepared to mount. Then up she sprang in her old deft way, easily throwing a leg over the saddle and managing to slot the unfamiliar sailor's shoes into the stirrups. Foxby accompanied her as she walked the horse round the Green, made a few turns and quickly regained her old confidence.

"Good luck, Miss," he whispered as she trotted away.

Teresa squeezed Sarah's hand and kissed a tear-wetted cheek. "We can do nothing more for her now. Go back home and I'll continue to watch over her, as always. I'll call on you if there's anything you can do."

Nance rode down Upper Orwell Street and onto St Clement's Fore Street. Everywhere was in darkness with hardly a light showing or a soul about, but with just enough moonlight to see between the buildings overhanging the cobbled streets of Ipswich. The horse knew the way and was untroubled by the shadowy appearance of the odd walker, or even the night watchman ringing his bell and crying, "Past two o'clock and all's well."

She rode along Bridge Street and skirted the black, moon-reflecting tidal basin by Stoke Mill, and as she passed between the bridge's stone parapets she could just make out one of the windmills on the hill ahead, silhouetted against the sky. Whenever the moon shed more light on the way, she urged a brisker trot. She went through the first turnpike uneventfully, paying the toll Foxby had given her, and was then clear of the town and heading for Tattingstone on the road to Colchester. On she rode, letting the horse choose its pace along a road it had pulled the Turners' carriage many times. When the occasional cloud obscured the moon and it was no longer possible to see the road, it slowed to a walk, but as soon as light filtered back it was fast-trotting again, sometimes cantering, its hoof beats on the stone and clay-hardened surface breaking the silence of the night. She passed Bentley Mill and approached the second turnpike near Grove Farm, not far from Tattingstone. The drowsy keeper, surprised to find a lone seaman riding through the night, asked where she was going. "Manningtree and the Stour," she replied, "then on to Harwich to rejoin my ship." He thought it strange that anyone should make such a wide detour, when from Ipswich he could have ridden straight to Walton and caught the morning ferry. But he took the toll and opened the gate.

About three o'clock, near the Bull Inn at Brantham and seven miles out of Ipswich, she met the night coach from London, the guard's penetrating refrain on the post horn announcing it as the Royal Mail that stopped for nothing and nobody. Prudently, she drew rein and waited beside the narrow carriageway. The tipsy coachman took little notice but at the rear the alert guard, an Ipswich man, raised his blunderbuss, suspicious of the solitary rider. As they passed he peered closely at her in the smoky pool of light from the coach lamp, her mount catching his eye: a strawberry roan-grey with a distinctive white shim on its forehead. What business had a sailor riding such a horse in the middle of the night? He clambered forward to speak to the driver.

"I'll wager yew a guinea – no, ten to an ounce o' baccy – tha' thar Tar was ridin' Jonathan Turner's coach geldin'."

With her attention firmly on the horse and the road, Nance's mind was clear and sharp, her demeanour calm and purposeful, her spirits almost serene as she passed the sable hedgerows, arching elms, deserted heath, darkened mansions and a wayside mill with its stationery water-wheel. For a while, her attention was so intense and contemplative that she all but forgot the awful nature of her mission, of riding a stolen horse. Now well on her way, and with Cabern ever in mind, excitement welled in her and she was flush with anticipation of their meeting in a few hours.

As she rode through Manningtree the sky brightened and, with Ardleigh far behind her, dawn broke. With the road clearly visible, she could canter moderately uphill and faster on the flat, over earth or grass where possible for easier going. Soon she was within sight of the ramparts of Colchester's Norman castle, then passing below the town walls towering above the road to the south. By eight o'clock she had cleared Chelmsford and by eleven was within a few miles of London.

Eventually, she cantered along Old Ford Road and passed by Bishop's Wood, reaching Bethnal Green village before turning right onto the cobbled streets of Mile End, New Town and Whitechapel. The distinctive sight of the London Hospital was now to her left on Whitechapel Road. All around stretched a growing patchwork of lanes, alleyways and new residences.

It was now noon and the road was a noisy, colourful sight filled with every sort of horse-drawn conveyance. Smock-frocked wagon drivers with long whips steered their high-piled loads to the hay market in Whitechapel Street, whilst brewers' draymen on trundling, bar-rel-laden wagons competed with high-wheeled carts, Hackney coaches and the occasional stagecoach. Drovers herded cattle, sheep or swine, and hawkers shouted or sang their wares on crowded pavements as market women balanced baskets on their heads. The centre of all activity was the market and it was said that one could furnish and provision a house and plant a garden, all with goods from Whitechapel Market.

Looking for somewhere to eat and rest – and perhaps sell the horse – Nance spotted a coaching inn and livery stable on the north side of the street and trotted into the yard. She was stiff and sore through not having ridden for so long. The Bull Inn was one of the first watering-holes for travellers entering this part of London. Nance noticed that as each coach approached the guard blew a five or six note refrain on the post horn to announce its identity to the inn's staff, porters and Hackney coachmen. The place seemed respectable enough, with one prominent notice that all weapons were to be handed over prior to admission, and another that the slapping and tickling of wenches was strictly forbidden.

The signs were clearly intended to allay the traveller's fear that, like so many inns, this might prove to be a den of thieves. They were as dishonest as the landlord, who set out to fleece each visitor royally. In addition, there were the smashers who passed on counterfeit coins in change, and porters who hovered around new arrivals, ready to snatch up any unattended luggage and dash out onto the crowded pavement. In short, all the inn's employees were into extorting, smashing and robbing together, later pooling their swag and each receiving his share. This, then, was the establishment where Nance hoped to sell the horse.

The London mail coach rolled into Ipswich soon after four o'clock. The guard, mulling over what he had seen and knowing Mr Turner personally, borrowed a horse and rode to the Norman House. After persistently ringing the bell, he convinced a sleepy maid that she should wake the master and within minutes an equally sleepy Jonathan Turner, a cloak about his nightshirt and hastily-donned breeches, was leading the way to the stables. In answer to his repeated banging and shouting, the flustered coachman Jake descended.

"Tha' owd nag was chargin' round the field fur nigh on half an hour last night," he grumbled. "Damned brute woke me up. I'd just dozed off agen when some idiot woke me by trottin' his horse round the Green at two in the mornin'." He came to Chaser's stall. "Alawk, 'em's hopped it! I swear I dewn't know how, sir, the door wuz locked."

"Obviously someone has stolen him," said Turner, noticing the trail of scattered straw. He turned to the guard. "Whom did you say was riding him – a seaman?"

Jonathan Turner was a man who could make things happen quickly. A printer was roused from bed and by seven o'clock handbills were printed offering twenty guineas reward for the stolen horse. This was a sixth of its value, but a year's wages for most people. By eight, a post-chaise ordered by the Turners to carry them south was pulling away from the Green. With a speed of twelve to fifteen miles per hour and a change of horses every ten to twelve miles, it was the fastest transport of the day.

Upon Nance's arrival at the inn, she and especially the valuable horse with its fashionably cropped ears and bunged tail were subject to the landlord's careful scrutiny. A seaman would presumably not want to keep a horse for long and there was the possibility of buying it for less than it was worth; she had ridden it lightly so to the ostlers it did not resemble an animal that had been ridden sixty-eight miles in a night. Whilst she ate breakfast, an inspection was carried out and a top value placed on it of one hundred and twenty guineas.

The portly mine host began in person the softening-up process accorded every customer deemed worthy of special treatment. Was everything to his honour's satisfaction and did he have everything he required? He lavished praise on the Navy, on every Tar who served king and country so magnificently, and waved over an underling who was a former seaman who had sailed with Admiral Rodney when he had been the first to break the line. When he retired with a polite bow, returning to the yard to inspect the horse again, he left them to talk of their respective service in the fleet. He did not have long to wait.

"The lubber ain't no seaman," reported the man. "He don't know a gallant from a royal, or a lanyard from a belayin' pin."

This confirmed what the shrewd landlord had suspected from the beginning, that the horse was stolen, and he considered his options. Buying a stolen horse to sell openly was not one of them. It would have to be disguised, given a new identity with a forged warranty, then taken to another part of the country to be sold at a country fair. But all that was risky. Horse thieves were hated and as likely to swing as anyone.

On the other hand, there was bound to be a reward for the return of such a fine animal. So why not detain the man while enquires were made? The horse was in fine fettle, but judging by the dust on the rider's face and clothing, and his bleary eyes, he had ridden long and far and must surely be in need of all the welcoming services the inn had to offer. He ordered a parish constable to be summoned and returned to Nance to play the perfect host.

Jonathan Turner, accompanied by Frances at her insistence, acted on the mail-guard's sighting and decided to follow the road to Colchester, enquiring at the tollgates along the way. The keepers recalled the lone rider, especially the one near Grove Farm. On the assumption that the rider's destination was not Colchester, where the trail appeared to go cold, but probably London, the Turners decided to travel the distance.

The turnpike trail led all the way to Bethnal Green village and they entered Whitechapel soon after three o'clock. At the Magistrates Court in Lambeth Street, Turner reported the theft and agreed to be bound over to prosecute, should the thief be apprehended. The handbills, some already distributed along the way, were now despatched by runner to every inn, livery stable and horse dealer in that part of London.

Meanwhile, Nance had rested, washed and had her clothes carefully brushed by an obliging maid – who had begun to wonder whether this was an unusually fair-looking seaman or possibly not a man at all – before returning to the parlour.

The constable called as requested, but had heard no report of a horse being stolen. Still, the circumstances did appear suspicious and he decided to examine the animal, interview the suspect and ask to see the warranty.

"Ridden far have you, sir?"

"From Colchester," she mumbled, instantly nervous.

"Do you have business in London?"

"Noo, I'm lookin' fur a berth."

"Now what ship would that be?"

"Oh, I dewn't have noo particular one in mind. I'll look fur a man-o-war."

"What will you do with the horse?"

"Sell 'em." Her voice was scarcely audible and her hands were shaking as she began to consider properly for the first time the likely consequences of her actions.

"Do you have a warranty?" asked the constable.

"Why noo, not with me."

The constable carefully looked her up and down. "Now who would buy a horse without a warranty?"

"I did have 'un," she assured him.

"Might I ask how you came by the horse?"

"Bought it in Colchester yest'day, sir."

"Then where's the warranty?"

"I've wholly mislaid it. I'll write fur another."

The constable knew by now that the story was false. "I have to tell you, sir," he declared firmly, "I'm not satisfied and must ask you to accompany me for questioning before a magistrate."

"But I've done nothin' wrong," she stammered.

"Then you can explain everything to the beak."

"But I cont, I won't—"

"Then I'm arresting you on suspicion of being in possession of a stolen horse. Come along, sir."

She was taken in charge and brought to the Magistrates Court and minutes later one of the handbills was delivered to the inn and shown to the landlord. "Twenty guineas reward!" he whistled. "Not bad for a couple of hours' work."

As soon as the constable heard of the Turners' arrival and saw the handbill, all became clear. Nance was taken to a room, by now weeping and shaking with fright, to discover her late employers facing her. The most terrible moment of her life was at hand. Frances could only gasp with incredulity at her former servant in her ridiculous seaman's outfit.

"You?" she gasped, her composure for once almost completely shattered. "You stole the horse?"

"Oh ma'am, oh my good lady," sobbed Nance hysterically, wringing her hands. "I didn't mean ta, I wholly didn't. It wuz ta save Rob.

Oh my good lady, what has yar poor servant done haa'ter all yar charity and kindness? Oh, I wish I wuz dead. God take me now!" she cried.

"You may well stand in need of His mercy before long," said Frances reprovingly, but without malice. "Now, I think you'd better tell us everything, in particular Cabern's part in all this."

"He didn't dew nothin', but 'em's in the Fleet Prison fur debt." Her bosom heaved as she fought for breath and tears splashed over her flushed cheeks. "I only took the hoss ta sell and pay the fine, then Rob would have paid yew back, I swear."

Frances looked at her equally incredulous husband and each knew the other's thoughts. She turned to Nance, her coolness regained and now more sorrowful than angry, feeling pity for the poor, distraught and panic-stricken creature before her.

"Nance, give me your hand." She did as she was asked, dropping to her knees and reaching out to take, limply, the hand of her old mistress which she bathed with tears. "Nance, you have committed a heinous crime, but my husband and I forgive you. But come now… the truth and nothing less. Why exactly did you take the horse and who else was involved?"

As the Court was still in session, she was brought before the Bench straight away where Mr Turner declared that he no longer wished to prosecute. But he was reminded that he had been bound over to do so. Nance then had no option but to plead guilty and was committed to Newgate Gaol on remand, pending transfer to Ipswich. Newgate had been described by Henry Fielding as, 'A prototype of Hell…'

Nance was conveyed there in irons by carriage and taken into one of the turnkey's lodges that stood either side of the Keeper's House. Once inside, the irons and all personal effects were removed. She was led through a dimly lit, forbidding passageway to one of the wards that surrounded the Women Felons' Quadrangle facing the Sessions House near Ludgate Hill. The little money she had brought with her was enough for some food but not bedding, and certainly not a private cell, so she was taken to a communal ward.

Nothing could have prepared her for what she found there. Drunken women, a few half-naked, lay on the filthy stone floor without so much as a blanket. Some sang bawdy songs or quarrelled, screamed obscenities or even fought each other; one or two whose minds were lost tormented fellow prisoners with their ravings, writhing on the floor or trying to climb the walls. There was the foulest stench imaginable, hanging near the ground like a fog and which the roof ventilators were quite incapable of removing. At intervals a solitary tallow dip relieved the gloom with its meagre light. Pillories stood at one end.

Nance soon discovered that felons without money were expected to work and the usual occupation was beating hemp. Male warders supervised them and any shirkers were locked standing up in a pillory and sometimes whipped. Above them was inscribed a sign, immortalised by William Hogarth: 'Better to work than stand thus.' Emotionally and physically exhausted, Nance sank onto the bare floor and fell asleep.

When she awoke to the living Hell all around her, she closed her eyes despairingly and willed herself asleep again, but strange dreams intruded with faces from the past. They gazed at her in surprise and welcome as she wandered across a verdant meadow with cottages, copses and streams, the brightness of the light almost dazzling. Puffy white clouds floated in a bluish sky, whilst gentle ethereal voices near and afar joined in an uplifting choir. As she wandered along a winding pathway, drawn towards some unknown destination, more familiar faces flitted before her. She was sure that one of them resembled her mother. They appeared momentarily and then were gone. Ahead of her, the most inviting of cottages beckoned amidst a pool of sunflowers and hollyhocks.

A lady, her golden hair cascading in ringlets over a shimmering white gown, was walking amongst the flowers, examining each one and holding it to her nose, while a blackbird sang from the bough of an apple tree. Curiously though, her expression appeared sorrowful and she even paused frequently to dab away a tear. She moved so gracefully, Nance thought she must be a lady of high rank yet when she half-turned towards her Nance realised her profile resembled Sarah. She dismissed the thought – even if she did somehow live on, Sarah would never aspire to such elegance… and yet… Now she turned fully and her face registered astonishment, joy and then sadness all at once. Nevertheless, she beamed a welcoming smile.

"Why, Nance! Nobody told me you were coming… oh, I see you're still in the body."

Nance was astonished and speechless. Could this really be her own dear sister come back to life? Sarah came to the gate and held out her hand, more relieved than happy, but radiant with love as she lapsed into her old way of speaking.

"Yes Nance, I'm yar owd big sis as loved yew in times agon and allus will!" She took Nance's hand, pulled her closer and kissed her cheek lovingly.

Nance somehow knew now that she was still asleep, yet this vision was all too real. She found her voice.

"Sarah, it is yew!" She laid a hand on the gate and pushed it a little, but a firmer hand and a wedged foot prevented it from opening.

"Noo, Nance," she said gently, "yew marn't coom in."

"But I must. Yew dewn't understand, I'm in terrible trouble."

"Yew can look," said Sarah sympathetically, with moistened eyes, "but yew marn't coom in. It's not yar time."

"Sarah, yew must let—"

"I durst not."

Nance seized the gate and tried desperately to force it open but the vision faded as an unseen force lifted her up and bore her away. She awoke, no longer in a flowery meadow but on hard cold stones amidst scenes of bedlam, breathing again the hellish stench of Newgate. She felt a sharp pain from a kick in the ribs.

"Show a leg there!" cried a gruff turnkey. Obediently, she staggered to her feet. "We've got new accommodation for your ladyship. Come with me."

A walk through dank resounding passageways and up some steps brought her to a relatively clean cell in which a little daylight from a barred window fell on a decent bed of straw. The open-bar door clanged shut behind her.

"Do what you have to," the turnkey ordered over his shoulder as he left, "the visitors arrive in five minutes." Visitors? What on Earth did he mean?

As soon as details of her escapade appeared in the newspapers, many men and not a few women wanted to see for themselves the enterprising woman who had ridden nearly seventy miles in a night. They began arriving at the gaol and asking to be let in. (This 'distinction' was usually reserved for criminals such as highwaymen, sure to be hanged, or traitors for whom a worse fate awaited. The keeper charged, of course, for viewing the prisoners.) Within minutes a dismayed Nance saw through the bars the passageway filling up with an inquisitive and fashionably-attired public.

The embarrassment and pain of it all felt worse than being in the communal ward. In rural Ipswich, being on the wrong side of the law was a disgrace, yet here in the capital she found herself famous, a sort of female Dick Turpin or Jack Shepherd. She knew that she would almost certainly hang, so these fine ladies and gentlemen were deriving sadistic pleasure from looking at a poor working woman who was going to swing.

Thankfully, her ordeal did not last long. As the horse had been stolen in Ipswich, it was decided to return her there to stand trial at Suffolk Summer Assizes so she was conveyed, shackled in a prison coach, to Ipswich Gaol. Inevitably a crowd gathered to see her admitted but here she could at least receive visitors she knew, although Matty no longer wished to be associated with his disgraced sister and her father was not well enough to come.

One who did arrive soon was Frances Turner. Her husband had made enquiries and she was able to tell Nance the whole story, one that made her almost as much a victim as a criminal. Firstly, Cabern was not in gaol and his whereabouts were unknown. Foxby, a smuggler and known horse thief, had been one of Cabern's henchmen long enough to learn something of his activities and forge his handwriting. When he'd heard of Nance's skill with horses, he devised a plan that held little risk to himself. If she had succeeded in selling the horse, the London address she was meant to visit was a disorderly house in the infamous rookery of St Giles near the Seven Dials, a place notorious as a criminal hide-out. There, just as Teresa said, she would have been robbed.

Frances impressed on Nance the importance of being as truthful as possible, and not to attempt to excuse herself in any way. Stealing a horse, after treason, counterfeiting and murder, was about the worst crime anybody could commit. After all, a properly cared-for and privately-owned horse had a working life of some twenty years and losing such a valuable animal could spell ruin for small businessmen.

Unfortunately, juries were usually made up of just such people and none of them would be sympathetic to a horse thief. Still, if her story prompted any leniency, Nance might hope that her sentence would be commuted to transportation.

CHAPTER 16

DEATH SENTENCE

The Suffolk Summer Assizes were held at Bury St Edmunds and were preceded by a solemn procession with as much pomp and splendour as the High Sherriff, Hamilton Comfrey, could provide. For the crowds the atmosphere was like a carnival, whilst for the defendants the likely verdict was death. Visiting judges and lawyers were shown the abbey ruins by their hosts and proudly reminded that the town's motto included the words *Cunabula Legis*, or Cradle of the Law[2].

All too soon for Nance, the day arrived for her trial. The presiding judge was Algernon Maxwell, Lord Baron of the Court of Exchequer. Jonathan Turner sat on the grand jury and also appeared as a reluctant prosecutor. In court, too, were Frances Turner and Dr Abbett, appearing as character witnesses, and Old Zebedee in fast-failing health. He sat in a daze, understanding little of the proceedings save that something terrible was about to happen to his beloved daughter.

In an age of elegance, where manners, dress and the social graces flourished, prisoners were at an immediate disadvantage. Having been

---

[2]   This refers to King John's barons' oath to enforce Magna Carta on this very spot.

confined for perhaps months in dark, unsanitary and overcrowded cells, they emerged blinking and shuffling into the light. Deprived of washing facilities and clean clothes, they stank so much that jurymen and court officials held up scented handkerchiefs or nosegays as they passed. Weakened by hunger and lack of exercise, their hair matted and faces white with caked dirt, most stood in the dock as though already condemned. There were some two hundred offences that carried the death penalty, such as a theft worth forty shillings or more; occasionally a sympathetic jury might value the stolen goods at a shilling less, thus sparing the offender the gallows.

Sarah and Teresa were also present. They had watched over Nance in the cells, accompanied her into the courtroom and now stood beside her in the dock. Unable to help in any tangible way, they could only pray. In contrast to other defendants, Nance was well-groomed thanks to Frances supplying her with clean clothes, soap and water and a comb. She curtsied to the judge and then to the court.

"How will you be tried?" she was asked formally.

"By God and by my country," she replied in a nervous, barely audible voice. The charge was read out and she was asked how she would plead. "Guilty, my Lord."

Lord Maxwell seemed hesitant.

"Are you certain? Is there nothing that can be said in extenuation?"

"If it please yew, my Lord, I am guilty."

"You do understand…" there was a long pause, "…that there is only one sentence this court can pass?"

"I dew, my Lord."

"Then have you anything to say why sentence should not be passed upon you?"

She opened her mouth as though to speak but remained silent. The tension rose as all eyes turned upon her whilst her own were fixed upon the judge. He peered at her penetratingly and his face wore a formal though not unsympathetic, quizzical expression. A grey, curling moustache emphasised his solemn, down-turned mouth in a face framed by an enormous wig that extended to the chest. Voluminous red robes, trimmed with ermine and flowing-lace cuffs, increased his already sizable bulk by half as much again.

"My Lord," she began at last, delivering in a halting voice the speech she had carefully practised and memorised under Frances' tuition. "I have noo excuse ta offer, my Lord, and noo reason ta give, why the law should not punish me as I deserve. I am truly sorry fur what I have done, but I do not beg mercy or forgiveness. Were I the person then tha' I am now, I would niver have stolen the hoss. But steal it I did. I ask only tha' yew commend me to God's mercy, fur I would not beg of this court the mercy I do not deserve."

The courtroom listened in perfect silence whilst Maxwell turned to High Sheriff Comfrey and said something softly. The other emphatically shook his head. The judge then enquired whether anyone present wanted to speak on the prisoner's behalf and Jonathan Turner rose from where he sat as prosecutor, apart from the jury. Amidst general murmuring he followed the usher and approached the Bench, bowed low, stepped into the witness box and took the oath. There he stood for a moment, head bowed and eyes downcast as though in deep contemplation, while silence settled over the courtroom and tension began to build again. Then he raised his head, drew himself up and respectfully but firmly addressed the judge.

"My Lord, I appear before you and before this court as the prosecutor of this unfortunate woman. I was bound over to prosecute and it was clearly my legal and moral duty so to do. However, my Lord, that duty now discharged, I appear before you now as her defender. I have been her employer, one for whom she performed most excellent and loyal service. And I am also a father, the lives of whose sons this woman saved."

He paused and glanced appealingly around the court, ensuring that every eye was upon him before continuing to address the judge.

"My Lord, I do not seek to excuse the crime yet I plead for mercy toward the prisoner in these most solemn and dreadful proceedings. If I may beg your Lordship's indulgence, I should like to say a few words on the prisoner's behalf by way of explaining the offence and its very extraordinary circumstances. Some four years ago, Mrs Turner, a lady known to many of you—" he paused to indicate his wife with a magnanimous gesture, "—took the prisoner into service. She performed her duties promptly and diligently and soon rose to become a most capable and trusted servant. She also cared for and supported financially her aged father when he was no longer able to perform his labours.

"Not only that, but without regard to her own safety she saved the lives of one of my sons from exposure in a river on a winter's night and a second from drowning in a deep-water pond." The courtroom buzzed with mutterings and exclamations as Jonathan Turner raised an arm as though to quieten the room. "Nay, my Lord, there is more. She also saved a boy from a rogue bull on St Margaret's Green by courageously interposing herself between him and the charging beast." The chattering rose excitedly until order was called.

"Therefore your Lordship will wish to know," he continued, "how a person of such selfless courage and exemplary character could be induced to commit such a heinous crime. I can answer that question in two words – Robert Cabern." He half-turned to the jurors and the packed benches. "Yes, Captain Cabern, formerly the infamous smuggler and now the courageous seaman who distinguished himself in Admiral Earl Howe's action off Ushant." The muttering of voices grew louder again, Cabern's reputation being well known to all. "The prisoner has had a long acquaintanceship with that man, much, I regret, to her disadvantage. However, in all respects the relationship was entirely proper – were it not so, Mrs Turner and I would not have suffered her to remain in our service.

"On the pretence that Cabern was imprisoned in London for debt, the notorious horse thief and convicted felon Foxby deceived this poor unfortunate creature into thinking her lover was starving to death for want of twenty pounds. He persuaded her to 'borrow' the horse, as he put it, and ride to London where she was to sell it and use the money to obtain Cabern's release. Cabern was then supposed to repay the value of the horse to me.

"Needless to say, my Lord, had she only approached me I would have helped her and made the necessary enquiries. Instead of that, she recklessly went ahead with this hare-brained venture. Yes, it was with a complete disregard for the law yet with all the heroism and selfless devotion she has ever shown toward a fellow being in distress. She rode to London just as selflessly and boldly as she dashed to the rescue of those three children, braving quicksand, deep-water and a rampaging bull."

He wiped away a tear with a handkerchief, then another, and prepared himself for the final appeal as he waited for the chattering to die down.

"My Lord, I most humbly appeal to you and to this court for mercy on behalf of the prisoner. I may know little of legal matters but I am practised in the performance of public duty. The law indeed has a duty to punish the guilty but, as I understand it, also to show mercy to the unfortunate. My Lord, I would have presented her with the horse rather than see her stand here. And were it even now possible, Mrs Turner and I would not hesitate to take her back into service this very day."

He bowed deeply and respectfully to the Bench as murmurs of approval filled the room. In another world, yet a heartbeat away, Sarah and Teresa smiled to each other in hope.

Frances Turner now came to the witness box, speaking in words charged with emotion, her clipped London vowels contrasting with the rural, almost musical chattering that lingered after her husband's address. She began by endorsing her husband's speech (which, in fact, she herself had composed) and went on to address the judge in her capacity as an employer.

"I have never known a more devoted, courageous and diligent servant than the prisoner you see before you. Nor have I known a more wronged, abused and ill-used creature. It is the wickedness of man, my Lord, that has placed her here and not any criminal inclinations. They do not exist in her for I have never known her to utter an unkind word or perform a dishonest deed. I stand before you, my Lord, as a humble suppliant and do most earnestly entreat you to show mercy to one who is sinned against, rather than sinning, and deeply wronged, rather than having done wrong."

She paused to allow these words to take effect before delivering her final well-chosen and deliberately challenging plea.

"Justice, my Lord, is the highest ideal to which man in his imperfect state may aspire. But the quality of mercy is divine. Therefore I appeal to you, as the earthly representative of an infinitely just and merciful God, for mercy for the wretched creature who stands before you. Within her breast there beats a most generous and unselfish heart, and her every action hitherto has been driven only by duty, filial love and the most selfless devotion."

At that moment, the courtroom window was pierced by a shaft of bright sunlight and Sarah and Teresa watched it creep along the well of the court and then shine on Nance, her head bowed. Was this providential, an answer to their prayers? Frances took full advantage of the tableau and gazed appealingly towards Maxwell. There were further murmurs of approval, this time louder, and a round of applause followed.

Dr Abbett also took the stand, speaking warmly and with sincerity as he recounted Nance's bareback ride by carthorse to summon him after her mistress had suffered a fit.

"Her presence of mind undoubtedly saved her mistress's life. It was I who recommended her for service to Mrs Turner – indeed, even now I would not have the least hesitation in taking her into service myself. I have observed her at first hand to be a most caring and dutiful daughter, a devoted sister, a loyal and a hard-working servant. If she has a fault, my Lord, it is that she is too trusting, too willing and therefore all too easily deceived."

Being a respected man of the community, and one whose medical skills were greatly valued, Abbett now played his trump card.

"My Lord, I myself have spoken with all the ladies and gentlemen present before you about this matter. And if I may presume to speak on their behalf, I would say that we appeal as one to your Lordship for mercy."

As he made his final bow, the courtroom gave its vocal and visible assent with a further round of applause lasting several minutes. Maxwell turned to whisper to the High Sheriff, but Comfrey's only comment was, "I trust your Lordship is suitably moved."

"Never more so!" he groaned. In all his years on the Bench, he had never encountered a case in which such powerful representations for clemency had been made on behalf of a defendant who was clearly guilty and who confessed as much. For a moment, he regretted the position he found himself in as his mind fought silently for a solution. After several moments of uneasy silence he addressed Nance.

"It is reason that speaks and the heart that pleads… but justice forbids. The decision is not mine. I have no option but to pass the sentence decreed by law—" there was an outcry of objections around the courtroom and it took a few minutes for order to be restored, whilst Maxwell covered his head with the dreaded black cap, "—but I undertake that this very night I shall make earnest representation to His Majesty the King on your behalf. Have you anything further to say before sentence is passed upon you?"

"Noo, my Lord."

"Nancy Auldfield, the sentence of the law is that you be taken to the place from whence you came and from thence to a place of lawful execution, there to be hanged by the neck until you are dead. May God have mercy on your soul."

Nance simply curtsied to the judge and to the court and was taken down to the cells. Her father wept as never before and wished that he might also die.

That evening, the outer doors of the grand dining-room at Windsor Castle opened onto the terrace where couples strolled, either in quiet conversation or captivated by the receding, streaky glow of a cauldron sunset. Inside, the King and Queen entertained friends beneath a forest of crystal-reflected candles that turned the approaching night into daylight. The centre of attention was the novelist Frances Burney, a personal friend of the Queen, who had been invited to speak about her recently published novel. The King was recovering from a bout of porphyria, often mistaken for madness by the ignorant, and with affairs of state completed for the day he merely wished to relax in the company of friends.

Because of his recent strange behaviour, however, many in the room felt uneasy in his presence and hovered nervously, fearful that some innocent remark might incur his displeasure. So when a messenger from the Home Office arrived, it really seemed that the congenial evening hoped for might be at an end. The inner doors opened and the messenger advanced solemnly to the threshold on tiptoe, as though the highly-polished floor were made of ice. He removed his hat with a flourish, held it close to his solar plexus and made a low, sweeping bow until his back was almost horizontal as he waited to be acknowledged.

"Come!" said the King tetchily. The man advanced and produced a document bearing the seal of the Home Secretary; it contained Maxwell's request for the royal prerogative of mercy. "Gather round, ladies, gather round," invited the monarch. "England's most talented young authoress will tell you all about her new novel. The title of it is—?"

"If it please Your Majesty, it is entitled *Camilla: or, a Picture of Youth.*"

"I look forward to hearing about it on my return." He drew back the chair he had just vacated and invited her to sit, which Frances did nervously. The messenger made a low, sideways bow to the Queen, then followed the King into an anteroom and waited while he seated himself to read the request. Meticulously, he read Maxwell's summary of the trial. Then, after pausing some considerable time for reflection, he read it again.

The King took up a quill and wrote that by his will and pleasure the sentence be commuted at Maxwell's discretion. Returning to the dining-room, the company instantly rose and he occupied a hastily vacated chair beside the Queen. He appeared thoughtful as he addressed her.

"That seaman we spoke to at Portsmouth, m'dear, aboard the *Queen Charlotte* – the one we commended for devotion to duty… What was the name of the young woman he was going to marry? Was it Auldfield, what, what?"

"Really, sir, do you expect me to remember the name of every seaman's woman?"

He searched his memory again and appeared satisfied, muttering to himself, "I think it was Auldfield, what?" He continued to ponder the matter some moments more while the guests maintained an embarrassed silence, then muttered "Auldfield" again, before the Queen's cold stare prompted him to change the subject.

Maxwell received the reprieve from the Home Office, conveyed by Royal Mail and special messenger, in court the next day and he immediately commuted the sentence to seven years' transportation.

But long periods of time elapsed between the sailing of one convict transport and the next, especially those carrying women, and it would be another two or three years before there was another. Nance would have to serve those years in Ipswich gaol although, if her conduct there was free of trouble, he intended to release her from the remainder of the sentence.

However, the reprieve presented a problem for the Keeper of Ipswich gaol, Thomas Baxter. Running a prison was normally a profitable business but what was he to do with a prisoner who had no money and yet would require feeding and clothing for years? The National Penitentiary Act called for 'labour of the hardest and most servile kind' so Baxter intended to send for Nance the following morning, both to inform her of the reprieve and to enquire how she might pay for her confinement.

In the condemned cell, though, knowing nothing of recent events, Nance was trying to come to terms with her fate, estimating the passing hours of darkness by how much of her little tallow dip was left. Irrationally, she fancied that by reckoning the minutes she might make time pass more slowly, delaying the fatal hour so that she might savour the remaining moments of life a little longer. She clung to hope. What if the hangman happened to be indisposed… or there were a reprieve? Yet locking-up had been hours ago and there was still no news.

The chaplain's words still haunted her. "Had you but served your God with anything like the passion you served another, He would not have led you into temptation and abandoned…" But then Rob had not abandoned her, he never could. Perhaps he really was in custody somewhere, or had simply not heard of her arrest? Yes, perhaps he might yet hear of it and be present in the crowd, then she could glimpse him for the last time before they parted for ever.

So lonely and forlorn did she feel, that she could only surrender to the religious impulse of the soul, reading aloud the written prayer with the last flickering of the tallow dip. And as she knelt down, thoughts of Sarah came to mind again, only now they were not so easily dismissed. After all, she had seen her sister's face in that basin of water – and if her sister did somehow live on, then so might she. Then again, as a convicted felon, what reason was there to think that an afterworld would be any better than this one? No, Sarah was long dead and soon she herself would be dead too.

Driven to distraction all day by the constant hammering as the scaffold was erected, and sick with worry at the night's rapid advance, she went over the gristly details again in her mind: the walk to the scaffold and the final moments of life. What would it be like, the sudden drop and jerk of the rope... would she feel any pain? Pray God the hangman would have the right length of rope! Too short and she might just hang there, being slowly strangled; too long and – horror of horrors – she had heard of others being decapitated.

Well, she would soon be dead anyway. What was it like being dead – an oblivion to be wished for, or would she become a ghost like Sarah? She had seen her face in the basin, but no, she couldn't possibly be alive in any way, could she? Not actually living, of course – after all she was in her grave – but perhaps a ghost, such as were known to haunt places where gibbets stood or unhallowed ground. At least Sarah's body was safely buried and not dug up by resurrection men, so she might still be resurrected when Gabriel blew his trumpet on the Last Day. As for Nance though, there was no guarantee her body would be preserved, more likely buried in an unmarked grave in the prison grounds – that is, if not sent for medical dissection. That was the worst possible outcome for, without a body, how could she possibly be resurrected? How could the Lord Jesus, in Frances Turner's words, 'raise her up to live the life eternal' if she did not have a body? Then again, what did it matter being dead anyway, if she knew nothing about it.

Despite all these thoughts in her tortured mind, she somehow became aware of a gentle presence, like a silent breath enveloping her, saying that things would not turn out as badly as she feared. Exhausted and emotionally drained, yet a little comforted by this soothing feeling, she slumped to the cold stone floor and gave in to sleep.

When she awoke it was already daylight and the full horror of what was about to happen instantly returned to her. And all too soon, the dreaded footsteps and clanking keys announced the turnkey's arrival. When he unlocked the door, though, she was pleasantly surprised to see him alone – no chaplain, no hangman – and even more so when he took her not to the chapel for the execution sermon but to the Keeper's House where she was ushered into Baxter's office.

It was a pale, disconsolate and fearful creature that stood before him. Purposely, he left her standing while he attended to some papers. But when he looked up, the sight of her did not inspire him with confidence that she was fit for any work. In a flat, disinterested voice he read aloud the reprieve, paying her no particular attention and barely raising his eyes as he announced the commutation to seven years' imprisonment.

"Only seven years?" she gasped. "Oh, gramercy, bless yew, sir!"

As the light returned to her eyes and vitality to her limbs, she suddenly seemed to him a very different class of prisoner from what he had expected.

"You once worked for Mrs Turner, I believe?"

"I did tha', sir."

"Doing what?"

"Everythin', sir. Cookin', launderin' an' housekeepin'."

"And what will you do here for the next seven years?"

"I'll earn my keep as I allus has done," she replied with a little pride now that her mind was relieved. Her answer came as a pleasant surprise: a prisoner who actually wanted to work! He stood up and for the first time she noticed his fine physique; under six feet and in his early fifties, he was nevertheless strong and muscular. Despite this rugged appearance and the unenviable nature of his office, though, he was also known to be a mild and humane man. He now walked round the desk and inspected Nance more closely.

"Did you say you've done laundering?"

"I have, sir."

"Then listen to me." He told her in no uncertain terms exactly how he wished his gaol to be managed. "I run a tight ship with no slacking, an' I will have cleanliness – can't abide filth. An' I will have discipline. If you can bring some order to the miserable skivers here, I'll see you rewarded. If not, I'll have the skin off their backs an' you'll rot in irons."

"Sir, I be a hard worker an' as good as any man."

"Then we understand each other."

251

He summoned the turnkey. Instead of the sullen way in which prisoners usually left his presence, he was gratified to see her curtsy politely and raise a smile.

Working in the laundry proved a good move. Much of the work was in the open air facing Keeper's House, in the yard that divided the female felons from the debtors. As she hung out the washing or draped it over heavy linen-horses, she could gaze up beyond the twenty-two foot, spike-topped walls at the sky and imagine herself as a bird taking wing. Her hard work and organisational skills turned a profit for the laundry, and she was rewarded by being made a trusted prisoner with her own cell, significantly better than the communal ward. She made friends among the prisoners and persuaded them that it was better to work and eat properly than idle away their days, starving and asleep on the floor.

As she lay on her straw mattress at night, an unseen visitor knelt beside her, pleased with her sister's quieter state of mind. Her nature seemed more purposeful and resolute now that she was removed from Cabern's influence, freeing her to become the responsible and industrious person she would always otherwise have been.

Sarah examined her closely as she lay there peacefully and planted an ethereal kiss on her cheek. Yet she found herself still sensing some darkness, her intuition divining that, somehow, something was not as it should be. She persevered until she could see, in a series of abstract images, a pathway of possibilities ahead. It led to a reunion and a deep love for someone – thankfully, not Cabern. But, not far distant, was a great obstacle… What could it possibly be? She went deeper still and there it was again before her inner eye – the vision she had seen on her deathbed of the hangman's noose!

She drew back, fearful and anxious, and returned to where Thomas was making the rounds of a garden that now extended beyond the bounds of his mansion and had become, effectively, a country park. He led her to a mossy seat beneath the trees and peered deeply into her knowing and despairing eyes. He could read in her mind everything she had just witnessed, including that terrible vision.

"Are you sure this is the future," he asked at length, "and not merely a possibility, or even an unfulfilled event consigned to the past?"

"No, it is in the future," she replied firmly.

He searched his mind carefully for any way by which things might go wrong but could only observe that Nance was at least safe in gaol and there didn't seem any possibility of her condemning herself again there. He gently held Sarah's hand and whispered words of comfort.

"Bless you, dear Thomas," she said, managing a wry smile. They remained there side by side until the evening light took its usual brief departure and twilight just as briefly covered the land. Nearby among the trees, a grey-haired and deeply-lined beldam with a bent back, as though still shouldering many burdens, sat wrapped in contemplation. Attracted to the park by its peacefulness, she occasionally raised her eyes and smiled at the couple. They rose and returned her smiles as they walked past arm in arm along a shadowed pathway, lit by a starry firmament, back to the house where Sarah remained with Thomas until the light, comforted by his protective embrace.

Nance was deeply saddened by the death of her father, for which she blamed herself. Frances, who visited regularly, came to console her; Matty had not come once, nor had she heard anything from John. With her new-found religious belief, which she felt had worked in winning the reprieve, she prayed fervently that Cabern would hear of her confinement and visit her – but there was no news of him. Yet all was not lost, she reasoned, if only she stayed in gaol without being transported.

Although she herself did not know it, in the course of time her sentence would have been reduced and she would be released. Her passionate and unpredictable life might have become one of normality, perhaps even with a place in service again. Her past, however, was about to catch up.

Male and female prisoners were not rigidly segregated in the gaol but felons and debtors were. Only Nance, as a trusted prisoner, was allowed into the debtors' quadrangle to deliver and collect laundry although she was not to linger there or converse with anyone. One day, as she strode through the wards with a basket of linen on her head she glimpsed a profile, partly hidden by a pillar, that seemed strangely familiar. She paused and quietly inched forward, trying to see without being seen. The man, sporting a beard and pigtail, looked like Cabern, but surely he couldn't be? Mindful of her orders, she lowered the basket and peeped round the side of it. At that very instant he turned round and they were face to face; she shrieked, the shock of meeting him again making her drop the basket, spilling its contents.

The shock registered on a higher plane of life too but without joy. On the contrary, the returning image of Cabern and his presence in the gaol only confirmed Sarah's worst fears. So that was the significance of the noose she had seen on her deathbed, in the tea leaves and on her visit to the gaol. Just when everything had seemed to be turning out for the best…

CHAPTER 17

ESCAPE!

Shh!" ordered Cabern, keeping his wits whilst equally astonished at their meeting. He stepped forward quickly and put a finger to her lips. "Don't let on that we know each other." Nonchalantly, he dropped to his knees and helped her pick up the scattered linen.

"Why be yew in har, Rob?" she whispered.

"Debt. And you?"

"Stole a hoss."

"Why?"

"Ta get yew outta gaol!"

They finished picking up the linen and she replaced the basket on her head, her mind spinning with thoughts of how she might be alone with him. The only possibility seemed to be the high wooden fence that separated the debtors' quadrangle from the yard where the washing was hung out to dry. They would not see each other but might converse through the fence without being noticed. As she walked away, she whispered, "By the yard fence."

In the following days they both contrived to be there as often as possible. Nance took to hanging out all the washing herself from a basket placed against the fence, whilst on the other side Cabern sat with his back against it, pretending to read an outspread newspaper. Their conversations were brief but informative. She related her own sorry history and learned that he had been caught storing contraband and punished with a huge fine. Ironically, he had after all suffered the fate that Foxby had dreamed up. Without the means to pay the fine he had been, with a strange legal logic, imprisoned until he could. However, debtors were often pardoned after two years and now, having been transferred from another gaol, his time was almost up. Nance was overjoyed that soon he would be able to visit her legitimately as a member of the public.

Having been pardoned in early springtime, he did just that. To avoid being recognised he came clean shaven, exchanging his seaman's pigtail for a lubber's tong-curled hair and calling at the gaol in the frockcoat of a journeyman. He introduced himself as Nance's brother, John, and was shown into her cell. When the turnkey shut the door and left, they waited until his receding steps disappeared and then she threw her arms wide to embrace him. She was now well into her thirties, he a few years older, but they felt and acted more like the youngsters they had been so long ago. Aflame again from head to toe, a smile lit up her face and her coal-black eyes sparkled. He, similarly in thrall, was an awkward youth again with all his old expectations, especially the desire to wed this spirited creature. They held each other tightly as though fearful of losing one another yet again. She smothered him with wet kisses that he returned, lifting and whirling her about like the young mawther of long ago. Eventually, they sank onto the bed, transported, until a glance at his pocket watch soon signalled the visit's end.

"If only I could somehow leave here," she moaned as the turnkey jangled his way along the corridor. If only, he mused as he left. Ever since their earliest meetings, something or somebody had prevented their being together but now at last she stood within his grasp – well, almost. If she could only escape and be over the wall, he would take care of the rest.

The next week or two saw him making the rounds of his more dubious acquaintances, especially former guests of His Majesty. The lock had not been made that could not be picked, they assured him, but the real difficulty would be in scaling the prison wall and negotiating the projecting spikes of the chevaux de frise. Nance had the means to climb the wall – a linen-horse could be used as a ladder and a clothesline could be fitted with an improvised grappling-iron; the spikes would have to be capped somehow. As for the lock, Cabern experimented to see if a bung could be used to prevent a bolt springing home; it could then perhaps be eased back with a metal instrument.

Later that month, 'John Auldfield' paid another visit to his sister. This time he had with him, hidden in his coat, cork caps for the spikes and a cork bung for the lock. He also brought a cake containing a jemmy with a curved, tapered point at one end and a claw at the other. She was enthusiastic as soon as she learned of the proposed plan. Once out of her cell, she would climb a chimney beneath the roof of the Women's Ward, climb onto the roof, make her way along to Keeper's House and let herself down by a clothesline into the laundry yard. There, the materials for the final part of the escape would have been safely stored in the yard shed.

The attempt would be made when Baxter and the other women prisoners had left for Bury, for the Spring Assizes, provided there was enough moonlight. When Cabern left, Nance was never so determined in her life, even when stealing the horse, to succeed and be away with him. In the following week she examined every inch of the escape route that she could access by using her position of trust, and prepared the necessary materials. A clothesline was smuggled into her cell and stuffed within her mattress. With her fingers, she measured the length of the bolt in the cell door to calculate how much bung would be needed, and managed to obtain grease from the kitchen to work into the lock so that it moved more freely. Hooks from the kitchen were bound together and fashioned into a grappling-iron. Finally, she measured how far up the prison wall she would be able to climb using one of the triangular linen-horses.

The night came with a clear sky and just enough moonlight to be able to move around. Before being locked in her cell, she stuffed the trimmed cork into the bolt socket, excitement and anticipation prevailing over any fear. The turnkey checked to see that she was present, then closed and locked the door; he found that he couldn't turn the lock the whole way but satisfied himself that it was shut. Nance waited until his receding footsteps ceased and the outer door was locked before beginning work with the jemmy. With practised motions, she used the tapered end as a lever and the door jamb as a pivot to press against the bolt, moving it a little every few seconds. Eventually she had the bolt pushed almost fully back – but it would move no further.

Watching on helplessly were Sarah and Teresa. They wished, hoped and prayed that the attempt would end here.

"She's done nothing wrong until now," wailed Sarah. "But if she tampers with the lock, it'll be obvious and Baxter will know she tried to break out."

"It's worse than that," sighed Teresa. "I've just learned that there's every chance of her being pardoned."

"What?"

"Judge Maxwell's been making enquiries about her. If reports are good, and as you say they would be, he intends to release her at the Summer Assizes." Scarcely had she spoken when Sarah grabbed her arm.

"Look, she's trying to force the lock. Oh, why don't you stop her?"

"I cannot, it's her choice. She has free will and I cannot take it from her."

"Nance," bawled Sarah, "Nance, for pity's sake, no…" but as before her words dissolved in empty air.

This time, though, Nance did sense her sister's presence. It made her pause and look around but then, overcome by determination to be with the man she loved, she dismissed it as pure fancy and resumed her work. Her guides resigned themselves sorrowfully to watching her condemn herself for a second time. They saw her use the jemmy's tapered end to prise up the metal cover of the lockbox. When the gap was wide enough, she slipped in the claw-end and heaved with all her might until she ripped the plate off the box. With the mechanism exposed, it was child's play to pick the lock and slide back the bolt. She paused and listened intently for any sound, but there was none.

It was now past midnight and throughout both gaol and town the weary mortals and their beasts lay fast asleep. Only Sarah and Teresa kept watch as Nance, carrying the jemmy and mattress containing the clothesline, tiptoed silently along the pitch-dark corridor. She passed empty cells, came to the chimneypiece at the end of the passageway and squeezed into the hearth; above her, two iron security bars prevented access to anyone except the tiny boy-sweeps but she knew that one was already loose and she used the jemmy to attack the mortar that held it. The mattress was dragged under the chimney to smother any sound of falling debris that might awaken the turnkey, asleep in his lodge below. Finally, by chipping and digging away at the brickwork, she loosened the bar further and wrenched it free. Now, not only was the way up the chimney clear but she had a second tool in the shape of the two-foot iron bar. She tied the end of the clothesline about her waist, tucked the bar into her belt and placed the jemmy between her teeth.

Feeling for the ledges and handholds used by the climbing-boys, she began the ascent and climbed until she could see the starry sky through the chimneypot. A few feet below it, at what she guessed would be the level of the attic floor, she examined the brickwork with her fingers for any cracks in the mortar then got to work with the jemmy, prising loose the mortar until a number of bricks had been dislodged. Now she could use the iron bar to free them, reaching through the growing hole and lowering them onto the attic floor. Pieces of masonry that fell down the chimney landed silently on the mattress. The chimney wall gradually gave way under her onslaught until the hole was big enough for her to squeeze through and stand in the attic itself just below the roof.

Still working by touch alone, her jemmy and bar made short work of the roof's wooden laths and the nails that held the slates in place. These she carefully grasped and pulled inwards with scarcely a sound. Every step of the daring venture had been carefully planned with Cabern and repeated over and over in whispers until she knew it by heart. She pulled up the clothesline and wound it about her waist then hoisted herself up through the hole she had made in the roof to emerge into the moist night air.

Stars were midway in their course and the moon cast just enough light to see by as she eased herself out and onto the sloping roof. With hands and legs outspread like a giant spider, she began to descend the last few feet. But a loose slate gave way and she slid down towards the parapet…

"She'll kill herself!" cried a distraught Sarah as Teresa tried to comfort her.

Nance made a grab for the slate but missed and it slid over the edge, seconds later shattering in the yard below. For a moment she held her breath, but there was no point in waiting for any response – there was no going back. With hands and chest pressed firmly against the roof, and feeling through her shoes for the parapet's edge beyond which lay a sheer drop, she edged her way along to Keeper's House. There she unwound the clothesline, fastened it to a waterspout and let it drop onto the roof of the laundry shed far beneath before climbing out over the parapet and shinning down the line, hand over hand to the shed roof. A jump of a few feet remained and she was safely on the ground. Breaking into the shed with the jemmy to retrieve the cork caps, grappling-iron and some improvised rollers proved no obstacle. Now, however, came the most dangerous and difficult part: negotiating the chevaux de frise.

She dragged out a linen-horse, inches at a time so that it made hardly a sound, and manoeuvred it on rollers across the yard before lifting it so that it stood on end against the outside wall. A second clothesline was tied to the grappling-iron, then she climbed the linen-horse as far as she could. Grasping the line tightly, she whirled it round and round and let the iron fly up towards the broken spike, just visible against the moonlit sky. The hooks failed to catch… Holding her nerve – she had come so far – Nance made several more attempts before the iron caught the central bar of the chevaux de frise and she could pull the line taught. Up she climbed, wrapping the line around a foot for each step, until she arrived just below the spikes.

Holding onto the wall with one hand, she fitted the caps over the spikes either side of the broken one before reaching through the spikes with the other hand and grasping the central bar. Pausing to breathe calmly before the final steps, she eased her way up the rest of the wall to lie across the broken and capped spikes. With the line tied to a spike and wound around her waist, she kicked herself off, turning a somersault and bringing her legs over her head and down on the other side of the prison wall. Then, at that most critical instant, she lost her grip, fell from the spikes and dangled twenty feet above the ground…

"She's truly mad!" cried Sarah, becoming even more distraught. Teresa held her hand for comfort but they could only watch on grimly.

"It's times like this," observed Teresa quietly to herself, "that a spirit guide wonders why they do it."

Nance edged her body round until she faced inwards and could grasp the top of wall, then she unravelled the line about her and let it drop into the darkness where unseen hands caught it and held it taut. Descending was the easiest part and within moments she had slid down and was on the ground, black with soot from the chimney, but held firmly and lovingly in Cabern's arms.

"By Heaven, woman, you deserve the seaman's kit I've brought you. You shinned down that rope like a true son of the sea."

"Darter," she corrected. "An' yew should have seen me a-gooin' up it."

Hurriedly they fled the gaol, crossed Helen's Wash and crept into the garden of a private house where he had hidden a scrip; for the second time, she dressed herself as a seaman. With Cabern also in seaman's dress, they took the Woodbridge Road and were soon crossing Rushmere Common, leaving Ipswich far behind. Flushed with success and happiness, she sang as she tripped along:

"What though our friends our absence mourn,
we with all honour shall return.
And then we'll sing both night and day,
over the hills and far away… far away…"

Within the hour they were passing The Bell Inn at Kesgrave and making for the heath. Having skirted the silent village of Martlesham, they walked on in the direction of Woodbridge until dawn found them on the banks of the Deben near the Mill Pond and opposite the Ferry House. The ferryboat would soon take them to the Sutton side of the river and beyond reach of any pursuer.

Seeing a character from Nance's past, Sorcy Solomon, walking towards them with an empty basket, they decided to stroll on as though complete strangers. Solomon had only seen Cabern once before and then in the dark, so he could be any seaman. His companion, though, with a pulled-down hat aroused Solomon's curiosity. There was nothing unusual about a seaman walking about at odd hours – but sailors generally looked upward and consequently wore their hat on the back of the head, never pulled down. Solomon eyed Nance carefully as they passed. The face was somewhat delicate for a seaman and dirty, too, which was also unusual; moreover, this seaman didn't walk with the habitual roll. He knew he had seen that face before. But he gave no sign of recognition and walked on in the direction of Martlesham.

The fugitives boarded the morning ferry, were rowed across and were soon in Sutton Walks and passing Ferry Farm. They were now in open country, a patchwork of deserted heath, common land and marshes that lay between Sutton and the River Butley. Cabern had brought bread and cheese and ship's biscuit so they would not have to call at a shop or inn until they reached their destination. This was near the North Vere where he had arranged a rendezvous with a Dutch smuggler. From now on they would rest by day and travel at night.

A passer-by in early morning spotted the clothesline dangling down the gaol wall and raised the alarm. Within hours, the whole of Ipswich knew and a crowd gathered at the gaol to stare and wonder how a middle-aged woman had the nerve to perform such a feat in the middle of the night. Baxter, hastily summoned from Bury, was at first astounded and then a worried man since he faced a heavy fine for the escape. The apparent ease with which the cell door had been opened placed the turnkey under suspicion and, as the keeper was ultimately responsible, some might even think that he himself had connived in the brazen escape. Local magistrates were hurriedly informed and parish constables despatched to make enquiries.

It was late afternoon when Solomon walked into Ipswich and on to his sailboat, moored by the jetty near Castlegreen. Frances Turner happened to be visiting from the Norman House and called out to him from the garden wall.

"Are you sailing on the tide, Master Solomon?"

He nodded, came over to stand beneath the wall as they exchanged greetings.

"Yew'll not niver guess," he then said, "who I saw this mornin', Ma'am. At least, har or har double."

"Whom did you see?"

"Yar owd servant, the one as stole the 'oss."

"Not—"

"Ay, Nance Auldfield, the one as coom for the job har. Had a demon in tow then, she did. I knew then right enough she wuz a wrong 'un."

"And where did you see her?"

"Sutton Ferry, Ma'am."

"She's just escaped from gaol. I think you'd better come inside, Sorcy, while I send for a constable."

As they waited, a second servant was despatched to inform Baxter and soon both he and the constable were taking careful note of everything Solomon told them. Shortly afterwards, the inevitable handbills and posters were distributed, offering twenty pounds reward for the apprehension of Nance, said to be travelling with a male companion assumed to be Cabern.

Baxter was skilled in the pursuit and recapture of escaped prisoners. Moreover, they appeared to be making for the coast and, hailing from Sudbourne himself, he would be following them on home turf. He returned to his house in the gaol, armed himself and was soon riding to the river where the ferryman's description of the height and build of the smaller seamen with a delicate and dirty face seemed to confirm it was Nance. He stabled the horse, crossed the Deben by ferry and took the road towards The Plough Inn, where he stayed the night. But of everyone he asked, none had seen the pair. The trail was cold.

He went over every possibility in his mind of where they could be making for. Not inland since they were dressed as seamen. A port or fishing village made sense because seamen were plentiful at such places, so Aldeburgh might be their destination. But they were on foot. They must surely be making for the sea and a waiting ship, perhaps at Bawdsey where Cabern had had associates in the past. Still, wasn't that a little too obvious? There were more than twenty miles of deserted beaches where a ship might safely stand off and on all day. He would have to begin at Bawdsey and travel up the coast, making enquiries as he went.

The next day he rode a hired horse to Shottisham, Alderton and Bawdsey and back again, seeking out each parish constable along the way. It was at Hollesley that he met an unusually zealous one called Barnabus Johnson. Unlike so many other unwilling volunteer constables, this man performed his duties well and arrested the occasional rogue or pickpocket with the aid of his specially decorated truncheon. He also kept the magistrates informed of anything of importance, from criminal activity to those who had failed to attend church. Johnson was, in fact, the nearest thing to a professional police officer the county had and Baxter could not have found a better associate. Hearing that Cabern was probably involved, and knowing his connection with smuggling, he suggested they enlist the help of the riding officers who were stationed nearby. So it was not long before Baxter was talking to their supervisor, Garrow Merryridge.

Far away and yet so near, a sombre Sarah followed her sister's progress in the garden pool's images, unfolding like scenes in a tragedy towards a seemingly inevitable conclusion. She saw Nance and Cabern making their way by night towards the North Vere and resting in each other's arms by day in sheltered places away from shepherds and labourers. Realising that Sorcy Solomon might have recognised her at the ferry, they stopped at a safe cottage used by Cabern's confederates where they each donned cloak and boots. Cabern also tucked a brace of pistols into his belt.

They skirted Stonebridge Marshes, arrived at Butley Ferry, and as dusk fell they stood on the opposite bank and were soon taking the path south of Chantry Marshes. As dawn broke over Dove Point, they hailed a passing waterman and paid him to row them across the Ore. With three rivers now behind them, they were approaching their destination and walking along the deserted shingle of the peninsular beside The Narrows to the beach agreed by Cabern for the rendezvous with the Dutchman. They could wait safely here until evening.

The area had long been used for landing contraband and Merryridge had useful informers. With three of his officers, together with Baxter and Johnson, he made his way to Orford Haven where their boat was housed. Leaving one officer on watch in case the haven was the intended rendezvous, the remaining men sailed the boat up the River Ore, passing within a few hundred yards of where Nance and Cabern lay concealed, then onwards. An old salt who had helped Merryridge before remembered two men that morning being rowed across the Ore to the harbour – so the beach was the pair's destination, right enough. Merryridge now knew that he was close to his quarry. He dropped two officers ashore with orders to walk back along the beach from the river's side while he, Baxter and Johnson, sailed north along the shore.

Towards evening, a sail was spotted far out in the bay and as the distinctive hull and rigging of a Dutch merchantman hove in view Cabern used the last of the sunlight to signal with a mirror. The flashes were returned and, as dusk fell, the Dutchman hove to and a boat was launched. Cabern acted with practised caution, anxiously scanning the beach and shoreline.

Nance, however, was jubilant and impatient. Just a few moments more and they would be on that boat, heading for the ship and Holland and a new life as husband and wife. A weak, hazy sunset streaked the sky below increasingly ominous clouds and a distant rumble of thunder could be heard. Reassuringly, though, the breeze rose only slightly and the uniform, feather-crested waves broke evenly on the shingle. It did not occur to Nance that there might be something in the offing far more terrible than a storm.

Sarah watched it all unfold and any hope she had that her sister might yet escape was dashed when she saw the trap about to be sprung. All she could hope for was that there would be no shooting.

CHAPTER 18

LORD, IN THY MERCY

Merryridge was in high spirits. He had seen the ship from the beginning, downed sail and mast and drifted near the beach. Only as twilight fell did he make sail again, steering for the beach opposite the Dutchman and arriving ahead of the ship's boat. A lightning-flash briefly illuminated the scene and loud thunder rumbled overhead. The two riding officers on land saw what was happening from a distance and waited at the head of the beach. As Merryridge approached the shore he fired a sawn-off flintlock, the usual smugglers' signal. Cabern saw its bluish flash and stood up with Nance, believing this to be the Dutchman's boat come for them. They walked to the water's edge…

But no sooner had the keel scraped the shingle than Merryridge sprang out followed by Baxter and waded through the surf. From behind Cabern, the two officers on the beach now stood, drawing their weapons and advancing at pace, their boots crunching the shingle. The challenge was made but Cabern's response was to draw his pistols. It was now so gloomy that the men could scarcely distinguish each other's features.

"Don't be foolish," shouted Merryridge as he cocked a pistol, now certain it was Cabern and remembering his promise to Nance not to harm him. "Surrender! You haven't a chance. And it's Nance we've come for, not you."

A beam of moonlight suddenly revealed the two men's faces. Whether what happened in the next moment was intended or not would never be known, but Cabern's finger rested on his trigger and the hammer fell. The ball tore through the folds of Merryridge's coat without hitting him and, instinctively, he returned fire. Cabern toppled backwards, dropped, and lay still. Nance shrieked and dashed forward to throw herself over him where she crouched defensively like a beast at bay.

"Rob, oh Rob!" she moaned. Clawing inside his waistcoat she felt a warm, damp shirt and her cries of grief became so wild that the hardened officers trembled. A second lightning flash revealed Cabern's blank face and sightless eyes. Even a new, prolonged thunderclap could not drown out her high-pitched scream. "Yew've killed 'em!"

"I'm sorry, Nance," murmured Merryridge, coming over to kneel beside her. "He fired first at me."

"Yew promised yew'd not niver harm 'em. An' now yew've killed 'em! Oh, my poor Rob, gorn... an' niver called me wife!" Her tear-soaked face a mask of grief, she tore at her hair and dashed her head on the stones before the officers seized and dragged her away but she broke free and rushed towards the sea. They restrained her again and the parish constable Barnabus Johnson, who had beached the boat, now approached her.

"Nancy Auldfield, late of Ipswich Gaol, I arrest you in the King's name." Her arms and legs were bound and she was dumped in the boat. Then the group pushed off, desperate to try and outrun the storm, pulling hard in the current and the rising swell to reach the haven.

While Teresa accompanied Nance, Sarah waited beside Cabern's body and as the life-force ebbed away she watched a second Cabern stir as though from sleep, stand up and look around. Realising that despite the darkness he could now see clearly the men in the boat with Nance captive, he resolved to continue the fight and looked down for his pistols… only to be confronted with his own shadowy face, the eyes staring blankly, the limbs relaxed in death. He then became aware that another figure stood nearby. Strangely, and in contrast to the dark mass at his feet, Sarah's features and dress were sharp and colourful. (She had made her spirit body as dense and near-physical as possible in order to be seen by the Earthbound.)

"It's all over Rob," she said simply, almost coldly. "Come with me."

"No, I have to go after my woman," he cried, pointing desperately towards the disappearing boat. Then he hesitated a moment and shot her a quizzical look as though of recognition. "You look like her. Who are you?"

"I'm her sister," she said, still without emotion and stony-faced.

"Sister?" he gasped, looking her up and down. "But you can't be… Sarah? You're dead, all these years past."

"I'm no more dead than you – nor less alive, whichever you prefer."

Rain began to fall over the beach, yet instead of wetness he only felt a tingling sensation. Still unable, or unwilling, to accept the truth of what had happened, he continued to glance around in desperation and stumbled towards the water.

"No, you're telling me lies. Besides, you don't even speak or dress like her. Where are my pistols? I must signal the Dutchman and get after Nance."

"Thanks to you, you'll as likely see her soon enough."

"What's that? What do you mean?"

"She'll swing for this – and all because of you. You surely know that." Her voice was grim. Disgusted by him and feeling somewhat sick, she felt like leaving him to himself but remembered John and their conversation in the aftermath of the sea battle. Still, she was matter-of-fact, her expression without warmth. "Now Robert, are you coming with me or must I fetch others?"

Lightning jagged again and thunder crashed. Whilst her radiant features were unaltered, the face masked by death at his feet was momentarily clearly visible.

"I suppose you're right," he conceded, calming down at last. "I must be snuffed out or I wouldn't be lying there. I'll come with you."

Wordlessly, she led him by the hand into a curtain of light that dropped before them. It hung there briefly, then vanished leaving the beach empty save for the corpse of a smuggler, a hero and a villain and an indifferent lover, tossed by the incoming waves. A while later the boat and its occupants returned to the haven. Rain beat down heavily as, cold and bedraggled, they beached the craft and sheltered in the boathouse cottage.

Sarah feared there would be no mercy shown a second time and any judge would have no option but to reimpose the death sentence. Her peace and happiness seemed to be at an end and she wished only to hide herself away alone in her cottage, meditating the awful inevitability of her sister's execution. Yet Thomas felt her pain just as keenly and came to her straight away. He found her wrapped in the darkest melancholy, heedless of the now ruined garden that had formerly brought her so much joy. The head of every flower drooped, the rippling brook was still and silent and shrivelled fruit lay beneath naked boughs. Only the faithful birds remained, singing a soft lament.

Sarah could only look up at him tearfully, pleadingly, wishing beyond hope for the impossible, that somehow her sister might yet be saved. He embraced her tenderly and calmly seated himself opposite. She tried to speak but realised that he already knew her anguished thoughts. In a moment everything had been revealed to him and he even saw her vision of Nance, imprisoned and awaiting her fate.

"Is there nothing we can do for her?" she sobbed at last. "I'm so afraid. Hanging's a terrible death. As well as the unimaginable fear, it's such a shock for the spirit body to be jerked out of the physical like that – and sometimes the spirit cannot pass over properly. They can become Earthbound, or trapped between the worlds."

He looked around at the cottage interior which, unlike the ruin outside, was relatively unchanged. Her own inner light and energy were undimmed. It was an altogether finer energy than his, yet complementary to him, and her humble abode radiated it despite her forlorn mood. Inspired, he leaned forward to grasp her trembling hands and hold them fast.

"Don't, whatever you do, give up. As long as hope remains there is a chance of modifying the outcome. But lose hope and all is lost.

"Now, I've already given the matter some thought and made some enquiries. Even now, being here beside you and your heightened perception, I find I can think even more easily and visualise better. The impossible can become probable. Listen, it will be the same trial judge, Maxwell, and he may not be the best judge but he's fair. The sentence will have to be death—" she shrank back in fear again, "—but it could again be commuted."

"You mean another approach to the King?"

"No, I don't think we can count on His Majesty's good grace a second time. Besides, Maxwell already has discretion in this case. He is also a gentleman who enjoys a reputation as a careful and considerate judge. I don't think he'll risk jeopardising that reputation, especially as he has been careless with it already."

"What do you mean?"

"He has been rather outspoken about the rights of the common man, which did not endear him to more liberally-minded citizens. And remember, I was of the same class as Maxwell and I know how such men think. Nance's case will trouble him considerably – and perhaps I can help him reach a more lenient decision."

"Can you do that? I mean, is it allowed?"

"I think so… no doubt we'll soon hear from John if it isn't! Look, as the law stands she won't be charged with escaping from gaol but with the original crime of horse stealing, for which Maxwell has already shown clemency. We might be able to induce him to do so again. Well, we can but try."

"Bless you, Thomas. How did so simple and undeserving a creature ever come to deserve such a wise and noble friend?"

"How did I come to be loved by an angel?" They reflected for a moment before the absurdity of their flatteries brought the glimmer of a smile to both their faces. "Now remember," he added, "you must play your part if we're to help Nance. Have you ever done any acting?"

"Only once, in a passion play," she replied, taken aback.

"Perfect. I was a passable amateur myself. They said I made a fair Hamlet and a decently crafty Iago, although I believe Mephistopheles was more my style. Anyway, I think we should pay his Lordship a visit."

The gates of Ipswich gaol had again closed behind Nance and soon she would find herself once more in the dock at the Assizes charged, as Thomas predicted, with horse stealing. She would stand before the same judge who had sentenced and reprieved her three years earlier.

Frances Turner came to visit. She was distressed to discover that, in the eyes of many people, Nance was no longer an impetuous and passionate woman who had committed a single rash act but a seasoned criminal bound for the scaffold. Moreover, she was listless, pining for her dead lover and apparently unaware of having done anything wrong. What was there for Frances to say except that Nance must pray most earnestly for forgiveness and prepare herself to suffer the penalty decreed by law.

When Nance appeared again before Lord Baron Maxwell, she sank in a polite enough curtsy; and when asked if she had anything to say, admitted her guilt as advised by Frances.

"My Lord, I am guilty as charged an' have prepared myself ta suffer the penalty decreed by law. I would only implore others who face temptation ta taak example by me, an' remember the wretched situation in which my wickedness has placed me, an' niver ta stray from the path of righteousness. That is all I have ta say, my Lord."

Maxwell frowned. He consulted a passionate written appeal from Frances Turner, who was unable to attend, being heavily pregnant. In it she detailed again all the selfless and heroic acts performed by the defendant, more than once risking her own life and limb. Her husband and Dr Abbett also added their pleas, begging once more for clemency. At length, Maxwell delivered his judgment.

"Once again you have made full confession of your guilt and that is to be commended. However, considering all the circumstances, I should be failing in my duty to my sovereign, to the laws of England and to the liberty of her people, if I did not reimpose the sentence decreed by law." He paused and looked down, as though examining his own mind.

"I must add that, in spite of all the representations made on your behalf, I have seldom encountered one so undeserving of mercy. You stand condemned by your own criminal actions, which show you to be not only insensible of right and wrong but also utterly ungrateful for everything that has been done for you. You were placed in a position of trust by your prison keeper and your behaviour was initially exemplary – to the extent that, had you not succumbed to your former wickedness, I might now be considering releasing you from the remainder of your sentence." There were gasps in the courtroom and incomprehension even flickered across Nance's face.

"Instead of which," the judge continued, "I find you the author and perpetrator of another most accomplished act of villainy which, by its exploitative and selfish nature, also brought suspicion upon two innocent men. You therefore leave me no alternative but to reimpose the original sentence awarded by this court." He took up the black cap and Nance stood impassively as the sentence of death was passed for the second time.

When he retired to his rooms at day's end, however, he did not seem the severe and steadfast upholder of justice he had been in court. Just as Thomas had predicted, this case troubled him greatly. In spite of the woman's reckless and criminal behaviour, he could nevertheless see in her a trace of innocence. She deserved to be punished, yes, but perhaps not quite so severely since her guilt was more by association. Something in his mind told him that he was being too harsh by following the letter of the law.

But then, would others see it that way? The damage done to his reputation as a fair and liberal-minded gentleman, as Thomas had described, was fresh in people's minds. These considerations kept him awake far into the night. Finally, convincing himself that he had done what was right by law, he donned cap and nightshirt, placed a lighted candle beside the bed and knelt in prayer. Then he climbed in, snuffed out the candle, pulled up the bedclothes and abandoned himself to sleep.

He was soon in the depths of sleep, beyond the intrusion of dreams, his spirit body rising a little above the bed. As the night wore on, however, the troubles of the spirit lingered and distorted images came to mind as the brain processed haphazardly the previous day's proceedings concerning the prisoner Auldfield. His dream became especially vivid, the narrative seeming to suggest that, rather than his being the judge, indeed he was on trial himself with judgment being sought against him...

Then, in a corner of the room, he saw as plain as day a rising cloud of white mist. It began to build and take human form until it resembled none other than Nance Auldfield. She stood with head bowed and eyes closed, her hands clasped in prayer and with a noose around her neck. As he looked on, mesmerised, he also became aware of the bedside candle being relit and a gentleman in the robes of an advocate standing beside him. The figure was vaporous yet clear, if not solid then still very much alive. But he did not appear threatening at all – more, in fact, like a legal colleague come to debate with him on the matter of judgement.

"My Lord," began the advocate, his words ringing within Maxwell's mind, "does Nance Auldfield really deserve to die for stealing the horse, a crime which the owner has long since forgiven?"

The judge, not knowing now whether he was asleep or awake or indeed in some other world, nevertheless kept his composure and entered the argument.

"She is not to be hanged for stealing the horse but in order that horses may not be stolen... or, for that matter, that prisoners may not escape gaol. Justice must be upheld and seen to be upheld."

"But, my Lord, you recommended mercy before, did you not?"

"That is true."

"And were you not upholding justice then?"

"I was indeed."

"Then is she not similarly deserving of mercy now?"

"No, because she abused the trust placed in her – the trust I myself placed in her too."

"But she was not charged with escaping gaol, only with stealing a horse, the crime for which you originally commuted sentence."

"If persons are not hanged for horse stealing," Maxwell said, feeling the need to remain stubborn, "horses will continue to be stolen."

Even as he spoke, at this moment a shaft of ethereal light fell upon the upper part of the baleful figure, still with the noose around her and hands clasped in tearful supplication.

"Not by the prisoner, though," retorted the advocate, "nor indeed by any who follow her example. She has been most contrite – and was twice prevailed upon by others' wickedness. She deserves to be punished, yes, but surely not by snuffing out the light of life itself – which, may I remind you, my Lord, you intended to preserve previously. It is a most final judgement, to extinguish this light that can never be relit."

As Maxwell considered these words, the shaft of light broadened and illuminated the woman fully as she lifted her head towards him with imploring eyes. At that instant a third misty figure joined them and even as the emboldened advocate bent closer to Maxwell, a restraining hand reached out to his shoulder. A silent reprimand shook his whole being as though it had been bawled in his ear, "Enough!" He turned to find a displeased John beside him.

"But—" he pleaded.

"This charade has gone too far. Bring it to an end!" Sheepishly, Thomas nodded and dropped to one knee.

"I beseech you, my Lord," he continued in softer, humbler tones, "do not, as the Bard said, put out the light – this light that so often has shone as a beacon of hope for those in peril. Rather, my Lord, return her to God's ever merciful spiritual light."

He fell silent and remained kneeling for a moment, head bowed, before dissolving away with Sarah. John stepped forward and held a hand over Maxwell, willing him to relax into sleep once more. Then he too departed.

Maxwell sank back, at one moment all but asleep whilst at another half awake, all the while a persistent plea of 'Don't put out the light' giving him no rest for the remainder of the night.

When he awoke at dawn, fully rested, he noticed that the candle he distinctly remembered snuffing out had burned to a stub. All he could recall of the night's events was dreaming of the female prisoner he had sentenced to hang, and hearing someone say, "Don't put out the light." Then the thought again came to him that he, as much as the defendant, had been the one on trial – followed by the powerful and self-serving thought that people would not think him a gentleman for refusing what others had so earnestly pleaded for.

Standing up and feeling strangely not quite alone, he went to his writing table and rummaged through court papers until he found the one he wanted. Then he took up a quill. As he wrote, he spoke his thoughts aloud as though to any who might be listening.

"She is indeed punished if she be transported, and that is scarcely less than loss of life. Some die on the outward voyage and many do so there at journey's end. Should she by some miracle survive, and even be pardoned, as a woman there is no chance of her coming back." He finished writing, glanced about him and as an afterthought muttered, "Lord in Thy mercy, let me be." From that moment, any thoughts of another's presence ceased and he felt at peace.

Later in court, he announced that after further careful consider-ation of all the representations made, he was again commuting the sentence, this time to transportation for life to 'Parts Beyond the Seas', the legal term for the New South Wales penal colony. Transportation appeared little better than a death sentence to Nance, though. With Cabern gone forever, execution had almost seemed preferable for now she faced a living death, a lonely and loveless existence on the other side of the world, exiled from her native land.

A relieved Sarah returned thankfully to her sad little garden, only to be confronted by the consequences of its long neglect. It even resembled the grounds of Thomas' mansion when she had first seen it. As she knelt there among newly-sprouting weeds, she became aware of peering eyes. Her brothers were at the gate together with some well-meaning neighbours and her mother and father were also approaching. Mark looked scornfully at the garden, or rather what was left of it.

"Yew ont half catch it when the master sees it in tha' state," he chuckled. "'Em'ul be wholly bate!"

"Looks like a tempest's hit it," smirked Albert. "Proper bumbastin' yew'll get."

"Stop your blabber both of you," ordered Beth, full of vitality as she strode up, "an' let the poor mawther be!"

She swept past them into the garden followed by Zebedee. In a sense they were still the parents but they had long since shed their years and Beth appeared similar to Sarah. It was as much as a dear friend rather than a former parent that her mother counselled her. They were so close that neither needed to express themselves in words, but Beth chose to give her daughter a gentle but firm reprimand, the gist of it being that Sarah's task was done. Her other daughter, no less dear to her, had made her choices in life and must be allowed to follow them.

No, Sarah must not – as John had told her more than once – try to live life for her. She could visit from time to time and gently influence her sister, one way or another. Otherwise, Sarah herself had a life to lead and must not be forever worrying about another's. Besides, Nance had someone better qualified to guide her – that was Teresa's province, not hers. Come what may, soon enough their dearest Nance would eventually come to stand at this very gate. When the mother had finished, the father's loving embrace further soothed Sarah's troubled mind.

Her spirits soon revived and the garden struggled back to life, repainting the earth with living dyes and banishing the weeds. Every flower and bush, as though rejoicing at their mistress's recovery, budded and bloomed and breathed with new fragrance. The stagnant brook cleared itself and purled once more into a gentle flood whilst from the apple tree, already fruiting, the loyal birds chattered with joy.

Back in a world of harsher realities, only family and Frances Turner were allowed to visit Nance in her cell. Her uncle and step-aunt came with the children and tried to comfort her, as did Frances. She, however, had another motive in mind too. She was a keen botanist who would have loved to study the flora and fauna of Terra Australis but, as a woman, was excluded from the Royal Society and any such opportunity. Perhaps now she might receive reports on what the new continent was like, since Nance had acquired some botanical skills whilst working for her, had an eye for detail and could write well enough to describe accurately everything she saw.

Moreover, a new purpose in life was what Nance needed, a mission that would enable her to rise above the wretched existence she imagined for herself as a mere convict. Human consciousness requires a focus and a mind constantly set on its own misfortunes, as was

Nance's, merely sees them grow until it becomes entirely disturbed. Accordingly, as the time for departure drew near, Frances gave her books, clothes and other necessities including a little money, along with every encouragement to make the best of her circumstances by seeking out and collecting interesting specimens.

In May, Nance was driven to Portsmouth by carriage with two other prisoners, Abigail Harris and Jemima Hargreaves, all in irons with the blinds down and guarded personally by Thomas Baxter. She was taken on board the *Nile*, a transport also carrying free settlers, and down to the orlop where she was confined with the other women in cages until the ship sailed. Only when Southsea Castle was far to larboard were they allowed on deck to see the last of England, their sadness tempered by the relief of breathing fresh sea air.

Captain Harbuckle solemnly read aloud to them the Articles of War that related to the rules of the ship and the penalties for any infringement. The voyage being licensed by the Admiralty, naval discipline prevailed and no officer at sea would tolerate the filth and squalor that prison officers might on land. From now on, the women were required to wash clothes, bedding and their bodies with seawater, and soon an assortment of feminine apparel fluttered from lines criss-crossing the ship's waist.

The journey would take seven months across two oceans, under some of the most difficult sailing conditions known, including gale force winds south-west of the Bay of Biscay. Then there were the awful ship's rations, the leathery salted beef, the weevil-infested biscuit, the cheese that crawled and the water that turned green before clearing again (though by way of consolation a little rum was sometimes mixed with it). At Tenerife they took on provisions and fresh water and were then borne westward by the snaking trade winds to South America, labouring awhile in the doldrums before crossing the line and sighting Sugar Loaf Mountain.

While in the São Sabastião harbour of Rio de Janeiro, the prisoners were again locked in cages and allowed on deck only under guard. In the stifling, humid, insect-buzzing heat there, discontent soon fomented into a resolution to mutiny and there was talk of breaking into the arms chest, overpowering the few seamen left aboard and making for the beach a hundred yards away in one of the ship's boats. Surely the Portuguese civilians would offer sanctuary, the well-dressed matrons they saw promenading along the palm-shaded avenues preferring their service to that of black slaves. Either that or they could offer themselves to the menfolk, bodies and all. Anything was preferable to their suffering below deck.

"Dewn't yew not know, have yew niver heard, mut'ny be the worst crime yew can commit at sea?" Nance warned her new friend Abigail Harris, grabbing her arm until she winced with pain. "They'll flog the hide off yew. They'll hang yew from a yardarm." Abigail wriggled free and wiped the beaded sweat from her face with a sleeve.

"I can't stand this bloody voyage, Nance. I'll go crazy."

"There be nothing worse than bein' flayed alive, or swingin' from a yardarm, an' more 'an likely both." She seized her friend again. "When they goo up on deck, make sure yew stay below – understood?" She shook her roughly. "Promise me!"

"All right," Abigail said sullenly, "I bleedin' promise."

Days later, the mutineers put their plan into action when the passengers were ashore, whilst Nance, Abigail and as many as they could persuade stayed below. Some of the women distracted the remaining seamen as the ringleaders ransacked the officers' cabins and stores. They failed to find the arms chest, but returned with an assortment of knives and makeshift weapons and overpowered the men. However, word quickly reached Captain Harbuckle thanks to a crewman who lowered himself unseen over the rail and swam ashore, and the mutineers, however desperate, proved no match for the returning captain and crew. The women were clapped in irons, tried by courts martial and swiftly convicted.

With the passengers still ashore, the boatswain ordered "All hands aft to witness punishment." Nance, Abigail and the prisoners who had taken no part in the mutiny stood huddled together, guarded by crewmen, as the offenders were brought forward. The captain reminded them that they had transgressed ship's rules and knew the penalty; however, instead of being convicted of mutiny, for which the punishment was death, they were being dealt with 'leniently' for the lesser offence of threatening an officer.

The first mutineer was led to an upturned grating and told to strip to the waist, exposing her back, whilst her wrists were bound to the grill. The captain read aloud Article 22, as the ship's company removed their hats out of respect for the King's command that any person striking a superior officer should be punished by court martial. The boatswain then produced a whip with which to deliver the sentence of three dozen lashes.

"Ship's company, on hats!" ordered the captain. "Do your duty, boatswain!"

The lash fell repeatedly across the woman's back, breaking the skin and leaving weals until the deck below was splattered with blood. Nance and the other prisoners cowered fearfully, and Abigail looked gratefully at Nance for sparing them the same fate.

"Cor bless yer, Nance," she croaked, giving her a kiss and swearing to remain faithful and true for life. When the bloody business was over and seawater thrown over the offenders' raw backs, they were taken below to the sick bay to have their wounds salted to prevent infection.

From Rio the ship re-crossed the Atlantic and within six weeks anchored off Cape Town, a small settlement dwarfed by Table Mountain and dubbed 'the tavern of the Indian Ocean'. Having taken on board stores, the *Nile* rounded the Cape of Good Hope and began the final and most hazardous part of her voyage, sailing eastward into the Roaring Forties. Every time the regular shock of wave against bow made her rise up, she seemed poised on the edge of an abyss; every time she descended, the waves forced the bows under and the rushing sea engulfed the deck, submerged the battened-down hatches and forced water through every gap all the way down to the hold. Mountainous waves hit amidships, threatening to set her on her beam end. Gale-force winds blew relentlessly with a wailing, high-pitched whistle, lashing sheet and sail and sometimes breaking spars, forcing hapless hands aloft to cut them loose.

Below deck, a dank mist hung everywhere leaving everything moist to the touch. As fearful, sleepless passengers huddled in heaving bunks listening to timbers and masts creaking continuously, life down in the clammy and dark orlop was as nigh unbearable as nature and man together could make it. Water sloshed round the women's feet and any poor soul who collapsed exhausted was tossed about like a marionette.

In one of the passenger cabins, Elizabeth Dickson, a free settler and the mother of two small children, went into premature labour. Her horrified husband Andrew dragged himself stumbling along the rolling deck to the captain's cabin, only to be told that the ship's surgeon was indisposed and none of the other crew had any medical knowledge. Perhaps, Harbuckle suggested, among the convicts could be found one or two who might be able to help. Dickson followed a lieutenant down to the hold where groups of soaked and sickly women hugged each other for warmth. When asked by the lieutenant, none had any knowledge of midwifery; yet Dickson was instinctively drawn towards one of them.

"Will you help my wife?" he pleaded. "She's in labour and needs a woman's hand."

Nance raised her eyes and couldn't help sympathising with the poor man in his anguish. Still, what could she do?

"If I can be of help, sir, I'll dew it. But taak my friend Abi too – she knows more 'bout havin' babies."

"Is that true?" Andrew turned to her. "Will you come?"

"I've seen babies come, sir. There ain't much to 'avin' a baby. I'll do what I can."

The three followed the striding, upright lieutenant and made their precarious, rolling way to the Dicksons' cabin where, in a dim pool of light from a hanging lamp and watched anxiously by two frightened children, was a woman on the bunk, grimacing with pain and clenching her fists. The two convicts lurched towards her, grabbing the furniture and each other for support, then pulled back the bedclothes to begin examining her. With a wry smile, for a moment her pain forgotten, she struggled to speak above the ship's groans and the warring elements outside.

"Why, my dears, you're wet through, both of you."

"Thus noo matter ta us, ma'am," said Nance.

"I've still a while to go," said Elizabeth, again grimacing with pain. "There are clothes and towels in the trunk over there. Do dry yourselves and put on mine."

The women turned to an embarrassed lieutenant who nodded, bowed stiffly and left along with Andrew who took the children away and closed the door. Unseen, anxious souls from the other side of life joined them, including Teresa and Sarah. Nance now again sensed her sister's presence and remembered how she always came to mind at perilous moments. Yet even if she were somehow present, how on Earth could she help now?

Nance and Abigail stripped, dried and dressed themselves while Elizabeth's contractions grew more painful and regular. It was evident that the birth was imminent and Abigail suggested the lady should stand up. The ship's listing, shuddering and plunging made standing unsupported impossible so the convicts held onto her and eased her out of bed. Although she couldn't walk, to encourage the baby to push downwards, the motion of the ship had the same effect. They seated her on the edge of a chair, wedged against the bunk as an improvised birthing stool, and prepared for delivery as Elizabeth's pain became almost unbearable.

"Push, ma'am, push!" encouraged Abigail.

"Come on, ma'am, push! Yew's nearly thar," echoed Nance. Sarah drew as close as possible to her sister and whispered, 'Come on, Nance, ask for help.' Though unheard, the thought had the desired effect this time and Nance found herself muttering, "Law help me, I dewn't want ta hurt noo one…" Instantly, she felt herself influenced by something, or someone, and her hands guided. Slowly a wet, pink mass emerged and she eased it out tenderly, gathered it in her arms and held it up by the feet before smacking it carefully across the buttocks. The child's mouth opened and a first cry of life was heard.

Nance passed the baby to Abigail and helped its mother back to the bunk, where she cleaned her and covered her with sheets. Intuitively, she placed a hand on the woman's brow and felt a strange energy – surely not hers? – pass through her fingers. Elizabeth felt it too as a soothing, healing warmth. Before long the floor was swabbed, Abigail had placed the baby in its mother's arms and Nance was opening the door to Andrew, announcing that he was the father of a healthy boy. He entered with the children following and saw by the weak yet positive smile on his wife's face that all was well.

"She'd make a good midwife with our help," observed Teresa.

"I think," agreed Sarah, "my sister has found her vocation."

As the rough passage continued, both Nance and Abigail were retained as nurses, spending most of their time in others' cabins and only returning to the orlop to sleep. By December they had reached calmer waters and sighted the new continent. The *Nile* hugged the southern coastline, navigated the Bass Straight, entered Port Jackson and dropped anchor in Sydney Cove.

A new home

CHAPTER 19

SYDNEY COVE

When, in 1769, Captain James Cook had landed in an unknown bay on the south-east coast of New Holland, it was following one of the rare deluges that temporarily transform the continent's most arid parts into a luxuriant display of nature. The extraordinarily wide variety of unknown flora he found, dense herbage and meadowland watered by falling streams, suggested the name Botany Bay. With the transportation of convicts to America ended and the failure of an African penal colony – and with the gaols of England full – the British government decided to found a new colony there.

A few years later, under the command of Captain Arthur Phillip, a fleet set sail with the first convicts and anchored in the bay in January 1788. What they found was marshy and sandy soil completely unsuitable for crops and little freshwater, with no trace of what Cook had promised. Moreover, the aboriginal inhabitants were no less unwelcoming, advancing with shouts of "Warra, warra!"[3] When a spear

---

[3] "Go away!"

thudded into the sand before Phillip, a soldier discharged his musket into the air and the natives retreated; but there was no choice other than to seek a more suitable location. Captain John Hunter sailed with other officers in three open boats some nine miles northward in search of Port Jackson, where he found a natural, deep-water harbour with plenty of fresh water. Phillip then led the fleet there and anchored in what he named Sydney Cove.

Nance's first sight of her new home raised her spirits for the first time since being on the run with Cabern. On the west side, some dozen houses and gardens extended to the water's edge, below rising meadowland and a tree-lined hill crowned by a windmill. To the east, taller trees shaded more houses, barracks and barns, all surrounded by meadow or herbage. The governor's two-story mansion and nearby white houses with their carefully tended, giant geranium-filled gardens looked wholly English.

On her first evening ashore at convicts' muster, she watched the sun sink to the horizon and turn the light blue waters into a fire-flecked azure, then reddish copper and, finally, deep orange as they reflected the shafts of sunlight that radiated like flashes of cannon-fire frozen in time. What strange land was this where even the sea burned like a conflagration?

She spent the first two days helping to land the ship's stores before coming to the notice of Jim Grayson, the commissary responsible for their issue. Learning of her domestic experience, he took her into his wife's service, principally as cook. When Mrs Grayson was absent, she would be free to travel at will provided that she obtain a pass and attended the regular convicts' muster. Nance was overjoyed to find familiar garden stuff of all kinds. Wheat mixed with a little Indian corn, the two staple crops, made excellent bread so she was able to bake and eat much as she had at home. Soon she was able to write to her aunt and uncle that she was comfortable in her new surroundings, well-liked by others and even treated with some respect as the Graysons' cook.

Life was not so good for others around Sydney and surrounding settlements, such as Parramatta, Toongabbie and along the Hawkesbury River. Convicts either worked for the government or for the free settlers, who only had to provide food and clothing. Gangs were forced to break rocks for road-building, or to turn hard soil with hoes rather than ploughs, or to fell heavy oaks with axes for ten hours a day. On Sundays they were read the Bible and required to attend church parade.

Male convicts were generally resigned to serving their time or hoping for a pardon, either to become settlers themselves or work a passage home to England. The women had little chance of being able to achieve either. Those convicts judged the most dangerous were termed 'magpies', wearing arrowed yellow jackets and toiling in chains. For some, an even harsher place awaited them – Norfolk Island, a thousand miles out in the Pacific – having been marched to the cove for transportation, linked by chains passed through iron collars around their necks. The colony's first coal miners had their heads shaven and carried coals from first light until dusk.

Never far away were the red-coated, pipe-clayed guards of the New South Wales Corps with their muskets, although their purpose was more to prevent native attack than an escape. After all, where was there to escape to – into the bush, over the unexplored Blue Mountains or across the Pacific in an open boat?

Nance wrote regular letters to the Fosters, to Frances Turner and to Dr Abbett. In one, she even requested that they send her the newspaper accounts of her gaol escape, a feat she still recalled with pride in spite of the tragedy that followed. Such letters were composed over the course of weeks, sometimes months, and often concluded hastily because it had been reported that a ship was about to sail. When away from Sydney, she would walk tens of miles in order to place the letter in the hands of a captain, whose ship probably had several other ports of call before reaching England, whilst those writing from England would have to find a ship bound for New South Wales. It could be two years or more before a reply to one's letter was received.

The heat of Sydney was becoming unbearable since much of the woodland that protected the growing township from the periodic warm winds off the Pacific had been felled. Without stout leather shoes, the sand was hot enough to scorch the feet. So after eighteen months working for the Graysons, Nance was happy to be reunited with the Dicksons when she went as lying-in nurse to Elizabeth and helped her with the difficult birth of another child. Andrew Dickson had been granted one hundred acres at North Richmond on the Hawkesbury River, east of the Blue Mountains. So highly was Nance regarded there that, when Andrew Dickson was appointed Superintendent of Public Works at Parramatta, she was left alone as overseer on the farm at Richmond Hill. It was a charming spot with peaches, pears and apricots in abundance and, at harvest time, the fertile river flats were covered by rippling wheat. To the west, the famous haze that gave them their name hovered over the Blue Mountains. The sky displayed many hues of blue and then there were those incredible fireball sunsets.

The Dicksons saw her as 'one of the family' and rewarded her with her own livestock, all kept on their farm without charge. For some while now she had been a convict in name only; she received no wages but had board and lodging with payment in kind and some remuneration. Indeed, for practical purposes she was better off now than she had ever been, even in her younger days at Amberslea. However, with only male convicts for company she felt lonely there, and not even the good things of her new home could diminish a growing homesickness. She secretly yearned to return to England and hoped, in a year or two, for a pardon.

After some time, Nance began to fulfil her promise to Frances Turner to report on the country and send back specimens of flora and fauna as well as native artefacts. Anything she could not collect she begged from settlers, who thought her mad for wanting to preserve dead insects and animal skins. She also wrote to Dr Abbett of the indigenous natives' savagery. Recently, a settler had been found with both arms and legs amputated halfway, the sole survivor of a party of nine including women and children, all murdered by 'the blacks'. Governor King ordered the New South Wales Corps to pursue and shoot as many of them as possible.

Although horrified by such outrages, Nance found herself wondering what the real causes were, whether it were not comparable to an ill-treated dog turning on its master rather than savages delighting in violence. After all, no-one had bothered to make a study of them, if only to find out how they managed to live successfully in the bush with apparently none of the problems suffered by Europeans. As a woman alone, she might have to live in close proximity to these people and pass among them on her travels. So she set about befriending the few who ventured near the settlements and they in turn introduced her to others.

One woman she found particularly friendly was Mama Ngandi. Known as 'the wise one' by her people, she seemed to be able to commune with the spirits of the dead; she certainly saw beyond the physical world and knew more than she let on. Befriending her proved a wise move because, if she liked you, none of her people would harm you. Nance was soon able to travel long distances without feeling threatened or intimidated, and was able to obtain by barter or by gift more precious specimens for her old mistress. Transporting them to England proved no easy matter but many were eventually received by an overjoyed Frances Turner, now an author, editor and aspiring botanist. In gratitude, she sent more than one chest to Nance with as much as they could hold to make her life more comfortable: writing materials and books, needlework and dressmaking tools and all kinds of cotton, linen and silks.

A new governor arrived, William Bligh, with his daughter Mary and her husband, Lieutenant John Putland. Bligh was a man with a mission. Ever since the arrival of the First Fleet, the behaviour of the New South Wales Corps had been notorious, and not just towards the natives. The only free men besides the settlers, the soldiers virtually did as they pleased and as there was little else to do they farmed the twenty-five acres of land each was allotted and became entrepreneurs. They would purchase entire ships' cargoes and sell them at inflated prices, especially the rum. Bligh had been ordered to break the monopoly and end the trafficking.

The soldiers' commanding officer was Major George Johnston, an uncouth and ruthless yet successful career soldier who had only contempt for his civilian paymasters who were obliged to employ him. Not content with exploiting the convicts, he had to be prevented from also using the natives as slave labour. Predictably, he regarded the new governor not as his superior but an enemy; in return, the quick-tempered Bligh judged him an insolent upstart and a bad soldier, who failed to instil discipline and was himself a greedy profiteer. Johnston was supported by John Macarthur, a former soldier turned wealthy entrepreneur and land owner whose illegally exported Royal Merino sheep grazed the best pastures in the colony.

Nance had unsuccessfully petitioned Governor King for a pardon but she still cherished hope and wanted to find out all she could about the new governor so that he might be favourable toward her. For a while, she had worked for Harry Richardson, a loyal and trusted government employee, and his wife Catherine; like others, they had come to regard her more as a friend than a servant. Harry knew a great deal about Bligh, who was justly proud of his own achievements.

Late one Christmastide evening, she sat in conversation with Harry and Catherine over a glass of wine in their candle-lit parlour to hear of Bligh's role in one of the most remarkable tales ever from the days of sailing ships. Richardson carefully lit a long clay pipe and settled back in his chair.

"Sailed under Cap'n Cook, he did, on the *Resolution* – that is, 'til those thievin' savages in the Sandwich Islands did for the cap'n with their spears. It was Bligh who brought the ship safely home, an' him as drew the maps. But he received not a ha'p'orth o'credit.

"Still, the Admiralty needed to keep him. See, breadfruit had been found on the isle of Otaheite. It were nutritious as bread with none o' the bother o' bakin' so the government wanted to use it in the West Indies as cheap food for slaves – but how to get it there? That was Bligh's job, it were to be carried on the *Bounty* in his cabin. He still weren't a full cap'n, only actin' like, an' he had no marines to enforce order. He were a hard taskmaster, though, cursin' an' swearin' at his crew like the divil hisself but reluctant to have 'em flogged. An' did they respect 'im? Not a bit."

Harry Richardson paused, knocked out his pipe on the hearth, repacked it with tobacco and lit a paper spill from a low-burning candle. The flame jumped, grew small and flared up as he drew and puffed out clouds of smoke. Nance recharged their glasses and listened attentively.

"When they arrived at Otaheite, Bligh had to wait five months for seasonal weather afore he could navigate and map the Endeavour Straits. An' while they were there... well, the crew took a fair likin' to the local lasses an' their lieutenant, Fletcher Christian, was the worst o' the lot. Fornicated his way round the whole island, he did!" He began to chuckle but was checked by his wife's icy stare. He bowed and nodded by way of apology. "So then Bligh had as fair a bunch o' useless, idlin' loafers for a crew as ever sailed one of His Majesty's ships. Bligh did what 'e could, bawlin' 'em out, but Christian led 'em in mutiny. He forced Bligh an' nineteen loyal officers and men into an open boat in uncharted waters a thousand leagues from civilisation, an' abandoned 'em to their fate."

He paused again, lowered his head and appeared lost in thought as he came to the climax of his story. By now the dying candles were giving up the ghost and soon only a single flame was left to animate the storyteller. Catherine and Nance leaned forward, spellbound.

"Well," he continued, "by dead reckoning and just goin' by memory, he navigated that boat for more'n three an' a 'alf thousand miles, never more than a mile or two off course, to Timor in the Dutch East Indies. An' 'e only lost one man, killed by natives on Tofua. On another occasion, 'e were commended by Nelson hisself." He settled back in his chair and folded his arms.

"So, husband," observed Catherine, "what kind of governor will he be? There's talk that Johnston and the soldiers hate him."

"Well, m'dear, Bligh's a man as knows all 'bout mutinies…"

They were about to find out just how resolute the man was. Just a month later, the Richardsons were among the invited guests at the governor's table, whilst Nance ate in the servants' hall. Bligh's daughter Mary, in mourning for her husband who had recently died of tuberculosis, dutifully welcomed the guests as lady of the house and then withdrew to the garden, kneeling at her husband's grave. Around 6 o'clock, with the evening sun still bright, her reverence was disturbed by the strains of *The British Grenadiers* and the tramp of four hundred redcoats marching along Bridge Street with Johnston at their head. He intended to pre-empt any action Bligh might take by seizing any papers that could be used against him. The soldiers approached the garden gates with fixed bayonets, marched through and fanned out to surround Government House. Mary ascended the steps of the entrance and turned to confront them.

"Traitors, rebels," she shouted, as the vanguard climbed the steps towards her. "You have just walked over my husband's grave. Now

291

you come to murder my father." She pointed to her chest and cried, "Well, do your duty, my brave soldiers! Run me through, stab me to the heart!"

Johnston ordered the first man to arrest her but she simply attacked him with her rolled-up parasol, bringing it down smartly on his plumed stovepipe shako and knocking it off. The others paused, uncertain how to react to this furious lady of rank, but with their officer swearing at them they advanced. She fought off another four men before an officer slipped behind her, grabbed her and hoisted her off her feet. Nance heard the commotion and ran to the door of the grand dining-room with Teresa at her side, aware of the danger and anticipating what was about to happen. Johnston entered, brushing aside startled guests, and Bligh turned to him with characteristic rage.

"So, it's mutiny is it? I'll have every man jack o' you court-martialled, flogged and hanged!"

He was red with uncontrolled fury, eyes rolling and arms flailing, as he advanced on Johnston with a flurry of oaths, oblivious of the ladies present. Any seamen would have been terrified, but these were mutinous soldiers with fixed bayonets.

"Arrest that man!" ordered Johnston, pointing at Bligh.

Nance was outraged that the one man who could pardon her might be deposed and her old temper exploded. As the helpless guests watched, she pushed through the soldiers now surrounding Bligh and sprang defiantly in front of him, stretching out her arms as a shield.

"Yew let our gov'nor be!" she bellowed. The soldiers levelled their bayonets but hesitated, as before, unsure how to proceed.

"Get that bloody woman out of here!" ordered Johnston. Reluctantly, two of them lowered their weapons and stepped forward to try and drag her away but she stood her ground.

"Let goo o' me yew frackshus, moot'nus ninnies!"

Harry Richardson attempted to intervene, only to be pinned back against a wall, a musket across his chest. Still the soldiers hesitated. Then they grabbed Nance by the arms and frogmarched her to the door.

"I'm the one you want," thundered Bligh. "Unhand her, you poxy, whoremongerin' sons of bitches! I'll see you hanged from the highest yardarm in the fleet!"

Nance was hauled to the door and pushed down the steps to collapse in a heap, her head dizzy, body bruised and face bleeding. Harry and Catherine Richardson, ejected with the other guests, helped her to her feet and persuaded her to come away. Bligh's thunderous voice could still be heard as the soldiers fell upon him and dragged him from room to room looking for evidence. The ransacking of Government House continued until the day ended beneath an angry flame-rolling sky.

Bligh and his daughter were placed under house arrest with guards mounted by the doors and gate. Yet the loyal settlers, including Richardson and Dickson, did not desert him and kept him supplied with all his needs. As Nance was on friendly terms with both families, she often took Bligh food and laundry, brushing past the gauntlet of guards. Because of the social gulf between them, she and Bligh did not converse yet it was clear to him that she possessed the qualities of courage and loyalty that he valued above all others. She still cherished hopes of a pardon – but Johnston stripped Bligh of all power and governed in his place.

The next couple of years brought further disasters for the Hawkesbury settlers, especially terrible floods that destroyed many crops. In the wake of a bush fire, a hurricane devastated the surviving crops, tearing them up by the roots. Then the warring winds whipped up the densest of rainclouds that first showered the land with hail the size of grapeshot and then unleashed a deluge of water that swelled the Hawkesbury beyond its deepest banks. The flats were inundated to rooftop height and settlers clung to chimneys hoping for rescue as furniture, uprooted trees, drowned livestock and men trying to swim their horses were swept along in an ever-widening flood.

From a hill that was now a riverbank, Nance spotted a family of five clinging to the roof of a floating barn, held fast only by a giant tree stump. Also watching on were Teresa and Sarah, who had left her sister's welfare in her guide's hands until now.

Her bond with Thomas had become even closer, her friends had multiplied, whilst those feeling drawn to seek her help seemed never ending. Whether she played the perfect hostess on Thomas' estate, received spiritual seekers at her own retreat, socialised with her peers or meditated soulfully in her own expanding consciousness, her life could not have been more fulfilling. Moreover, unlike on Earth and however much there was to do, it was never too onerous and there was always 'time enough' in which to do it. Only an occasional pang of regret at not seeing Nance cast a shadow over this otherwise ideal existence. Teresa's summons, therefore, had overjoyed her even though danger beckoned for her beloved sister.

"I had to fetch you this time," said Teresa. "She'll try to rescue those people herself. We can't let her. This time we – you – must stop her or she'll drown."

Nance couldn't stand idly by, like the little crowd already gathering, and inhumanely watch a whole family perish. A rescue had to be attempted. She found two long lengths of rope and knotted them together, tying one end to a boat and the other to a tree. When two men nearby refused to help, convinced it was too dangerous, she declared that she would go alone and stepped into the boat. Even as she did so, a thought came to her, this time as clearly as though spoken aloud.

"Aren't you getting a little old for this?" It definitely seemed to be a woman's voice, although there were none nearby, and she couldn't help thinking of Sarah. Sister or not, real or imagined, what she said was true. Nance's ageing body was no longer the one that had dashed to rescues years before, had ridden to London in a night and had scaled a prison wall. Besides, although she could row, this was no Orwell but a torrent. Nevertheless, she sat down and reached for the oars.

"No, don't!" came the voice again. "Make them do it, not you."

She raised an oar and prepared to push off from the bank, but cast a long, lingering look of desperation in the men's direction. Finally shamed into action, they agreed to go as long as she remained behind. While onlookers paid out the line, they battled against the current until gradually they had manoeuvred themselves alongside the barn on the downstream side. With one oar dug into the tree stump to hold the boat steady, the other man crouched and lifted his arms to receive the three children, one by one, before helping down the parents. Nance watched from the bank with soulful, steadfast eyes, as though commanding their every action and willing them to succeed.

The family safely aboard, the two men rowed for their lives praying that the line would hold until they made landfall. Charles Cornwell and his family warmly thanked their rescuers – and Nance, whose part in it all had been seen.

When the new governor, Colonel Lachlan Macquarie, embarked for New South Wales, he took with him the 73rd Regiment of Foot to replace the disgraced New South Wales Corps. Like Bligh, he too had a mission but also a vision and with Bligh safely back in England, along with Johnston and Macarthur, he was free to pursue it. Transportation was usually for life so therefore, he thought, the colony should not just be a place of punishment but a decent place to live in. There must be hope and the genuine promise of a fresh start and a worthwhile future. His first task was to relieve the Hawkesbury settlers and protect them from further flooding by moving them to higher ground by creating the five 'Macquarie Towns' of Richmond, Wilberforce, Pitt Town, Castlereagh and Windsor.

It was here that he encountered a man in late middle age who greatly impressed him. A former Suffolk farm labourer, Jethro Merryridge had come out as a free settler and been granted fifty acres of land. Knowledgeable about agriculture, he had built up his farm and bought increased acreage, only to lose everything in the Hawkesbury floods and having to begin all over again. He was innovative in his methods and made good use of convict labour, encouraging his men to learn as well as work so that, as emancipists, they might manage farms of their own. This was what Macquarie wanted to hear although he hesitated for a moment, smelling alcohol on the man's breath despite it being not yet noon. (Jethro had indeed been drinking for many a year. It was not because he particularly liked rum – who did? – but because it helped deaden the pain of a life without Nance.) Nonetheless, he promised Merryridge further land and invited him to become a magistrate and to be his representative at Windsor.

Before they shook hands and parted, the thoughtful governor asked why the man had never married. He replied that, in the old country, he had loved a wonderful, adorable creature but she had loved someone else; since he could not stop loving her, he couldn't give his heart to another. Macquarie said that he understood, yet suggested that Jethro Merryridge ought to marry for company's sake. Jethro nodded his acceptance and they shook hands.

"A word of advice," added the governor at the door, "from a wiser, albeit rusticated old jungle-wallah like me – watch the rum, laddie!"

Macquarie was a good administrator and initially popular with the settlers, but they soon resented his liberal attitude towards convicts and his intention to integrate emancipists into the community. Many settlers refused to dine with him at Government House, but not Merryridge, and an unlikely friendship between an old military man, who had spent much of his life in India, and a sometime farmhand-turned-farmer began to blossom.

Nance was also farming by now, renting a plot of fifteen acres, half of it still covered by trees, where she tended thirty sheep, forty goats and thirty pigs guarded by two dogs. She was becoming modestly prosperous and hoped that the money she earned would pay for a passage home if she could obtain a pardon from the new governor. Yet she remained unknown to him whilst the very people who might recommend her ignored him.

She still saw her old employers who were now also her friends, including the Graysons, the Dicksons, the Richardsons and the ones she had helped save, the Cornwells. Another frequent visitor to her farm was her old friend, Mama Ngandi, with her unrivalled knowledge of plants and animals. And now her thoughts about the future began to change…

She still walked to Sydney when there was a ship with mail from England, and saw there a town of brick and stone rising with new roads and pavements. One day she visited the very spot where she had first landed more than a decade previously and, sitting there gazing across the cove, she began to wonder what might await her in the old country. She would have to seek work again but was nearly fifty years old. Her family was long gone, but perhaps she could live with her uncle and his children – though would they really want her? Would even Frances Turner want her, as an ex-convict?

What, then, would another change of sky hold for her? Loneliness and poverty more than likely, and a sad old age on parish relief if not in the Poorhouse… Surely life here, where she had real friends, was preferable to an uncertain one there and, besides, Australia was changing. It was fast becoming a country and she was one of those helping to build it! No, better by far to be relatively well-off here than a pauper back in Amberslea.

With a pardon, though, she could mix socially on a more equal footing and she decided to speak with Catherine Richardson about it on her next visit. She thought this an excellent idea and had a suggestion: yes, the stand-off between settlers and the governor was a difficulty, but there was a new magistrate in Windsor who might help her. He seemed to be on friendly terms with Macquarie and a word from him could be the best possible recommendation. She would mention it to the other ladies and, the next time one of them met the magistrate, he would be invited to hear from them how much they owed Nance and the respect in which she was held. In fact, Catherine made a special journey to see Merryridge and presented him with a petition signed by all the ladies and their husbands. He was astounded.

CHAPTER 20

THE NEW ADVENTURE

Could this Mrs Auldfield really be his Nance? When Catherine had left, Jethro settled back and recalled those far off days at Abbeyfield Farm. He still corresponded with his family and for a while they had mentioned Nance – when he had enough money, he had intended proposing by letter and paying her passage to join him – but after her disgrace there was no further mention of her and he had assumed she married Cabern. He knew nothing of her trial, imprisonment and transportation, so how could this be the same person?

He drove his cart to Richmond and drew up by the gate of the little homestead on the hill where the dogs' barking alerted Nance to the arrival of a tall, well-heeled gentleman striding up the path.

"Do I have the honour of addressing Mrs Auldfield?" he asked. He wasn't sure that he recognised her at first, much altered as she was by age and experience. He too was changed, having grown to maturity in this new world.

"My name be Auldfield, yes, sir." He certainly recognised the accent.

"You're from Suffolk."

"Born and bred."

"Mr Merryridge of Newbourne, at your service," he beamed, removing his hat and bowing respectfully. She stared at him knowingly, incredulously.

"Not Mr Jethro Merryridge?"

"Why, yes… and you… You're—"

"Yes, Mr Merryridge. I'm Nance Auldfield."

For a moment they stood silent, in awe of the impossibility that they should meet again here. Then sheer excitement and exhilaration overwhelmed them. Nance's eyes swam with tears of joy, her cheeks reddened and she tottered as though about to faint. He steadied her by the arm and gently guided her indoors and to a chair.

"Mr Merryridge—" she began.

"Jethro, please," he corrected.

"I cont not call yew tha'. Yew be a gen'l'man now, an' I—"

"For you, I shall always be Jethro, the labourer from Abbeyfield Farm."

As he spoke, she noticed the same look in his eye she had seen that evening in Piper's Vale when he had declared his love for her. She noticed something else too. Though lined and sunburnt, heavier and with thinning hair, in her eyes he still cut the fine figure she remembered. Yet as they talked, she became aware that his appearance was somewhat emaciated. Why the yellowish skin and eyes? And now that he was seated, she could see his ankles were swollen. What, she wondered, was causing this? His voice recaptured her attention.

"But how on Earth did you come to be here?"

"Stole a hoss – dewn't ask why. It wuz all soo stupid."

"You must have had a reason," he said sympathetically.

"I did it ta save Rob. So I thought. But thus all over with. He's dead."

"I'm sorry, I didn't know. My brother writes to me occasionally, but he's said nothing of you or Cabern for many a year."

A strange calmness came over her as she prepared herself to relate her long, sorry history. From this kindly soul, she was sure there would be understanding rather than condemnation for he had always been steady and considerate with none of the excitability of Cabern. Jethro wanted to know the whole story, so she talked at length and made tea, then talked some more and made more tea. All the while he listened carefully and anxiously, the pain clearly visible on his face as he seemed to be himself living all the ordeals and sufferings she had undergone.

It was well into evening by the time she'd finished. The sun dipped from an orange sky and the shadows lengthened in a benign nightfall as the gently swaying oaks merged beneath winking stars. As he finally stood to return home, he hesitated on the threshold, loath to leave her.

"Don't you worry, my dear Nance. If anyone deserves a pardon, you do."

"That's sweet of yew, Jethro," she added, not wanting him to leave either. "Yew came ta my rescue once afore."

"A long time ago, Nance."

She picked up a lantern, placed a lighted candle inside and handed it to him. Still he hesitated. She glanced at the path and the track beyond, from which all traces of day had disappeared.

"If yew dewn't get a-gooin' soon, Jethro, yew ont be a-coomin' back." A bolt from the distant past struck her mind. 'I said tha' once afore ta someone,' she thought. The spherical glow from the lantern framed his warm, loving smile, then he turned, walked briskly through the gate and mounted the cart. He hung the lantern on it, took the reins and, with a final wave, trotted into the night. All the way homeward, his thoughts were so full of Nance that she seemed all but real beside him. As for those dewy black eyes, they had plainly shown as much love for him as he still felt for her.

As for her, sleep was a long time coming as she lay thinking of him and, especially, of a remote and dear past. Why had she not accepted his proposal then? With no Cabern, she would have married Jethro because, she knew, she had loved him all along. Only her infatuation with Cabern had blinded her to the truth. How different life would have been – she might be asleep with Jethro right now on their own farm in England, perhaps as parents of grown-up children. But now he was a gentleman and she was disgraced, so it could never be. She sobbed far into the night, salting the pillow with tears.

Jethro lost no time in making the rounds of the new towns and taking statements from everyone who knew Nance. Then his horse and cart were soon travelling the newly-built road to Government House where Macquarie heard his eloquent appeal for a pardon. A large bundle of papers was placed before the governor from which Jethro produced sheet after sheet, each testifying to Nance's services as nurse and midwife, and to further acts of charity and bravery.

"Nevertheless, answer me one question," interrupted the more prosaic Scotsman, not without a trace of impatience. "What is your personal interest in this woman?"

"I wish," said Jethro proudly, "to take her to wife. She's the one I spoke of earlier, the one I always loved yet thought never to see again."

"As a magistrate, though," Macquarie observed, his expression unchanged, "ye canna very weal marry a convict, can ye?"

"No, sir."

"Then I had better make her a free woman."

"Sir, you will make me the happiest of men!"

Macquarie wordlessly took a quill and began writing, painfully slowly, while Jethro slipped round the desk and waited anxiously at his elbow. Finally, the governor sprinkled the paper with sand, carefully folded it and poured the sand back into the container. He started to hand it over, but paused.

"I'd like to meet this remarkable woman. You and Mrs Merryridge must dine with me one evening."

Jethro made a low, sweeping bow and strode triumphantly from the room holding aloft the precious paper. It was late in the evening when he returned home so he paced the veranda, sipping rum, and contemplated the comfortable homestead he would soon share with his beloved Nance – a humble home, greatly blessed. This certainly called for a celebratory toast before retiring. Before daybreak, he set out for Nance's homestead.

To the west, the majestic Blue Mountains seemed clothed in a clearer azure than usual by an auspicious Heaven, as though inviting angels to travel Earthward on the rays of a rising sun. One inhabitant of the ether who did visit was Sarah, summoned from her home by Teresa to witness, for a change, a happy occasion for her sister.

Nance concealed her earlier private sorrow and was glad to see him again, leading him into the parlour. Nothing could have prepared her for the inexpressible surprise and joy of opening and reading the paper he handed to her. It was an absolute pardon, bearing Macquarie's signature.

"Oh Jethro, oh my dearest Jethro. I am free at last!" She threw her arms around him, hugging him with profound gratitude, then danced around the room, re-read the pardon and hugged him again. The weight of all these years fell away. The horrors of the horse ride, of the gaol and the court, of Cabern's death beside her and of the transport ship… all dissolved.

"I've, ah… one more surprise for you," he said nervously.

"Another, soo soon – wha' could tha' be? I cont stand noo more excitement fur now. I must sit afore I fall."

"First of all," he began, struggling to find the right words, "do you still like me? I mean, as a man… after all this time."

"Like yew? Law bless yew, I could love yew ta dead!"

The rays of the morning sun now streamed through the parlour window and bathed his face with new light. It was his moment of destiny, yet he felt strangely awkward and afraid. Beside them, a sister's loving eye kept eager watch, her heart filled with joyous anticipation.

"You remember that evening in Piper's Vale?" She smiled in reply. "And do you remember what the clumsy woodcutter asked you?" Her face now suddenly betrayed fear as she realised what he was about to say. "He asked you to marry him and said he would never love another."

"Soo yew did, Jethro," she said hesitantly, beginning to tremble with uncertainty.

"I kept my promise, Nance. I've always loved you, perhaps more than you knew." He dropped to one knee. "Nance, will you—"

"Noo, please dewn't," she begged. "Ask of me anything but tha'. I'm not fur marryin'."

The realisation of what she was saying came over him gradually, until it penetrated his defenceless heart like a dagger. He lowered his head with incomprehension and remained there, silent and motionless. Even the unseen presence was dumfounded. Sarah, just as helpless, could only watch in despair as her sister prepared to let Jethro and her one chance of real happiness slip from her grasp yet again.

At last, he rose slowly and wordlessly took her hand, kissing it reverentially as she looked askance, before stealing silently away. He mounted the cart and departed as though dead, giving the horse the reins to find its own way home. There, a broken man, he dragged leaden feet inside, locked the door, collapsed in a chair with a bottle of rum and drank himself insensible to everything.

Almost immediately, Nance had realised the enormity of what she had done or, rather, not done. The pain and sorrow of every previous misfortune that had so recently been lifted from her were as nothing compared to the despair now overwhelming her. She stumbled out of her house and walked blindly, not knowing where, hatless beneath the blazing sun and reeling as though also drunk. She prayed that the earth might open up and swallow her, and this little plot become her tomb. Then, exhausted as though the life force itself were ebbing away, she sank to the ground and crouched, head between her knees, on a broad rock.

She didn't notice the clip-clop of horse's hooves and an approaching cart, but the driver noticed her. A lady reined in, applied the brake and carefully lifted her long skirts clear of the wheel as she alighted. Catherine Richardson knelt beside the pitiful, forlorn creature and put an arm round her. Two reddened, inflamed eyes flickered briefly in recognition before squeezing out further tears.

"Nance, whatever's the matter? Pray tell me and I will help you in any way I can."

"Please," she wailed, "I cont taak yar charity noo more."

"Charity? Nonsense! Look what you've done for my family and for Elizabeth Dickson more than once, and so many others, not to mention the Cornwells. We'd all likely be dead if it weren't for you." She slipped an arm underneath Nance's shoulders and helped her to her feet. "You're coming home with me."

On the way, they passed the Dicksons' home and Catherine stopped to tell them what had happened. They hurried outside and carried the still distraught Nance into the house, where a new maid dashed into the parlour, gasped in astonishment and fell at Nance's feet. She was Abigail Harris. Mindful of having forgotten her place, she nevertheless looked imploringly at Elizabeth.

"Oh ma'am," she cried, "I'd have been in terrible trouble once if it hadn't been for Nance!"

"That seems to be what everyone says," agreed Elizabeth, turning to Nance. "My poor dear, what on Earth has happened?"

"It… it be Mr Merryridge," she sobbed. "He wants ta marry me."

They helped her to a chair and Elizabeth and Catherine sat beside her, each holding a hand, while Andrew stood nearby, feeling somewhat helpless. Naturally, they asked how this could possibly be the reason for such grief and despair.

"Because I love 'im wi' all my 'eart an' soul. But I said noo 'cos I'm not good enough fur 'em. He got me a pardon—" she paused, gulping for air between sobs, "—but I'm soo far beneath 'em. I've not much money, certainly noo dowry… an' I'm old an' ugly an' 'e be a fine gen'lman."

The women exchanged forlorn glances and it was now up to Andrew to take the situation in hand.

"The colony's most famous midwife," he declared, "is more than good enough to wed Windsor's new magistrate. As for your appearance, you are still a fine-lookin' woman – I am sure the ladies here can enhance what nature has achieved. Why, by the time you leave here, you'll be a bride fit for a governor! And as for the other difficulty, I promise you a dowry to match."

"But, sir, I cont niver taak sich charity."

"Then answer me truthfully one question – what value is to be placed on human life?" She shook her head, puzzled. "I speak of the lives of all the people and babies you've saved, and much else besides."

"I'm sure I dewn't know, sir."

"Neither do I. So there'll be no more talk of charity. Oh, and there's just one condition."

"What'd tha' be, sir?"

"That you write to Mr Merryridge this very hour accepting his proposal of marriage."

The tears flowed again, this time in rivulets, as Nance dabbed at her face and tried to smile while thanking them profusely for their kindness. With Andrew's guidance she put quill to paper and penned a note accepting Jethro's proposal of marriage. Then she folded the paper, sealed it with a kiss and then a blob of wax, and handed it to Andrew.

The next few days saw much activity at the Dicksons' homestead. Abigail Harris took extraordinary pains to transform the appearance of her old friend from a somewhat ageing matron into a desirable bride. Her greying hair, combed mercilessly straight, was carefully dyed and curled with tongs, her face was massaged and exfoliated whilst wooden dentures filled the gaps. A new wardrobe completed the metamorphosis before the former servant and convict took her first uncertain steps, now with a distinct gleam in her eye, in a new life of freedom.

Tending her little garden, long since restored to a whirlpool of colour and overflowing with fresh blossoms, Sarah's sensitive spirit was again burdened with feelings of impending doom. She went to Thomas' garden and knelt in silent contemplation by the scrying pool. Its calm waters were darkened and ruffled by an ominous wind as though auguring an approaching storm. Then, as the surface settled, an image appeared of Jethro's homestead and a woman shouting and hammering on the front door. Others joined her and a man put his shoulder to it, forcing it open. Wedged under the door was a folded note with its seal intact, which Sarah's intuition told her was her sister's letter. She watched as they entered the house and went into a room lit by a single candle where Jethro lay partially clothed on a bed, in obvious distress. In the blink of an eye she was there beside him, surprised to find others of the spirit world there too, including Teresa.

"It's his liver," she said, "or rather what was the liver. It is no more."

An emancipist, a doctor following his former profession and who had cared for Jethro on Earth, sat at the bedside shaking his head sorrowfully.

"Too much rum, I'm afraid, over the years. The tissue was already badly scarred and that last drinking bout put what was left beyond recovery." Sarah looked at Jethro's yellowing skin, swollen ankles and general emaciation.

"Is there nothing we can do for him?"

"We have done all we can. As you know, we can heal up to a point but we cannot alter the course of nature. He won't last another day, perhaps not even the night."

"Oh no, poor Nance!"

That evening, crushed by fate's cruellest blow yet, a silent Nance arrived for what would probably be her last meeting with Jethro. Rather than dwell on sad reality, they talked of the past at Abbeyfield Farm, of how they would sneak away to lie together in the long grass and meet 'by accident' while running errands, and how Jethro had climbed out of the window that night to escape Mr Knoller.

"Providence," she mused, "has surely played a part in our lives. But this be the fate we've created fur ourselves – or, rather, I have."

"No… I shouldn't have left you… when I did," he said, his voice hesitant and barely audible. "I should have been there at your side… when you needed me most."

As the night wore on, with Nance kneeling by the bed, he lapsed into unconsciousness only to awaken in the early hours and look around as though aware of another's presence.

"What can yew see, Jethro?"

"Nothing… nothing. Strange, though… I thought I saw Pa. He died many years ago… must be a trick of the light."

A fever took hold and she watched him become more and more distant, lapsing in and out of consciousness. Finally, his eyes opened and gave a final flicker of recognition, gazing beyond her towards the doorway.

"Is that you Pa? It's good to see…" he murmured, before a final sigh escaped his lips, his eyes became sightless and his body motionless.

The tragic figure of the new arrival haunted the Temple of Healing's colonnade, blind to its ethereal beauties and deaf to every sound – even to Sarah as she tried to console him. His only thoughts were of the world he had just left and of Nance – his lifelong love, his other nobler self whom he had lost and eventually found, only to lose again so swiftly and with awful finality. How she must be suffering this very moment.

"Oh Nance," he wailed, "how I wish I'd died before we ever met, than die and cause you such unspeakable grief." The lush translucent foliage, the sweet fragrances and the orchestral ripple of the fountain only highlighted by their contrast the black despair that enveloped him. "Nance, how I wish I were snuffed out completely, rather than live on in spiritual purgatory without you!"

Sarah, growing impatient and tired of being ignored, stood herself face to face with him and fixed him with eyes that would not let go.

"Why wish for annihilation when there is none? And even if there were, how would that help poor Nance? She is indeed suffering terribly, perhaps more than you imagine, but rather than contemplate death why not show her there is still life for both of you?" The words shocked him out of his mood.

"How could I possibly do that?"

"There is an old black woman she has befriended, Mama Ngandi. The woman is about to return to our world and is on her way to Nance to bid farewell. The Europeans don't appreciate it but the woman is a mystic. She can see the spirit, including us."

"But how will that help?" he asked despairingly.

"We can communicate through her."

"Through an aborigine, a naked savage?"

"Still British, I see, judging by appearances. Beneath that so-called primitive exterior, I assure you, flourishes a noble soul far more evolved than yours. She incarnated to help her people and she's probably forgotten more about the true nature of humanity than the white man has ever learned, or probably ever will. But there's no time to argue. Her earthly sun is about to set – and Nance's too, if we don't hurry."

He still seemed helpless, downcast and dithering.

"For Heaven's sake man, stop wallowing in self-pity and come with me – now!"

She grasped his arm roughly, held him tightly and together they stepped from the soft ether into the heavier, denser atmosphere of an earthly evening with rough ground beneath their feet. They arrived at Nance's homestead just before sundown and saw a dark-skinned visitor awaiting her return. When Nance arrived, she first checked that the animals were securely penned and then was about to open the front door when she heard a woman's harsh whisper.

"Missish!"

"Who's there?" she asked, startled and a little afraid.

"Missish Auldfield!" The woman, naked except for a loincloth, stepped from the shadows, her dark eyes peering intently from beneath long, dusky brows. A short fringe of greying hair, white in places, showed her advanced age yet a wide smile, engaging and dynamic, was evidence of a still youthful spirit.

"Why, Mama Ngandi. Why be yew out soo late?"

The woman stood still for a moment, silhouetted against the blue and crimson sky, streaked with darkening cloud.

"Me go walkabout."

"Goo far?"

"More far. Me wanta go back own country. When sun jumps up, me go an' not come back. You big womanfella, you plenty kind. You laikin old woman an' me not forget. Me come ta say 'tank you'."

"But why yew goo? Sing out loud, Big Mama."

"Me all alone now. Big fella Ngandi bilong-me, little fella bilong-me, Papa, Mama – all gone to dreamtime. Me all-time cry. So me go ta dreamtime soon, but old bones rest in own country first."

The sky darkened as the globe of fire slipped further beneath the streaky clouds, painting bush and woodland a burnished copper. Mama Ngandi turned and looked wistfully at the fiery scene as though seeing it for the last time. When Nance asked her where dreamtime was, she took a moment or two to answer, her eye seeming to focus on something, or someone, beside Nance.

"You bin there."

"I niver have—"

"In sleep, Missish. An' long ago when you in gaol. You see big sis."

The long-forgotten dream flashed into Nance's mind, of standing beside Sarah at a cottage gate. Could it be that it was no dream at all, that it actually happened?

"How d'yew know tha'?" she gasped.

"Big sis tell me."

"But how she tell yew?" Nance was incredulous, yet somehow a small hope leaped in her mind.

"She wit you now. Me see her. She tell me," said Mama, matter of fact.

"Sar—"

"Shhh! No speak name." She put a finger to her lips. "She in ta dreamin' now... must show respect. She no dead. No-one die." Mama was almost scornful. "We all come from dreamtime, white fella, black fella, an' all go back. She back in dreamtime... She laik you. You help white fella, black fella here, an' she help there."

"But where be this dreamtime?" Nance asked again.

"What whitefella call Heaven. All creature come from dreamtime, all go back. We say dreamtime but it have no time... all live today. Me old woman now but big sis bilong-you she say, 'Mama Ngandi, sing out plenty loud. What you say true.'"

"Sar—"

"An' she have big fella with her, big fella bilong-you."

"Jeth—"

"No name!" she hissed and covered Nance's mouth with her hand. "You can tink name, but no speak it! He laikin you plenty much, say he climb outta winder for you. Ten he shot, almost die for you. He wanta marry, but you love other fella, ten he come here. He still wanta marry. He in ta dreamin' now, but he wait for you... he have home all ready and heap big kisses. Ten he marry you."

Together they stood watching the airy lake of fire receding and the skies blacken until the stars, strangely close, hung like glowing lamps in the velvet darkness. All the while, Nance struggled to understand what she had just heard. At last she found her voice.

"Oh, dear Mama Ngandi, how can I iver thank yew enough?" The old woman smiled warmly and started to walk away. "Noo, yew cont not goo. I ont let yew. Yew must tell me more—"

"No. Sun lie down. When sun jump up me go walkabout, this time plenty far. Must go rest."

Nance pulled her close in an embrace and for the first time kissed her, as though holding in her arms her beloved sister once more. Then she slipped off her shawl and draped it over the woman's shoulders.

"Then fare ye well, Mama Ngandi. I pray we meet agen in a better place."

The evening meeting wrought a change in Nance, her grief tempered a little to a benign melancholy. She felt a bittersweet acceptance and a renewal of her old readiness to make the best of things. For somehow, someday, she now knew that come what may she would see Jethro and Sarah again.

She moved to the burgeoning town of Richmond, safely above the flood levels, where she opened a store. This was achieved largely due to the generosity of Frances Turner and one of her Ipswich friends, who had sent rolls of material of all kinds in a chest to make clothes and linen. Some she kept for herself, but mostly she sold them from her store while continuing to offer her services as midwife and nurse.

The last of her many patients was a shepherd with influenza who passed the virus on to her. From an initial sore throat and dry cough, she was soon perspiring heavily with a high fever; she retired to bed and slept awhile before waking early next morning, choking on mucous. The first sunbeams penetrated the window, tingeing everything a bright orange and then, as the skies turned lighter, a soft pink. As she lay there, aching throughout her body and breathing with increasing difficultly, another light began to fill the room, this time from within.

She saw, or thought she saw, a woman at the foot of the bed, who bore the likeness of her mother as she remembered her from childhood. Breathing soon became agony, but breathe she must if she were to hold on to life. Even as she struggled, the now unmistakable face of her mother smiled as though in welcome. Nance was sure she heard the woman whisper her name. The face was soft and gentle and radiated a mother's love as she spoke again, ever so softly.

"Let go of the pain now, Nance, and come with me."

Nance raised herself on one arm and, to her surprise, managed effortlessly to sit up. Then she found that she could stand just as easily and, as for the pain, she no longer felt any. She could breathe easily too. In a moment she was held fast in her mother's loving and very real embrace and feeling the warmth of a tender kiss. Glancing back, she saw without surprise her own face on the pillow, motionless and at peace. Guided by her mother's hand, she walked towards a luminous curtain and passed through it into an avenue of shadow, pierced by a distant ray of light glowing ever brighter as they advanced. They emerged beneath the rustling canopy of a lush woodland grove where light rays darted through the gently swaying boughs.

Before her on a floral lawn she could see, though still as in a dream, many well-remembered faces from long ago. Old Zebedee stepped forward – old no longer, but green with age, as erect as in his prime and with the sturdy shoulders that had guided the crooked plough so well. Dazzled, her eyes unaccustomed to the brightness, she was overcome with love as he embraced her with a single word, breathed from his innermost being.

"Darter!"

Then she saw Sarah, in the bloom of womanhood and radiant with health. She had kept a watchful eye on many others she had known, when it was their turn to make the transition, helping them to where they needed to be, and now it was her sister's turn to be welcomed. She took her by the hand and introduced her to her brothers, the dear companions of her youth, Albert, Mark and then John, too, who had passed over on a sea voyage.

Her Uncle Foster then took her hand, as did a much altered aunt, and others stepped forward including Dr Abbett, flush with youth and with his customary bow. One after another they greeted her, a smile here, a fond embrace there of the many she had served, nursed or befriended. By far the most prominent was a dusky female in raiment so ethereal it seemed woven of light, yet even her radiance could not conceal from Nance's squinting eyes the unmistakable smile of Mama Ngandi.

Finally, at a distance and keeping to the shadows, stood one motionless and sorrowful figure with bowed head who, even in her dream-like state, she could not fail to recognise as Rob Cabern. Apart from Sarah, the others withdrew quietly one by one as though making way for someone special.

Meandering beside the grove was a crystal stream, its slow-moving surface like a mirror reflecting the overhanging trees so perfectly that they appeared upside down with their roots in air. From the opposite bank, the brightness was so intense that Nance could scarcely distinguish anything but a shadowed, motionless figure silhouetted against a blanket of light. She knew who this was. But as she stepped nearer the water and gazed down at some stepping-stones, the water reflected her hands, rough with cracked skin and streaky with protruding veins, and her aged, crumpled face. She hesitated.

"It's all right. Go on, Nance," encouraged Sarah, "step across."

Reluctantly, she placed a tentative foot first upon one stone and then another. Glancing down, again the toothless, ruined image of a lifetime's toil met her eye. Yet now, even as she watched, the reflection began to alter. The lines and wrinkles faded, the eyes brightened and the grey hairs darkened and curled as the years fell away. The withered, cracked and sunburnt skin metamorphosed into youthful, rosy cheeks.

She lifted her head, blinked and tried to focus on the figure coming to meet her. As he drew nearer, there was no mistaking the hearty smile of a swarthy and youthful Jethro of their past. Then she was on the opposite bank and slipping dreamily into his outstretched arms. His eyes looked soulfully into hers, just like when they had met furtively in those faraway days at Abbeyfield Farm. He placed an arm around her waist and ran his fingers through her shining ebony locks.

They looked deeply and penetratingly into one another's loving eyes – the mirror of one soul reflecting the mirror of the other – and their trembling lips met, blending their spirits as halves of an indivisible whole.

"Jethro," she breathed, still dazed after what seemed an age of ethereal oblivion. "Be this a fittin' epitaph fur a mawther as loved all wrong – an' a crone as couldn't think aright?"

"No, my dear," he whispered, "this is only the prologue to a great new adventure... only this time, we shall take it together and never part again."

If you have enjoyed this book...

Local Legend is committed to publishing the very best spiritual writing, both fiction and non-fiction. You might also enjoy:

AURA CHILD

A I Kaymen (ISBN 978-1-907203-71-8)

One of the most astonishing books ever written, telling the true story of a genuine Indigo child. Genevieve grew up in a normal London family but from an early age realised that she had very special spiritual and psychic gifts. She saw the energy fields around living things, read people's thoughts and even found herself slipping through time and able to converse with the spirits of those who had lived in her neighbourhood. This is an uplifting and inspiring book for what it tells us about the nature of our minds.

A SINGLE PETAL

Oliver Eade (ISBN 978-1-907203-42-8)

Winner of the national Local Legend Spiritual Writing Competition, this page-turner is a novel of murder, politics and passion set in ancient China. Yet its themes of loyalty, commitment and deep personal love are every bit as relevant for us today as they were in past times. The author is an expert on Chinese culture and history, and his debut adult novel deserves to become a classic.

CELESTIAL AMBULANCE
Ann Matkins (ISBN 978-1-907203-45-9)

A brave and delightful comedy novel. Having died of cancer, Ben wakes up in the afterlife looking forward to a good rest, only to find that everyone is expected to get a job! He becomes the driver of an ambulance (with a mind of her own), rescuing the spirits of others who have died suddenly and delivering them safely home. This book is as thought-provoking as it is entertaining.

PATHWAYS OF THE DRUIDS
Christopher J Pine (978-1-907203-61-9)

Christopher J Pine's wonderful debut novel is a brilliant blend of fantasy, myth, magic and history. An exciting adventure story for all ages. In AD 60, the Roman Empire occupies Britannia and the ancient culture and freedoms of the Celts are being destroyed. Guided by the Druid priests, Boudicca leads the Iceni in an uprising against Nero's forces but it's a losing battle. However, the Druids have a mastery of nature and skills far beyond those of the Romans. They devise a final desperate strategy to avoid slavery and summon their greatest magic yet to open a portal into an alternative world. One last Celtic tribe, the Ordoveteii, race to cross the threshold...

DAY TRIPS TO HEAVEN
T J Hobbs (ISBN 978-1-907203-99-2)

The author's debut novel is a wonderful description of life in the spiritual worlds and of the guidance available to all of us on Earth as we struggle to be the best we can. Ethan is learning to be a spirit guide but having a hard time of it, with too many questions and too much self-doubt. But he has potential, so is given a special dispensation to bring a few deserving souls for a preview of the afterlife, to help them with crucial decisions they have to make in their lives. The book is full of gentle humour, compassion and spiritual knowledge, and it asks important questions of us all.

REDEEMING LUCIFER
Lennart Svensson (ISBN 978-1-910027-20-2)

This extraordinary novel is a tale in the finest tradition of legendary deeds, a blend of esotericism, pure imagination and acutely observed historical fact. A Russian army captain and his trusted striker find themselves journeying through parallel, mystical worlds in an epic quest to find Lucifer, no less, and to heal the world of its ills. But first, an ultimate cosmic battle must be fought… This book challenges each of us to examine our life's purpose. Lennart Svensson is a Swedish academic and this is his debut novel in English.

BROKEN SEA
Nigel Peace (ISBN 978-1-910027-23-3)

In the summer of 1968, a carefree and naïve Roy is preparing for university, oblivious that the whole world is soon to be turned upside down. First, he falls helplessly in love with Eva. Unfortunately, she is Czech and her country is about to be savagely invaded by the Warsaw Pact. Can their love survive this struggle for identity, both personal and national? In the course of one year, every character is profoundly changed…

"5* Packed full of political tension… excellent characterisation and a gripping plot. Highly recommended." *The Wishing Shelf Book Awards*

These titles are available as paperbacks and eBooks.
Further details and extracts of these and many
other beautiful books may be seen at

www.local-legend.co.uk